W9-BFD-294

For further information on
Sufi Studies please write to:
The Society for Sufi Studies
P.O. Box 43
Los Altos, CA 94022

The natives are restless

by IDRIES SHAH

In airports, in hotels and on beaches, an Englishman stands out by reason of his dress, his bearing, his speech and his immunity to ridicule. As far as he is concerned, what an Englishman does is right, and to hell with everyone else.

JOHN RUSSELL
Portrait of the British:
New York Times Magazine, March 9, 1986

OTHER BOOKS BY IDRIES SHAH

Literature
The Hundred Tales of Wisdom
A Perfumed Scorpion
Caravan of Dreams
Wisdom of the Idiots
The Magic Monastery
World Tales
The Dermis Probe

Novel
Kara Kush

Informal Beliefs
Oriental Magic
The Secret Lore of Magic

Humour
The Exploits of the Incomparable Mulla Nasrudin
The Pleasantries of the Incredible Mulla Nasrudin
The Subtleties of the Inimitable Mulla Nasrudin
Special Illumination

Travel
Destination Mecca

Human Thought
Learning how to Learn
The Elephant in the Dark
Thinkers of the East
Reflections
A Veiled Gazelle
Seeker After Truth

Sufi Studies
The Sufis
The Way of the Sufi
Tales of the Dervishes
The Book of the Book
Neglected Aspects of Sufi Study

Studies of the English
Darkest England

Adventures among the English
– and Others . . .

The
natives are
restless
by
IDRIES SHAH

THE OCTAGON PRESS
LONDON

Contents

Foster's sweat-bathed face was agonised. 'It's those damned drums, Carruthers', he panted, weakly. He slumped back on the makeshift brushwood bed.

'Steady on, old chap.' The Commissioner suppressed a shudder as the compelling, primitive rhythm thudded in his brain. 'You know our mission. Headquarters sent us to help these people, no matter what it costs.'

He put the water-bottle to the trembling man's lips. 'Drink this, old fellow. Remember, the natives think that they own this jungle – them and the spirits.'

The drums continued their hellish pounding. The natives were restless all right. What would tomorrow bring?

Empire's Eve by John Stout

1

See Worri Mean?

Character

A character is only an entire character when
its elements disagree, when it contradicts its
expected behaviour . . . that is the essence of
success of the English . . . A character always
in character is no character at all.

Han Suyin: *The Four Faces*

I had been away from England for some months, and much of its
image seemed to have faded, even to the extent that I was
wondering whether some of my experiences there had really
happened.

The little grey man in the crumpled suit, sitting next to me in
the aircraft, soon put an end to all that.

'If the River Thames', he was saying, as the jumbo circled
London, 'hadn't been there, they could have made London
much bigger.'

'But', I said, 'I thought that London only came into being
because of the river. Capital cities do: centre of trade and
transport routes, defensive line, and so on.'

He looked at me blankly; or, rather, with that English look
which I knew so well, and which meant that I hadn't a chance.
But I don't give up so easily. I tried again. 'Berlin on the Spree,
Paris on the Seine, Cairo on the Nile, you know the idea.'

'Oh, that old thing!' He used the dismissive phrase which
marked him as an academic, and laughed, giving the short bark
of scholarly insouciance. I automatically read the clues, knew
what was coming now, and mimed the words of the next two

sentences as he spoke them. 'Is that old theory still about? Disposed of it myself, years ago. Paper before the Geopsychological Society, back in '53.'

Luckily my confusion was covered by the bump of our landing. The Professor was impressed by the pilot's skill, and thought that the other passengers' applause arose from a similar cause. He had missed the irony, having only boarded the airliner at Frankfurt. All the way from South-East Asia we had had terrible moments whenever the kite took off or landed: shudderings, thumps, grinding noises. The economy-class passengers had even been issued with free glasses of Nigerian Riesling. And our morale had not been raised by the pilot's voice from the public-address system. 'This is your captain speaking. We shall be taking off momentarily, and the next point we hit will be the coast of . . .' English is a tricky language if you don't keep your wits about you.

Still, we were now in good old England once again. The Professor took my hand in his clammy one and pressed a card on me. It read, 'Professor Emeritus Xylophone Jaberish, M.A., PhD, FIGS: Founder-President, International Geopsychological Society, London.'

I soon found that I was neither geographically nor psychologically prepared for England; too much had taken place in my life since I last saw it.

A man in overalls caught my arm and said, first in English and then in Urdu, 'Get moving, don't block the gangway.'

That was more like it: recognition of my existence by the terrestrial element. I made my way, pushed by eager tourists, marching stolidly behind the skein of travellers, eventually to arrive at a desk.

Everyone was standing docilely in line. They did not relish my placing myself at the head of the queue: a habit I'd picked up abroad, where Devil-take-the-hindmost is more current, and I made my way to more congenial company at the back, amid cries of 'Cheek!' and 'I don't know what things are coming to, do you?' invariably addressed by someone to someone else who did not know what things were coming to, either.

I was wearing a large pair of aviator-style dark glasses and a wide-brimmed hat as I shuffled up to the official and offered my passport. He immediately asked me to remove them. Before I'd done that, he handed the passport back. I waited to be dismissed. He looked at me and said, '*Don't* hold everybody up, Sir: they haven't got all *day*, you know.' Consulting my watch, I noted that it was nearly midnight, and so I answered cheerily that nobody at all, himself included, had much of the day left, anyway.

I was sensitive enough to see that that, for some reason, did not please him either.

There had been no car on the tarmac to whisk me through, bypassing customs and immigration: but, of course, there hadn't been any visible tarmac. Now there was nobody to collect my bags from the carousel. I had been spoilt by the cosseting which I'd got used to on a world tour. I picked up the cases myself, to carry them past the Customs people. Then one of them stopped me.

'Let's be having you, then.'

Having me? Oh, yes; English for 'I'll deal with you now'.

I said 'Nothing to declare, Officer.'

'Then why are you going through the Red Channel?'

'I didn't even know that I was in a channel. How do I get into some other one?'

'You step over there, and go through the Green Channel.'

'How do you do that, actually? And how do you mean, "Channel"? It looks just like the way out: like nothing at all, just space.'

He looked at me wearily. 'I wouldn't try to be a comedian, Sir . . .'

'I'm not going to. I'm a writer, you see . . .'

His colleague was more helpful, if less perceptive. 'Let 'im go, Bert. 'E don' unnerstan' a werd 'v English, ass aw'.'

'Thank you', I said; 'And I shall commend you to your superior.' His only answer was directed towards his colleague. 'See worri mean, Bert?'

I passed through an open door and found myself in a larger hall, teeming with people. Again there was nobody to take charge of me, no camera flashlights, or gleaming teeth, not a single garlic breath. Only a sense of anti-climax, almost of loss.

Then, suddenly, I was through, and in vociferous demand, as several men, each claiming to be a special cheap taxi service, each looking less like a taximan than the last, descended upon me.

My mind went blank as I tottered to a seat, by the wall, followed by the taximen. I saw pictures: remembered the time when one of my relatives had stumbled off the aircraft into this very hall not so very long ago. I had been there to meet him, but he was still bemused by his nonchalant reception.

He had just arrived (those were happier times) from Kabul, via Moscow, by Aeroflot. I had sat with him near this very spot, to allow him to get his breath.

After a few minutes, his eyes had come into focus, and then I saw that they had a faraway look. 'Dear Idries', he said, shaking his head slowly from side to side, 'you should not believe what they say about the Russians. They are definitely improving.'

'How can your Eminence say such a thing?' I asked, incredulity overcoming my natural restraint.

'By the evidence of my own eyes. Do you know, when people arrive at Moscow Airport, they are met by the Chief of Protocol. There is a red carpet, an inspection of a Guard of Honour, a brass band. I know, for that is what happened to me.'

Even then, I had known which I preferred, the Muscovite show or the English insouciance. I stood up and shook off the pirate drivers, shouting, 'I have no money, and I am a heavily-armed international terrorist!' They melted away with gratifying dispatch.

My ears went back into action automatically, and I heard the two English women to my left chatting.

'I really felt bad, dear, when I heard him over the announcement system. It was a *Spanish* pilot, could tell that by his voice. I thought, "Dear me, I hope he doesn't crash the plane", know what I mean?'

A louder voice, this time from the right, jerked my head around. A Spanish woman was talking to her husband, in the rapid-fire manner of Madrid.

'Of course I was afraid, *querido*: it was my first flight. But, as soon as I heard the Spanish voice of the pilot from the loud-speaker, I knew that our brave boy would bring us safely through all perils.'

Someone was having me paged. Obeying the announcement, I went to the telephone. It was my personal assistant, S. K. Dehlavi, who had gone on ahead.

'Thank goodness you are all right. Everyone seems to be crazy here.'

'You're probably the crazy one, Dehlavi. Why didn't you meet me? I've been fighting off the weirdest taxi-drivers.'

'That's exactly what I mean. Taxi-drivers. I'm still in London, and it's the rush-hour. I couldn't get one to take me to Heathrow. The radio-cab dispatcher says they're all there already.'

'Wouldn't be surprised. But you must have been able to find *one*? You just hail them, off the street.'

'That was the crazy one.'

'What did he say?'

'He thought you were several people.'

'How could he? He'd never seen me.'

'He seemed all right at first. Then he said, "Who're you going to meet at the airport?"'

'I gave him your identity: "A Koreshite, a Sharif of the noblest lineage and a son of Sirdar Ali Shah, and a grandson of the Great Nawab of Sardhana, and a scion of the Jan Fishan Khan, Lord of Paghman . . ."'

'And then what? Cut it short, Dehlavi.'

'Then he told me to get out of the cab, saying, "I'm only licensed to carry four, and that's six of you already!"'

'How long have you been in England, Dehlavi?'

'Only a week.'

'I'm surprised you've survived that long.'

In the East, if not anywhere else, one can't answer one's employer back; though poetic quotations are permitted. Sultan Khan Dehlavi contented himself with:

> In the shop of the sightless jeweller
> The shell, the stone and ruby
> Are as one . . .

Somehow I got to London – by tube train. I just made the station safely. I had had a narrow escape when a truck came roaring out of a tunnel as I was trying to understand the words on a huge sign which said: 'Caution – Frequent Vehicular Emergence'.

Although the weather was fine and sunny, I knew I was back in England by the conversation of my neighbours on the train.

An eager, well-dressed American opposite wonderingly remarked to his wife that English people did not seem to give their national anthem the respect that a patriotic hymn surely deserved. Beside me was a man in a tweed suit and scuffed shoes, who identified himself as a Cambridge academic.

'I could not help overhearing you, Sir', he said, 'and can perhaps offer a solution to your problem.'

The American seemed a little surprised, '*My* praablam? Oh, well, okay, shoot . . .'

'You see,' said the Englishman, 'the tune to which the words of "God Save the Queen" are sung is the last but one survivor of the identical anthems formerly used by most of the Germanic principalities: 1793, Imperial Germany, 1811, Switzerland, 1850, Liechtenstein. It was brought over here from there; and Liechtenstein still uses it. I fancy you also got "My Country 'tis of Thee" from a similar source. Hardly English d'you see.'

The American fell silent. In his place I would have done the same. Not being in his place, I asked the scholar to continue my education in Englishry. 'Is there more about the National Anthem?' I asked.

'Matter of fact there is', he answered; 'and a great deal is revealed by textual, musicological and historical study.'

'Such as?'

'Such as, though the tune as we know it is credited to John Bull, organist at Antwerp, it may have been by Henry Casey, author of "Sally in our Alley".'

What was John Bull, the archetypical Englishman, doing in Antwerp? I couldn't help wondering. But I wanted to clarify exactly why people might not stand up, from respect, when the anthem was played.

'I suppose the younger generation spurn it from iconoclasm, rather than because of its connexion with Antwerp or the hymns of defunct German principalities', I said.

'Well, it's got a longer history than that, this attitude', he told me. 'You see, the opening words are said to have been suggested by the Catholic hymn *Domine Salvum*, which meant that many Protestants felt it was unsuitable for Anglicans.'

'I see', I said, 'It was thought subversive.'

But I was running ahead too fast. 'Not entirely', he said; 'because of the words

> "Confound their politics
> Frustrate their knavish tricks".'

'Yes', I said, 'some people have said that this couplet is too hostile to foreigners.'

'I hadn't finished', he said, looking at me over his horn-rims.
'Sorry.'

'That's all right. As I was saying, the bits about politics and
knavery are thought to have been put in after the Gunpowder
Plot. They are anti-Catholic, not really anti-foreign. Fawkes
was English, after all.'

'Has anyone ever made a public denunciation of the National
Anthem?'

He gave me a severe look. 'Perhaps you do not recall the
Dean of Worcester's informing *The Times* that he would not
allow the second verse to be sung. It was, and I think I have his
exact words,

> "Un-Christian, indecent, disgraceful anywhere, in a church
> blasphemous, and in a cathedral a brawling obscenity".'

The American had leant over me towards the English don,
listening intently, a bemused look on his face. Now the man of
learning extended his neck towards him. 'You, Sir – would you
like chapter and verse on that?'

The American took a deep breath. 'I'd rather have a Mac-
donald's with ketchup on it', he said.

I buried my face in a newspaper, the *Daily Mail*. One and a
half million copies circulation . . . An article by Andrew Alexander. 'I am not sure that the average Briton wants (or should
want) to be as prosperous as the average American with all that
involves in terms of dedication to work and career. And there is
a great deal in the American way of life which no sensible person
would want to import.' Quite so.

Well, I thought, if the National Anthem really meant nothing
– and people from most other countries would find this hard to
credit – there must be *something* that did. I would keep my eyes
and ears open.

One of the best places to find out how the English think is a
London club. I have never spent more than a hour or so in mine
without hearing – in the drawing room or around a dining-table
– something new, interesting or relevant to the topics of the day.
The afternoon of my arrival back, I was treating my jet-lag with
a cup of coffee when I became aware of a conversation between
some other Members settled in the circle of armchairs around
me.

One of them was showing the others a photograph which he

had taken in Egypt at the time of the Suez Episode, which is English for a war. It showed a graffito on a ruined wall: PALE HOUNDS, RETURN TO THINE ABODES! Some Egyptian patriot, weak in English demotic but evidently the owner of a dictionary, had been doing his stuff.

'Of course', said the retired General, 'in my time it was "Go Home, Dirty British!", you know.'

'Well,' said the ex-Governor, to my amazement, 'there's not much wrong about that.' As I pricked up my ears, he sauntered to the library and returned with a large book, for which the other Members, accustomed to this sort of thing, had been patiently waiting. The Governor announced:

'*Two Thousand Years of London*, by C. Whitaker-Wilson, London 1933. I read to you from page 61:

"Soap did not come into general use in England until as late as 1824 . . . the point is interesting as an example of a common and indispensible commodity being of comparatively recent development."'

There was a general murmur of approval at this information. 'Must say that my time in the Colonies was a little after 1824', was all that the General felt like adding, 'Aw, aw, aw!'

So, I learned, cleanliness had been next to godliness for only a century and a half, almost as recently as the adoption of the Union Flag. That explained, perhaps, the old saying I had seen in Tilley's *Dictionary of the Proverbs in England*: 'Wash your hands often, your feet seldom, and your head never.'

The small group of Members had moved off to the bar, leaving the book on the table. I picked it up, wondering idly whether further study would show that, say, football was a deprecated sport in this supposedly football-crazy country. As if in answer, the book fell open at page ninety-eight, which records that football was actually made illegal in England by Henry VIII, Elizabeth I and Edward II.

That night I had nightmares about being soapless for a thousand years. Of course, if I'd kept up my reading, I would have known since 1962 what Nancy Mitford had said, in *The Water-Bottle*: 'true cleanliness is considered rather immoral by my compatriots.'

Except that, two decades later, the English changed again. In mid-1985 it was revealed in a research report that, although no more than 15% of the inhabitants of the island bathe daily, the average person takes 4.5 baths or showers every week.

And this document comes hard on the heels of another one, which tells how the twenty million households in the United Kingdom boil 1,825 million unnecessary gallons of water a year – as a by-product of teamaking; so there is no bias against heating and using water, as such.

It is more likely that there is a resistance to Indian ways. Dr T. G. P. Spear, in *The Nabobs,* a learned monograph on The English in Eighteenth Century India, has traced the custom of having baths to 'the Indian method of ablution', which 'had most struck observers in the eighteenth century'. This English bathing business, Dr Spear observes, 'is quite modern'. The Englishman, too, says our learned Cambridge man, used to consider whisky 'no gentleman's drink' until his compatriots in India, taste influenced by the fiery native arrack, took to it.

2

Up-Country

The Vice, not the Man

We must defye and abhorre the vices, but not
the man.

Tyndale: *Enchiridion*

Centuries before I (or, I dare say, anyone else) had started to
take an interest in the matter, the Angles and Anglekins had
metamorphosed themselves into The English. They had de-
tached, mentally, but not romantically, from the Saxons, who
hovered in the back of their minds, like the Pharaohs in the
consciousness of today's Egyptians. This divorce was effected
almost as effortlessly as the earlier one, from the Schleswigians.
For centuries now, of course, their cousins, the Teutonic Tribes
across the Channel, have only meant foreigners, like any others.
Distance has something to do with it: in the eyes of Londoners,
and others in the south where the power lies, 'civilisation ends at
Watford'.

And Watford, or somewhat north of it, just beyond the capital's northern boundaries, is in Hertfordshire – part of the old
kingdoms of Mercia and the East Saxons. South of Watford is
civilisation: and, by implication, north of it is not quite as
English as one would like it to be (for surely civilisation, like
God, is English) even though the name of the vanished Angles
lingers there – in East Anglia, for instance.

I journeyed north one day, by Inter-City express, rashly to
fulfil that very English ritual, an appointment to lecture before
the members of a Literary and Scientific Society.

Many miles beyond Watford, I was glad to hear an official say

18

that we were still in the same country; there is always the risk, for a traveller here, that he may overshoot his objective, and find himself in Scotland: England may be anything else, but it is not large.

The unintended reassurance was contained in an exchange between another man in the compartment and a ticket-inspector. Upon being asked why the employees of the railway were proposing to strike, the British Rail man answered, without hesitation: 'And why not, Sir? This *is* England, you know'.

I do admit to having felt some curiosity. Did he mean 'England, as opposed to a totalitarian state, where striking was forbidden'? or 'England, where people went on strike all the time'? Unable to decide, from an inspection of their faces, which of the two men would be the better one to question on the point, I decided to remain silent. Even though my fellow-passenger had said, in an even voice, 'Oh, yes . . . England', and I suspected that he was hostile to the idea of a strike, I remembered, perhaps just in time, an experience in London: and held my tongue.

I had said to a learned-looking man who was gazing at the Greek inscription beneath a statue, 'Excuse me, Sir: are you a Greek scholar?'

His answer ('No! I am an Englishman') had taught me not to ask direct questions.

To a foreigner, I reflected, the English can seem odd when talking about their English ethnicity. Some of them realise it themselves. 'In 1701', says Michael Duffy in *The Listener*, 'Daniel Defoe enraged many of his countrymen by daring to point out, in his poem "The True-Born Englishman", that they were the product of interbreeding among half the peoples of Europe . . . The message was unwelcome to a people who gloried in their distinctive English nationality and achievement to an extent which outsiders found insufferably arrogant.'

That might have been the case in 1701 but, certainly in my experience, English people often revel in the title of mongrel. Their Englishness does not stem from any particular kind of blood. Did Defoe's revelations cause a change in emphasis, from stock to something more mystical?

Perhaps the inner Anglean popped up, three hundred years ago, to deal with this complication . . .

No complications attended my arrival in the town where I was scheduled to speak. It was late at night, but I found the Station Hotel, where I was booked in, easily enough; it was at the station.

The rugged-looking, very large lady on duty, patting the curlers in her hair, seemed surprised that anyone actually wanted to stay there. 'It'll be that Mr Arkwright that booked you in, that's what it'll be', she said, finally, as if solving a particularly unusual mystery. She brightened up a little, however, when she said that I was too late to get any food; the kitchen was closed.

Her emphases, perhaps because of my unfamiliarity with the local pronunciation, seemed to fall upon the words in such a way as to suggest that the kitchen was something which should have been closed long ago. The expression on her face, if it would not have stopped a bus, might well have slowed it down.

I went to my room: Number Nine, a figure which often causes hilarity here, because of its associations with a pill administered by army medical officers. The amusement arises because any mention of excretory functions, or even of underwear, guarantees an English comedian's reputation as excruciatingly funny.

Strangely, for a place where there was no food, the room smelt of boiled cabbage. Over the washstand in the corner hung a mournful sepia picture of a stag at bay. I felt too hungry to take out my notes, but when I opened my briefcase in the absurd hope that there might be a forgotten chocolate bar inside (I never ate chocolate) a piece of paper fell out.

I had copied out some words from Stephen Leacock's *My Discovery of England*: about his lecture tours here. At one place the previous speaker had been Lord Haldane, talking on Einstein's Theory of Relativity. Leacock had said to the chairman that surely a general audience could not understand such a subject. The reply was 'they didn't understand it, but they all enjoyed it'.

That had been in 1922. Had things changed in half a century? If not, I told myself, I was safe. In England, this record seemed to show, you did not have to be intelligible to be popular. Surely this news would hearten foreigners who read my book.

There was another extract, which I'd typed out from the Frenchman Paul Blouet's *John Bull and his Island*, published a century earlier, under the pseudonym of 'Max O'Rell'. It supported Leacock:

'When John has paid his guinea, he enjoys himself, even if he does not understand a word.' Money for old rope: who wouldn't be a lecturer in a country like this? Who *couldn't* be? But there was more, which I had copied out to hearten myself in the limbo between my normal quiet life and the unknown terrors of the lecture in the North:

Madame Modjeska, the Polish actress, had played several principal roles in London theatres. She was asked, said O'Rell, to perform in a large London drawing-room. 'Striking a tragic posture, she recited something in Polish. The host and guests were lost in admiration [but] Madame Modjeska had given them, as a recitation, the numerical adjectives from one to a hundred.' Not quite cricket, though.

I was still hungry, but a little less apprehensive. My nervousness was not from stage-fright: I had addressed plenty of meetings before; but because of the wording of the letter signed 'Hon Sec', which had confirmed the fixture. It said, 'We look forward to the pleasure of greeting you . . .'

Now, as part of my research, I had been reading the excellent book on English native customs by a Continental observer, Dr H. Taine. He was not only a Doctor of Civil Laws, but an Oxford one, which meant that he must surely know a good deal about the English. And there it was, in black and white, on page fifteen. The Hon Sec had written that he wanted the *pleasure* of greeting me, and so did all the Members of his society. Here, in plain words, Dr Taine spelt out exactly what that 'pleasure' really meant:

The temperament of the people, he says, is 'violent and combative.' And pleasure, the key word in the Hon Sec's letter? 'Pleasure is a brutish and bestial thing.' What form would this brutish and bestial greeting take? Only a foolhardy Afghan, surely, would have essayed a journey here after such a warning.

I was still hungry. My eyes moved to the sagging bed, the atrocious stains on the wallpaper, the brooding object, like a dog's bed, in a corner, the light from the street-lamps trying to struggle through the unwashed window-panes . . .

I jumped up, with a cry of alarm, at the sound of a fierce hammering on the door. Many years ago I was taught (in another connection, as the police say) to adopt an attack stance as the best preparation for defence. I sprang to the door and threw it open, contorting my face into the necessary scowl. Let the bestiality commence.

The lady from downstairs, a grubby powder-blue dressing-gown over her nightdress, stood there with her fists in the air, ready to continue drumming on the thin door-panels. Her expression was one of even greater disapproval than before. Something unusual had happened, I could tell that at a glance: and I was undoubtedly involved.

It had, and I was: there was Someone On The Telephone for me. For a moment I felt really guilty, almost afraid. After all, nobody knew that I was here, did they? I had left no address in London; so how could they have tracked me down?

The lady, raising her voice shrilly from its usual metallic bark, galvanised me from this condition with the words, 'Well, come on then, you dozy devil!'

I shouted my name into the instrument as I grabbed it, skidding to a halt at the bottom of three flights of stairs. 'Thank God!' answered an unfamiliar voice.

'Oh, it's all right', I said, 'I got here safely,' when the man identified himself as the Onn Sekk of the Society.

'*No, I don't mean that.* Twern't in doubt, that. What I mean is, I can hear you've got a strong enough voice.' Strong enough? Oh yes. The fear, the lack of food . . . 'Thank you. I'm not too hungry yet. I'll be all right.'

'*No, I don't mean that*, not that at all,' said the Onn Sekk. 'I mean to *fill* the hall with. Had a lot of people from the South, you know. Don't seem to raise more'n a whisper, most of them. I speak as I find.'

I deepened my fine baritone a little, and assured him that all would be well.

'Gradely', he said.

'No. *Shah*'; must get the name right. After all, I *was* the Lecturer.

'Gradely', he repeated firmly. 'Call for you at half-past ten tomorrow. Name of Arkwright.'

'Thank you and goodnight, Mr Gradely', I said, unnerved.

'That were Mr Arkwright', said the lady, now at my elbow.

'Yes, he told me that. But who is Gradely?'

'Gradely, you poop', she sniffed, 'means "nice".'

Back in my room I lay down on the bed and drifted into a half-sleep. Mr Arkwright hadn't seemed combative and brutish: well, not very. And the woman downstairs hadn't actually shown a violent side. But perhaps they used weapons: penknives.

I had just recalled a passage in James Morier's *Adventures of Hajji Baba of Ispahan*, where an expert on England is briefing the Hajji: and penknives are distinctly mentioned:

> 'But is there not a certain tribe of infidels called Ingliz?' said I, 'the most unaccountable people on earth, who live in an island, and make pen-knives?'
>
> 'Yes, truly,' said the katib, 'they, amongst the Franks, are those who for centuries have most rubbed their foreheads against the imperial threshold . . .'
>
> 'But what have you heard of their government?' said I. 'Is it not composed of something besides a king?'
>
> 'Yes', returned he, 'you have been rightly informed: but how can you and I understand the humours of such madmen? They have a Shah, 'tis true; but it is a farce to call him by that title . . . he does not dare to give the bastinado to one of his own viziers, be his fault what it may.'

Well, the ruler might have no power, but what of the people? They were sometimes friendly and sometimes not. In 1841 two Parsees, naval architects, spent two years in England, and wrote a book about it. They were very definite on this matter. They might do anything to you; be for or against you, nobody could predict which:

> What makes the public cheer a man in the streets of England one year; the self-same public, or mob as they are called, will hoot the same person for years after.

Thus the words of the respected followers of Zoroaster, Jehangeer Nowrojee and Hirjeebhoy Merwanjee, of Bombay.

Of course, I was not English or even Indian, so perhaps the rules might not apply to me. The Parsees had addressed their warning to their fellow-Indians: 'And here we would inform our countrymen', they had said; and I was not one of them. But would the English mob know that? The passage continued:

The majority of the lower orders in England are very rude in their manners and behaviour towards strangers, whom they do not like to see in their country.

There would be nothing for it but to avoid the lower orders or behave as if I were not any kind of a stranger. They might even cheer me this year, and prepare to hoot me later.

It did not help much to find a scrap of paper torn from *The Lincolnshire Echo*, stuffed into a crack in the wall. The only legible news-story read:

Cries for help from a man clad only in his underpants and stranded on an island in the middle of a gravel pit were ignored because householders thought it was an escaped peacock.

I spent the night in an uneasy half-asleep. Dreadfully cold under my one thin blanket, a phrase from an English list of proverbs went through my head again and again: 'Cold weather and crafty knaves come out of the North, 1659'.

In the morning a tall, mournful-looking, red-haired and ageing figure appeared at the door of my room. He had something in his hand, but it was not a penknife. He handed it to me. I took it and saw that it was a green-painted, light metal object, with black spots, quite small and in the shape of a turnip. I was inspecting it with interest admixed with uncertainty, when he said, 'Whistle. Got it from a cracker at Christmas. We use it for signalling operator when to change slides in projector.'

After warning me that the whistle was almost irreplaceable – the next Christmas was eight months ahead – Mr Arkwright led me down the stairs and then to an enormous motor-hearse parked nearby. 'No other transport,' he said. 'Taxis all on strike.'

As we climbed in and settled onto the wide seat beside the driver, obviously intended for the undertaker's mutes, I tried to assume a jovial expression and start a conversation.

'Just as well there is no taxi,' I said; 'after all, wasn't it Marcus Tullius Cicero (106–43 BC) who wrote about the hackney transport over here? He said, if I recall it correctly, "Beware, in Britain, that you are not swindled by the chariot-drivers." Over two thousand years ago!'

I glanced at the Hon Sec's face. My jest hadn't gone down as well as I had hoped it would with a man of culture: Mr Arkwright only frowned. I'd thought that it was rather neat: linking taxis, Britain, a foreign visitor and, of course, adding the international touch.

As we sped through the streets, and I saw, on alternate lamp-posts, a picture of me affixed, together with an appeal to attend my lecture, I had a strange sensation. Sitting there, in a *hearse*, looking at my own photograph, being carried towards some sort of judgment. And being mocked at the same time, by my likeness, endlessly repeated. The impression of peril was not reduced by the silent figure of Mr Arkwright, sitting beside me, gazing gloomily at my face as if weighing me up for some fell purpose . . .

Culture vultures to a man, the no-nonsense audience at the Literary and Scientific Society exercised to the full their evidently well established right to stop the lecture whenever they felt like it, to ask questions. Nobody betrayed feelings of approval or the reverse: each merely settling back in the hard chair with mouth set and eyes straight gazing, when I had stumbled out my answers to such searching queries as 'What's "conventional" mean?' followed by a short account of their own opinions on a variety of matters.

'They speak as they find', the chairman whispered to me after each question.

When I had finished, there was dead silence.

I had the uncanny feeling, not for the first time in England, that I was among a tribe in one of the more rural parts of Afghanistan. Indeed, I had felt just this atmosphere before, among some Pamir nomads. I had given them a harangue, at their request: and both parties had discovered at the same moment that our opinions about the hereafter were dramatically at variance.

By some strange coincidence, I have discovered that Eric Newby found an echo of the Pamirs and the nomads of Afghanistan during his peregrinations in the English outback. He even writes (in *Something Wholesale*) of the 'mocking quality' of this association.

I sat down, trying not to look at the sea of faces, eyes riveted upon me, just like those Pamirian nomads.

Then a distinguished-looking man, wearing a monocle, checked suit and spats, rose to his feet. He spoke for some fifteen or twenty minutes, hardly drawing a breath, giving a stunningly accurate and beautifully articulated summary of everything which I had said. Then he added comments on my photographic slides and some choice reminiscences of his own.

'That's t'Major,' said the chairman, 'we always let him have t'last word.' And so they should, I thought: with a man like that, why had they bothered to import someone from the South – from anywhere, come to that?

When he sat down, never mentioning me, there was a storm of applause, in which I joined wholeheartedly.

As I left, my fee, mostly in small coins, jingling in an old plastic bag smelling of fish, and abstracted from the admission money, was handed me by the military man. I congratulated him on his ovation, and said, 'Why not give the lectures yourself? You're twice as good as anyone I've ever heard on the lecture circuit.'

He had a sense of humour. 'As for the clapping,' he said, 'you may care to read this, from David Yallop's *In God's Name*.' He had taken a dog-eared photocopy of the page from his wallet. Circled in violet ink were the words:

> The massive [Italian] crowds broke into loud and sustained applause. The Latin counterpart of Anglo-Saxon silence.

'Been through the Italian campaign meself', said the Major; 'decided to show the lecturers that. They never get any recognition up here, you know. People in the north don't like to encourage southerners, but they'll always give a local lad a bit of a hand. Of course, lecturers usually aren't much good. Speak as I find.'

I was quite touched. 'That's very nice of you', I said, though still a bit confused, 'but how about *you* giving the lectures, as I suggested?' I repeated that I thought he was a star performer.

'I know that', he said, graciously, 'but this society has an endowment; we have to spend the money somehow; in the rules, you know. Members like me are not allowed to have any of it, so we engage lecturers.'

'But you didn't pay me out of capital,' I said, holding up my fish-bag, 'I got these coins from the gate-money.'

'Ah, well, wouldn't do to break into our capital, would it? We're hard-headed realists up here in the North, you know.'

'Oh, yes, of course.' Perhaps I could puzzle that one out on the return journey . . .

I asked Mr Arkwright on the way back to the hotel in the hearse why they already had taken down my portraits from the lamp-posts.

'Lecture's over, pictures might do for another time. Leave them there and they'd get tattered in wind and rain', he told me, briefly.

In the entrance hall of the hotel the lady in charge sniffed.

'*Major* knew all about it, I suppose?' she asked. 'Always does. Now don't go complaining to me. They always do, you know. Lecturers.' The way she said the last word would have got her the part of Lady Macbeth at a Royal Shakespeare Company audition, against the stiffest opposition.

She refused to be paid in coins out of my bag of loot. 'Credit card'll do gradely,' she said.

She handed me a giant beef-dripping sandwich with sudden and surprising grace, like a dowager awarding a prize at a flower-show. I took it with a courtly bow as I toiled upstairs to pack. 'Buttie', she said.

'Gradely', I replied. 'Speak as I find.'

Something about the nature of the succession of events which I had just experienced sent my mind ranging into the past. As I settled down in the train, trying to make sense of life in England through its people's behaviour, I remembered a scene from many years before. In training as my father's secretary, I was with him in Ankara, drinking in the words of a grizzled, powerful-looking man whom everyone treated with awe.

Kamal Pasha Atatürk, the man who saved Turkey from anarchy after the first world war, glowered under bushy eyebrows, smoked furiously and gulped cup after cup of thick black coffee. Nearby sat Ismet Inönü, another great general and Kamal's close friend, later to become President of the Republic.

Atatürk, Father of the Turks, was speaking about the English.

'People say that the English are mad. But the best way to win and control an empire is to be thought mad. Has that ever occurred to you? Especially if you are not really mad. People humour the insane, and, before long, find themselves obeying them. In many countries, Turkey included, there is even more of a bonus. People here imagine that the insane are divinely blessed . . .' Gradely, Kamal Atatürk.

Certainly my London landlady thought *me* mad. Before I got home, she had had a message from the Hon Sec. 'He wants to know what you've done with the green spotted turnip that you were blowing through during your lecture', she said, suspiciously.

'Oh, yes', I said. 'That would be the one he got out of a cracker.'

'Crackers is right', she muttered, as she went off to her quarters, slamming the door.

These foreigners are all the same, you know.

3

The Natives are Restless

Free or Unfree?

It is the freedom to think which has made such excellent books blossom forth amongst the English.

Voltaire: *Reflections for Fools*

This soul's prison we call England.

George Bernard Shaw: *Heartbreak House*

His name was Isa bin Abdullah al Nasrani and that was the cause of trouble. People who know the Middle East will immediately divine that he was a Christian: 'Jesus, son of the Servant of God, a Nazarene' is, after all, what his name means. But, in England, he was tired of being treated like an infidel, or asked how many wives he had, where he had left his camel, and whether he was a real sheik.

Isa was from Lebanon, and proud of it: nothing wrong with that, but whenever he visited England the natives became restless because he was giving off the wrong signals. So, informed (or misinformed) that I was an expert, he came to me.

I quizzed him sternly. 'Do you touch people when talking to them? Do you eat garlic? Laugh immoderately or not at all? Look straight into peoples' eyes? Still wear winklepicker shoes or wide-bottomed trousers?' But, however much I probed, his answers were always No.

True, he was small and of Phoenician appearance; but so are many Cornishmen, as I assured him. He spoke English tolerably well, and people hearing him talk sometimes said things like

'Don't tell me – I know – you're from Derbyshire!' So that was all right.

In the end we decided that his cover was so regularly blown in England because he lacked the magic symbols which prevent people from digging deeper. When people said, for instance, 'Where do you come from?' he recoiled from saying, 'I've been in jail', as many English people would do, by way of jocular reproof at such inquisitiveness. And, of course, if asked his name, that only started the usual questions.

He had, in a word, no status in the eyes of the local tribe.

Very well, there was only one thing, or only one long string of things, to be done. Isa had to make a number of complete changes: nationality, name, appearance, qualifications, the lot.

He bought appropriate clothes at Horne Brothers and eschewed day-glo bow ties. That part of it was not easy for him, because these ties were the latest thing in Beirut at the time. Now for the more difficult stuff. He moved from Kensington, because too many Arabs live there, and shunned Bayswater and St John's Wood for similar reasons. He took a small flat in Plumstead. Solid, unfashionable, English.

A week or two later he came back to me. 'My friend, I need your help. Come with me to the lawyer who is collecting information for my official Anglification.'

Although I remembered the wise Afghan saying, 'A mouse-pelt will never cover a drum', (how could I help with official matters?) I went with him, to give moral support.

The lawyer (at £100 an hour) was Mr Simon Ap-Starman, in a good way of business near one of the Inns of Court, and highly recommended for this kind of thing.

When we were seated in his panelled office, he explained that it would be a good idea if Mr Nasrani were to apply for British Nationality as a Citizen of the United Kingdom and Colonies under the Nationality Acts: which he then read out in considerable detail. I am sure that, though he must have known the word filibustering, as an honourable man he did not have one eye on the clock.

'Of course', he said, after looking with approval at Nasrani's English clothes, 'it is not easy. I suggest that you do all you can to accumulate, shall we say, superficial plausibility.'

'Which means?' Nasrani was eager and, although rich, not unaware of that meter ticking.

'Far be it for me to suggest that appearances are everything, or, indeed, anything, in the eyes of officials in this country' said Mr Ap-Starman – though it took him longer to say it than it does to read – 'let alone those at the Home Office. But we can't be too careful'.

He suggested, in short, that Mr Nasrani might, after this little preliminary talk (thank you, that will be two hundred pounds, in cash) go away and collect supporting facts which might, after appropriate verification by Mr Ap-Starman, help to fill out his dossier for the Home Office.

So we did. By that I mean, Nasrani did. He spent the next few weeks reading the newspapers and talking to all the English people of repute whom he could find, to see what characteristics 'and other items' they had which he might acquire. One or two other Lebanese, some of them wise in these matters, chipped in with ideas at many a brainstorming session at their favourite restaurant.

Finally, I was once more called in to advise. Some of the ideas were unfamiliar, others downright potty.

'Now', said Nasrani, as we devoured halwa at the counter of the Phoeneciarama Kebab Takeaway, 'now, tell me how to buy an Oxford University Master of Arts degree.'

'Non-starter', I told him.

'But it is true that the MA is sold by Oxford, for a sum of money? In the Lebanon, an Oxford MA is something. It must be something, too, in England. I paid a man from Sidon a large sum for the information that you simply *buy* the degree. Do you deny that it is bought and sold?'

'Yes and no, Nasrani.'

'How can you have Yes *and* No?'

'You can in England. You see, Oxford University does bestow the MA, with little or no formality, on people for money . . .'

'Haa!'

'But only if they already have the Oxford BA, Bachelor of Arts, degree.'

'Ridiculous!' he hissed. But when I insisted that this was a fact, he accepted it with eastern fatalism. 'Very well, I shall get the BA after my naturalisation. It will help me to pass among the masses.'

'Not just among the masses', I assured him. 'But what else do you want to check out?'

Nasrani looked at his notes. 'I have to change my name.'

'Nothing easier', I said. 'What, or who, would you like to be?'

'I would like to be John Smith.'

'Too obvious', I said; 'all burglars give that name to the police, and it is often used for dubious purposes when registering at hotels.'

'I am not a burglar and do not intend to stay at hotels', he shouted; but I skilfully interrupted him with a Middle Eastern gesture which means 'You never know your fate', and he subsided.

'In any case', I continued, 'In England you can change your name by deed poll, but you can't change the part they call your Christian name, by law.'

'*Christian* name? All my name is Christian! I am a Member in good standing of the United True Catholic-Essentialists.'

'I mean your forename.'

'Why?'

'I'm not quite sure, but someone once told me that it is something to do with baptism. The name was given in a religious ceremony, and so it's sort of holy: you can't put it asunder, type of thing.'

'You are not joking with me?'

'No, Nasrani, honest.'

'Then these English are pagans at heart. To treat me, a Christian, thus . . .'

'Never mind', I said, hastily, because I thought that Near Eastern sectarianism would not help his cause one whit, 'you are a Christian, and "Isa" isn't too bad. People will think it is like "Asa", which they do use here. Just don't translate it, that's all.'

'Not translate it? That would be blasphemy! Why, I've got a good friend called Jesu Cristo . . .'

'I am sure you have, but he must be Spanish, or Latin American. They don't use that name here, think what you like about it.'

It was time to bring up what the English call heavy guns: documentation. Sometimes they call it chapter-and-verse. 'There is an English writer', I told Nasrani, 'called A. G. Gardiner. He was a great expert on England, and wrote a valuable

book called *Prophets, Priests and Kings*. In it there is a cautionary tale about how you can actually be ruined in England by
having the wrong kind of name.'

Nasrani leant forward. 'I must know this, and at once', he
muttered.

'I am trying to tell you. In fact, I shall give you the full,
authoritative text.' I took him back to my place and read the
passage out to him:

> '"When Mr A. C. Morton rose upon the firmament in Parlia-
> ment, he seemed to have a prosperous future before him.
> But one day a malevolent pressman in the Gallery dis-
> covered that 'A. C.' stood for Alpheus Cleophas. He pub-
> lished the fact to the world, and Mr Morton never recovered
> from the blow. He vanished in derisive laughter. His fate was
> sealed at the font."'

Nasrani let out a long sigh of relief. 'I understand. But I have
collected better names from reputable sources, and may adopt
one of those. How about "Bartholomew-Cholmondeley"?
Nigel Bartholomew-Cholmondeley is the hero of a very English
novel I bought recently.'

'Subject to two things', I said, relishing my role as adviser now
that something I really knew about had come up.

'And they are?' He looked at me like Hercule Poirot.

'They are, first, you must be able to pronounce it properly,
otherwise you'll be rumbled for sure.'

I paused. 'You write it "Cholmondeley", but you must always
pronounce it *Chumly*, or better still, *Chumm-ly*. You know the
sort of thing: just as "Featherstonehaugh" is always to be pronounced "Fanshaw".'

He practised it several times, and nodded, with pleasure. 'It
sounds good. Very English. "Chum" means "Friend", of
course; though in Turkish "Chumly" would mean "The Man
From Chumm".'

'Be that as it may', I told him, 'there is a further problem.'

'And that is the Bartholomew: you pronounce that *Byu*, I
suppose?'

'No, you do not. You pronounce it Bartholomew. Bartholo-
mew-Chumm-ly. I was about to speak of the hyphen.'

'But the hyphen is very aristocratic.'

'As a matter of fact, it is not. I have researched this', I said primly (because I had) 'and you have to be careful with hyphens.'

I then gave him a rundown on the matter, stressing that the origin of some hyphenated names in England was when the father of an heiress, having no male issue, had demanded that some (possibly fortune-hunting) would-be husband couple his surname with hers as a condition of agreeing to the marriage.

'The result is', I continued, 'that lots of people, especially those in the upper class who lack hyphens, look down on the hyphenated ones as johnnies-come-lately. Indeed, Tim Heald's *Networks* lists, in 1983, 500 surnames of the major families of England and Wales, showing that only 24 of the names – less than five per cent – are hyphenated. That means that you would, if hyphenated, have to confine yourself to certain sections of the community. You'd have to shun the upper class and aristocracy like the plague, Chumley.'

He thought he understood, or he said that he thought that he understood, so we left that matter. Now he had a name and might get a degree. 'Next question?'

'I'd like an English title.'

'You can't have one.'

'But I *want* one!'

'Too difficult.'

'All right, then,' he said sulkily, 'I'll have a foreign one.'

'I don't know about that', I said, guardedly.

But Isa knew better: he'd made enquiries, and that was how we found ourselves in the office of a certain title-broker not a hundred miles from Piccadilly.

Naturally, I had prepared Isa for various eventualities by making him memorise an appropriate quotation. It was from Ralph Waldo Emerson's *English Traits*:

> Everything English is a fusion of distant and antagonistic elements . . . Nothing can be praised in it without damning exceptions; and nothing denounced without salvoes of cordial praise.

Even if we were to negotiate for a foreign title, we would have to deal with an Englishman in the matter. A Norman-descended one, of course.

4

It's Those Damned Drums Again, Isa

What a Title Can Do

English people may be rank-conscious, but
most of them simply do not understand titles.
Someone took advantage of this to get a dig at
Lampson, the British Ambassador in Cairo,
whom nobody liked. Lampson had just
become Lord Killearn, and a colleague introduced an English lady to him under his new
title, guessing what would happen. Sure
enough, she gushed, 'How wonderful to have
you here, Lord Killearn! Thank goodness
they've got rid of that dreadful man Lampson
. . .'

Sir William Frazer-Tytler,
British Minister in Kabul.

As we made our way to the glass and concrete building, of the
kind called Prestige-Designed, where the title-broker had his
office, I couldn't help reflecting on the ironies of fate and the
peculiarities of man. Isa bin Abdullah wanted a handle to his
name. Yet, only a month before, an Afghan prince had arrived
on my doorstep waving a passport which described him only as
'Mister'. Kissing it in ecstasy he had cried, 'Free at last! Hotels
will not overcharge me now! People will leave me alone. O,
Blessed Mister!'

And there had been the time when, being interviewed in
London as the prospective lessee of a house, I had been asked
whether I knew anyone with a title. 'The Trustees, you see,

35

might be favourably inclined towards someone who could find referees of some consequence, say a lord or two, something of that sort.'

(That, in turn, reminded me of the time when a detective had come to question me about a missing parcel, supposedly delivered to my address. I had written a letter stating that it had never been received. The police officer had said, 'We have had a letter from a nob, the Sayed Idries Shah, saying that he hasn't seen it. Well, that lets *him* out. Now what about you?')

To hell with the Trustees, and with the lovely house that I had set my heart on, I thought, as my attention came back to the agent, who was saying, 'Well?'

'The only titled people I know in this country,' I snapped, 'would sign anything for a fiver. Is that what your Trustees want?'

He smiled as he showed me to the door. Had I won or lost?

Two days later I got his letter. I had been granted the lease . . .

And now I was edging into the world of titles again.

A title-broker, according to the man in the plush office where we now sat, was someone who brought 'unwanted titles and title-wanters together for mutual satisfaction'. If I had been inclined to wince at the way in which this was put, I was quickly reassured by the aspect and manner of the tall, distinguished and wholesome-looking man who sat facing Abdullah and me, at an undoubtedly authentic antique oaken desk. His greying hair was neatly brushed, his jowls a trifle full from good eating. His patrician forehead was unlined, and his horn-rimmed glasses sat upon his prominent nose with just the right assurance.

His name was Walter de Blanchemaine FitzGilbert: it said so on his visiting-card.

'I have been trying to buy the degree of MA', said Abdullah, 'but my friend Shah here says that it is not possible.' He indicated me with a wave of his podgy hand, which made my hair bristle even more than did the words. I could not let him get away with that.

'If I may interrupt you, Mr Abdullah', I said, 'I must remind you that I am an Easterner too. Your attempt at disparagement, implying that this gentleman can somehow outdo me, is a familiar gambit in the Levant: it will not work here.'

FitzGilbert held up his hands, palms towards us.

'Now, come, come, gentlemen,' he said, in a suitably deep, rich voice, 'this will not do. First, let us dispose of the academic titles part, and then we can get onto the interesting bits. You are both right. You can buy some degrees, but not all. There is no law in England, either, preventing you from using an MA obtained from a "degree mill", usually run by a man with an accommodation address, who just grinds them out. But such a piece of paper will cost you anything from £50 to £500, and will not be worth any more, than if you had had it printed yourself: which would cost, at most, about £5.'

'Then perhaps I could become a professor?' asked the Beirutian, still, for some reason (probably the desire for respectability or the powerful influence of the prestigeful American University of Beirut) pushing the academic idea.

'Professor', said Mr FitzGilbert, 'is a title which is at a strange point in its career. Two world wars have wreaked havoc. Formerly everyone was intimidated by German professors, but then everything German fell into disrepute, and with it professors – up to a point.'

He paused, and looked at the ceiling. 'So, in Anglo-Saxon countries, professors have almost become figures of fun. Seaside Punch and Judy shows are traditionally operated by "professors". In Latin countries, of course, "professor" simply means a schoolteacher, or a teacher of anything: and you know what status such people have.'

In spite of myself, and feeling that the slumping figure of Isa bin Abdullah needed some support, I chimed in.

'I say, I've been a professor myself. I flew from England to give my lectures, and I was on the front page of a newspaper, with a photograph, with the headline, "Professor Commutes to Geneva".'

Hardly had I had time to shoot him a look of triumph when he trumped me. 'Yes, exactly; you see what I mean, don't you?' He shot his cuffs. 'Most people in positions of power or authority in this country never attended any university; that's what foreigners can't understand. Continentals and under-developed people almost worship higher education. It's only useful, on the whole, for scientists and civil servants here: and they don't have the highest ranking. Did Shakespeare, Churchill or our own dear Queen ever go to a university, or become professors?'

FitzGilbert was warming to what was evidently a favourite theme. 'Why should anyone want to be a professor? Professors usually study what people – Milton, Napoleon, Sir Isaac Newton – said who never went near a university, let alone becoming professors. Have you never heard the remark, "He was intelligent enough to get into a university, but not intelligent enough to see that it was a waste of time"?'

He went on, 'If you gentlemen want to know how the English feel about professors, I may refer you to the "humbug" lines of Dean Mansell:

'"With a ceaseless Bug, Bug, Bug, and endless
    Hum, Hum, Hum,
Behold the great professors come!
Professors we
From over the sea
From the land where Professors in plenty be."

'And you may care to see this news item, which is quite recent.'

He opened a drawer in the desk and took out a bunch of cuttings. The one he selected, and gave us a photocopy each, was marked '*The Guardian*, 17 May 1977, p. 1, col. 1'. It said

PROFESSORS EARN LESS THAN STUDENTS
THEY TEACH:

Professors at Britain's leading music colleges receive lower rates of pay than their students charge when giving private lessons to eke out their grants.

Isa and I looked at one another aghast. 'You mean that they half learn something and then teach it *at a profit*?' I stumbled out. '*And* earn more than their professors in the process?'

'Hole in one,' said FitzGilbert: 'of course, it is traditional that all kinds of mere musicians are called Professor: you know the kind of thing – "Take it away, Professor!"'

I thought he was exaggerating, and made a mental note to check this out.

Later I looked up its possibilities in my trusty *Chambers's:*

Professor . . . assumed often by mountebanks, quacks, dancing-masters, &c.

But that was later. Now, Isa – in his frustration at the strange

atmosphere where no bargaining seemed possible, jumped up.
'What do you mean, "mere musicians"? I'll have you know that
I am a registered patron of the Eastern Mediterranean Song and
Dance League . . .'

'It may be all right where you come from,' said Mr Fitz-
Gilbert, 'but we English are not all that sold on music, actually.
Quite a minority interest over here. Of course, the Continentals
think music important, so they berate us for not bothering too
much about it.' Isa looked sullen. I, on the other hand, smelt a
piece of information for my researches into the English. I said,
'Have you a reference to cover that?'

'I'm a bit of an admirer of Heinrich Heine, you know', Fitz-
Gilbert said, 'and you'll find these words in his works; always
remembered them, must be twenty years now:

> "These people have no ear, either for rhythm or music, and
> their unnatural passion for pianoforte playing and singing is
> thus all the more repulsive. There is nothing on earth more
> terrible than English music, except English painting."'

FitzGilbert gave us the faint but positive look of triumph you
see on the face of the Englishman who has prevailed. 'All right',
said Isa, 'let's get on to the interesting bit you were talking
about.'

The title-broker smiled. 'That's better. Now, first of all you
must understand that continental titles are generally considered
more valid than English ones: elsewhere than in the British-
influenced world, that is. That's only abroad, so it does not
count much. There are good reasons for this. Titles such as
Baronet were actually invented here as a means of raising
money by King James in 1611, and that devalued titles a great
deal. Second, people have been ennobled for all kinds of things,
like giving money to political parties. The honours here do not
have the genealogical continuity of European ones.'

'I knew that', I told him, still feeling sour about the professor
business, 'because, in our part of the world, the authorities who
interest themselves in such things point out that both British *and*
Continental titles are very junior, in their estimation, to the
Eastern ones.'

He did not like that; I'd overdone it, and he glared at me.
'Only quoting', I said hurriedly.

'Quite. Well, now, if you want an English title, it will take a great deal of time and effort and so on. Continental ones are better organised. I can offer the following:

Dukedom,   £250,000
Marquisate, £100,000
Barony,   £10,000.'

He had it by heart, and looked at us, now beaming, like a man who has brought good news.

Isa whispered to me, 'Those are only his negotiating prices. I'm sure we can do better.'

I said, 'Tell us a little more and we'll think it over, and come back to you on this one.'

The use, like that of the phrase 'this one', in England always means a delay, but leaves the door open: as in 'I'll have to see the Managing Director about this one'. And 'think it over' means that the sales-pitch has not worked.

The broker was still affable. 'Yes, do so by all means, but remember, they come and go. In fact there is only one ducal title on the books at the moment, and it may sell at any time. Dukedom of Almendra Dulce, in fact, very old. But I'll give you an idea of how it works.'

How it worked, was a revelation to me.

Many Continental titles, FitzGilbert told us, can pass down only to legal heirs. But a legal heir includes an adopted son.

'Find a penniless duke or whatever, have him adopt you legally, no matter your age, and presto!' was how Mr FitzGilbert put it.

'And I get into the *Almanach de Gotha*?' – Isa had done his homework: up to a point. I decided not to complicate matters by airing my knowledge that the *Almanach*, though authoritative, was not comprehensive. You can be out of it and still titled. It did not list the Spanish nobility, and ceased publication during the Second World War . . .

'I guarantee it.'

'But', I asked, still trying to recover after the recent snub, 'how can people respect someone who has simply been *adopted*, and is not of the blood of the noble duke, or whatever?'

FitzGilbert gave me a pitying smile. 'Would you, Sir, dare to suggest that a man of rank would actually adopt anyone whom he did not feel to be worthy to inherit his title? Or, better put,

would you dare to suggest such a thing, and imperil the whole
structure of Western nobility?'

'No, I suppose not', I had to admit.

'I'll just jot down those prices – I mean honoraria', he said,
and pushed a piece of paper over to us.

'I would have liked an *English* title', Isa said.

FitzGilbert frowned. Instantly I recalled a passage in Herr
Kurt von Stutterheim's *Those English!*, in which he deals with
an Englishman's change of mood if affability does not have the
desired effect. If 'he sees that all his blandishments are failing'
says this otherwise admiring Teuton, 'the polite and kindly
Englishman is capable of becoming in the twinkling of an eye
one of the harshest people imaginable.'

Von Stutterheim had spent fifteen years in England studying
the natives. It was evidently one of his really tough customers
with whom he had to deal today. Something harsh was coming
up.

'Look,' said FitzGilbert, sitting bolt upright and fixing Isa
with a basilisk stare, 'you're not exactly first eleven, are you, old
son?'

'First eleven?'

'Yes . . . you're, well, foreign, aren't you, yourself? Let's face
it.'

Now Isa produced his googly, clearly designed to skittle both
me and FitzGilbert. 'People keep saying things like "you
shouldn't have a double-barrelled name," and "you shouldn't
have a foreign name." Very well: how about Prince Philip? I
have cuttings from the English papers which call him "formerly
surnamed Schleswig-Holstein-Sonderburg-Glucksburg."'

I said, 'Schleswig-Holstein is a magic word in Britain. It is the
Angles' ancestral land. Look it up in any book. It crops up all the
time.'

FitzGilbert nodded. 'And', I continued, 'only *some* hyphenated names are shotgun ones.'

The title-broker smiled. 'As for the Sonderburg-Glucksburg
part,' he intoned, 'that's subsidiary. Philip changed his name to
Mountbatten, a direct translation from Battenburg; *and* you'd
better not feel that you know better than royalty, old lad.'

Yes, I said to myself, he's English all right: got an answer to
everything. I wonder what he changed *his* name from? . . .

Isa was trying to fight back. 'I don't just want to be British, I want to be *English*. In our country, of course, *Britani* isn't disliked so much as *Inglizi*, but "in for a penny and you can run with the hares and hounds", as you say over here.'

FitzGilbert winced. 'Nobody can *become* English. You have to be born here for that. Get that straight right away,' he said.

The Lebanese winked and touched the side of his nose with his forefinger. 'Mediterranean or Central Europe born no good, eh?' He was smiling, and I sensed that he had got FitzGilbert onto the killing-ground. I knew that look from many a Levantine game of chess.

'That's right.'

'So,' said Isa triumphantly, 'Prince Philip, born in Corfu, Greece, as your gossip-columns keep telling us, is not English? All the Members of the House of Lords who are German immigrants are not English? I, Isa bin Abdullah al-Nasrani, cannot become English?'

FitzGilbert capitulated. 'All right, then. You can. But that has nothing to do with titles.'

Isa dug me in the ribs, delightedly. 'Did you hear that?'

'Best of British luck to you', was all I could think of, at such short notice.

Isa was in a good mood: he tipped the liftman as we left, having kissed the reluctant hand of FitzGilbert's receptionist.

'Yes, I think I'll have one of those' murmured Isa bin Abdullah as we passed through the simulated-marble entrance hall on our way to the street.

I felt a drumming in my head. FitzGilbert was an Englishman, and we were in England. So our experiences would be a valid part of my book. But buying a title? It was positively unEnglish. After all, you could not even buy English baronetcies any more. Was Isa going about things in the right way? Do the English approve of short-cuts? The drumming got louder.

'It's those damned drums, Isa', I gasped; 'soon the natives will be restless.' But he was not listening. He was repeating to himself, 'His Grace Mister Isa Bartholomew-Cholmondeley, Duke of Almendra Dulce . . .'

I just didn't have the heart to tell him how another foreigner, with far greater chances than his, had been driven to distraction by English ways and had felt himself compelled to fall back on one of his German titles. A monarch, no less.

But I rang up FitzGilbert and told him. The tale concerns King George III, who heard that a certain English gentleman would not take an oath of allegiance to him or even allow him to be named as king in his presence. After all, such people as James Hogg had composed ditties which were sung in the streets. This one, though in Anglo-Saxon Scottish, was much quoted by English people in George III's time:

> Wha the deil hae we goten for a King
> But a wee German lairdie?
> And when we gade to bring him hame
> He was delving in his kale-yardie.

The German king of the English had, however, absorbed at least something of the mentality of his new people. He had soon learned how to give back-handed compliments. He said, 'Carry my compliments to him, and say that I respect his steadiness of principles; or, as he may not receive my compliments as king of England, present them as those of the Elector of Hanover'.

FitzGilbert delighted, asked for the name of a book where this anecdote was to be found and the page number. Then he said, 'Love it! This should help shift a Jerry title or two'.

He was so pleased that I shared a new piece of information with him. I had found it in the *Oxford Dictionary of English Christian Names*:

'It is, indeed, by no means clear what [in England] a man's name legally is, whether there is such a thing as a legal name'. He found that very interesting . . .

As the Afghans say, 'An owl is known by its hoot, and a wolf by its howl'.

Isa went away and thought over the question of names, titles and Anglification, thanking me for my trouble. Three months later I received an invitation to a party from a baron. As I shook my host's hand I asked, 'How did you do it, Isa?'

'Quite easy, really,' said Abdullah; 'I discovered that there is no obstacle to your changing your name to "Baron" in this country – so I did it by deed-poll. Much cheaper than that dreadful lawyer and the de Gilbert or whoever he was, the title-broker.'

'Baron Isa', I said, 'yes, it sounds good. But "Isa Baron Fordham-Leyton" – what made you choose that name?'

'Easy enough when you know how', he grinned. 'I went to the library and found a reliable book, from Oxford; they must know what they are talking about. It is called *The Oxford Dictionary of English Proverbs*, and I found this in it, on page 280 in case you feel tempted to Anglify:

> '"In 'ford' in 'ham' in 'ley' and 'ton'
> the most of English surnames run"'.

'So I just ran them together: Ford/ham-ley/ton. It is simple, my friend, as the English say, when you know how.'

5

Sloonjin Summf

Minds like Ours

Minds like ours, my dear James, must always
be above national prejudices . . . as a people,
the English are very little indeed inferior to
the Scotch.

John Wilson, *Noctes*

I was sitting quietly, after a long walk, on a bench near the
Spaniard's Inn in Hampstead, linked by legend with Dick Tur-
pin the highwayman: one of the greatest of those armed gentlemen of the road whom my Afghan readers will recognise as a
typical Pashtun *Qati at-Tariq*. It was a beautiful summer's day,
and I wondered why the two men lurching towards me should be
arguing so fiercely, pulling one another about.

Finally they came and sat down on the wooden seat, still in
discord. The tall, craggy one was shouting.

'Did ye no' see tha' fillum? The one where the British sojer is
being spoken to bi tha' Jairman officer?' The Scotsman's voice
was hoarse and menacing.

'Ner, ain't never seen that.' The Cockney's voice was just as
loud.

'Well, laddie, the Jairman, fingerin' his wee pistol, shouts,
"Silence, English swine!" And the sojer, a wee little horn-
iegollach of a mon, looks him straight in the eye and hollers:
"*Scottish* swine, if ye please!" That's the kind of people we are,
ye Sassenach neep-eater!'

I had read that, by the letter of the law, it was still illegal to
wear the kilt in England, and that the Scots and English were

always at odds. Doctor Samuel Johnson was on record as saying that 'the noblest prospect which a Scotchman ever sees is the high road that leads to England.' The Cockney had an even sharper comment to make. He had pulled a cut-throat razor from his top pocket, and his hand was inching forwards towards the Scotsman's throat with it . . .

I, in the meantime, had taken out a notebook and was carefully recording the anecdote about the Scottish swine. Then I saw that both the Scot and the Englishman had stopped menacing one another and were gazing, suspiciously, at the pen in my hand. In each of their homelands there are certain circles where taking notes is one of the most inappropriate things that a man can do: unless he wants to advertise himself as a copper or a nark.

They had obviously been celebrating, before the breakdown in international relations, for the smell of whisky was very strong.

The huge Scot was the first to act. With a hoarse 'All thrawpol ye!' he scooped me up from the bench and threw me to the dusty ground. We sprawled there, struggling, while the northerner adjusted his great hands around my throat, with some artistry, preparing to squeeze when he had them set just right.

This was it, I thought. This was how I was going to die: I had often wondered about that, and now I knew. I knew how, and where. But why? Because I had been writing in a notebook; how very unexpected. Still as our Eastern sage Saadi had it, 'Life hangs on a single breath, and the world of existence is between two non-existences' . . .

As his fingers started, slowly, to tighten on my adam's apple, the big red face with its ginger stubble came closer and closer. From his twisted mouth came a long howl. It sounded like 'Ye Afghanistanian sloonjin summf.'

Afghanistanian? As I took that in, something in me, by-passing my reasoning faculty, made me laugh. I gasped, giggled, and finally roared until I thought my lungs would burst.

The Scotsman shook his head as if to clear it, and picked me up by the throat until I stood erect. Then he let go and I fell down again, still sobbing with laughter.

He bent down with a puzzled look on his face, and I nearly passed out from the fumes of his breath.

'Ye should be greetin' and no' laughin', ye stopid krittur' he roared. Then, baring his broken yellow teeth, he demanded to know what the joke was.

'It's nothing, really,' I gasped, when I could talk, 'it's just that what you take for an oath describes me perfectly. You see, I *am* an "Afghanistanian".'

His face cracked with a slow smile.

'Is that right? Och, ye're no' a Sassenach after a'. Ye're bonny fighters, me faither told me, ye Afghanistanians. He fought ye in the Khyber Pass. But you're only a little yin. No more'n a grilse, so you are.' He was right: I was very skinny in those days. But I was relieved: you always have mercy on a grilse, and throw it back into the river, to let it grow into a full-sized salmon.

His temper having subsided, the giant linked arms with the Cockney and they walked, arm in arm, back towards the public bar of the Spaniard's Inn. The Scot was already enquiring what his friend would like to drink.

Now at this time I had not seen the *International Thesaurus of Quotations*, compiled by Rhoda Thomas Tripp. If I had, I would have felt less trepidation: because the likely outcome of such an incident as this is spelt out, in the quotation there from Charles Caleb Colton:

> An Irishman fights before he reasons,
> a Scotchman reasons before he fights,
> an Englishman is not particular as to
> the order of precedence, but will do
> either to accommodate his customers.

The Cockney had dropped his open razor on the ground. I picked it up and held it in my hand, about to close it neatly, because many people in England do not like litter. Suddenly a shadow fell across me. It was that of a policeman.

I had learnt that in this country you always have to say something to the police. People with guilty consciences are always silent. Apparently this fact is taught at the police college.

Managing to grin, I looked him straight in the face and said the first thing that came into my head. 'Lovely afternoon, officer. I'm a Sloonjin Summf, you know.'

It didn't sound at all right, now that I had said it. The Policeman flexed his knees. 'If that's lost property, Sir, I'll hand it in at the Station,' was all he said, as he relieved me of the weapon.

Of course I had been worrying unnecessarily about being charged with Wandering Abroad With A Dangerous Weapon, or the like. Like everyone else in the country, I was protected by the dictum of Mr Justice Darling:

> The Courts of England are open to all men, like the doors of the Ritz Hotel.

A few minutes later I saw the Scotsman staggering towards me, his face wreathed in smiles.

'Ye're an ontallagont mon,' was all he said, as he lurched past.

To be called intelligent by a Scotsman, if you are not a fellow-countryman, is praise indeed. Most, if not all, Scots are sure that they are intellectually superior to any foreigner, and particularly anyone to be found in England. Some think that it is blood, not environment, nature and not nurture, that gives the Scots this useful advantage.

Lewis Spence, whom I remember well as one of my father's oldest friends, wrote masses of books in his Edinburgh eyrie about human beliefs: he was especially keen on Atlantis. In *The Problem of Atlantis*, which – like all his books – was published in England and had many more Sassenach readers than Scots, he explains why his fellow-countrymen are so effortlessly superior to the Anglo-Saxons:

'If a patriotic Scotsman may be pardoned the boast, I may say that I devoutly believe that Scotland's admitted superiority in the mental and spiritual spheres springs almost entirely from the preponderant degree of Cro-Magnon blood which certainly runs in the veins of her people.'

Cro-Magnon: Stone Age man. Evolved in Asia, and chased off the Neanderthals. There's a lineage to be proud of, I thought as I watched the shambling figure from the North hiccup its way past its gaping inferiors, the English natives.

And yet, flattered though I was by the Cro-Magnon's praise, there yet lurked in my mind a sense that I had been condescended upon. Could I retrieve my Anglean aplomb?

Oddly, to me, though not exceptionally in England, the very reverse happened. I began to recall how some English people regarded the people of Kent, my adopted county, as not even fully human.

No less an authority than the *Oxford English Dictionary* says so: KENTISH LONG-TAILS, it states, is 'a phrase embodying the old belief that the natives of Kent had tails.' Perhaps the learned Dutchman, G. J. Renier, was alluding discreetly to the people of Kent when he contrasts the English with 'normal humanity' . . . In his best-selling *The English; Are They Human?* often more thoughtful than is implied by what he admits is its 'catchpenny title', he says:

> 'Just as the common reserve of the Scots and of the English has led to the current mistake that there is an identifiable variety of mankind which can be called the British, these analogies have misled international thinkers into believing that there is no deep-seated difference between the English and normal humanity.'

Whatever that difference is, foreigners may be glad to learn that Dr Renier does not regard it as genetic. It can, indeed, be transmitted, though he does not tell us exactly how. What he does say is 'The world is crying out for the unity that transcends patriotism without destroying it'. Fair enough; but who will give it to us? Renier knows. 'Greater England', the Dutchman proclaims, 'points the way.' Whether his 'normal humanity' will be able to seize its unparalleled opportunity, only time will tell. The Scots may be able to help.

6

Bringing an Afghan

Charter

A glorious charter, deny it who can,
Is breathed in the words 'I'm an Englishman'.
Eliza Cook: *The Englishman*

In the United States, if you were to say 'I'll come tomorrow and bring an Afghan', people would be surprised if you arrived without a bedspread composed of crocheted or knitted squares. In England, the same phrase is taken to mean that the visitor is to be accompanied by a long-haired hound.

In Imperial times, it would have been a promise almost without meaning. Afghans were wild men against whom the British had, it is true, fought three wars. But, since they lived in a mountain kingdom beyond the North-West Frontier, remoter even than the domain of the wild Pathan tribes, nobody would be likely to introduce one into a respectable home.

Afghans also suffered from the strange aberration of not wanting to join the Empire, even though they were always fighting the Russians.

It must be admitted, though, that if I had rung someone in Kabul (yes, there are telephones there) and said, 'I'll be bringing an Englishman', it might have sounded almost as odd.

So Bringing an Afghan, even today, is not so much a sign of English eccentricity as a challenge to English ingenuity. When a film of the Third Anglo-Afghan war was being shot in England, genuine Afghans – mostly students trying to earn vacation money – were rejected as Afghan Native extras for crowd scenes because they 'did not look foreign enough'. But the casting director surmounted the difficulty. That is why, if your knowledge of foreign parts is partly derived from the screen, the little yellow men in that film may form your image of my compatriots.

When I moved into the country, I actually had the experience of being not foreign enough to be foreign, while a real native of these islands was considered too foreign to be British. Let me explain that.

I had moved into what was considered in the village to be the Big House and one day I dropped in for a sandwich at the inn which adjoins our property. The landlord greeted me with, 'Well, what's it feel like to be our Squire?'

'What do you mean; how can *I* be the squire around here?' I asked him.

'Well, then,' he said, polishing a glass and looking at me truculently, 'if *you're* not squire, who is?'

I turned it over in my mind. Then I thought of the people just down the road. The local policeman had recently said, speaking of them, 'Reckon they know the Royals, they do . . .'

'How about the Bloggses?' I asked, naming them.

The Landlord shot me a look of what the English popular papers call Dark Menace.

'The Bloggses? They cain't be squires hereabouts. Why, the Bloggses are Welsh!'

A lot of it concerns how you talk. Susan Crosland told in the *Sunday Times* how some English people intend to please when they say 'But you don't *talk* like an American', and seemed to imply that she didn't know how to handle unintentional patronising. At least, she called it insufferable; so I decided to rush to her rescue. I immediately penned the following:

Dear Ms Crosland:
I always read you with enjoyment, respect and admiration. Perhaps you will forgive the impertinence of a stranger writing to you.
In your piece in the ST today, you talk about people saying 'You don't *talk* like an American': and the problem when such remarks are unintentional. I've often had the same difficulty myself. This is what I do:

ENGLISH PERSON: 'But you don't *talk* like a foreigner!'

MYSELF: 'Oh yes, I do, I assure you. Whenever there is sufficient demand.'

I have noticed that this acts as a put-down in the case of hostiles, but does no harm to the ingenuous. It also scores with whoever is listening.

I am glad to be able to report that she approved, and says she may well adopt the tactic.

You don't have to be English to profit from the English mentality. Now and then there may be an unexpected cachet for you, as an Afghan I know discovered not long ago.

This friend of mine was booked in at a large, very traditional, hotel in a German city. He was about to register at the reception desk when a huge, full-length portrait of a gorgeously-attired grandee caught his eye.

'Who's that?' he asked the elegant assistant manager.

'That, Sir, is the Elector of Saxony. In former times, as you may know, the Holy Roman Empire had seven of them. They date back to 1356. They were kings, in fact. We still accord the hereditary successors of such people royal honours.'

Now my friend had recently acquired British nationality. Not only that, he was on the electoral register. So he was entitled to vote, and was free to describe himself thus, should he so wish. As an elector.

In the space on the hotel's register reserved for 'occupation' he therefore wrote, in block capitals and as the Assistant Manager watched, the words ELECTOR OF LONDON, ENGLAND.

That got him the red carpet treament: no trouble was too great. The Assistant Manager at once proved that when he spoke of royal honours, he wasn't lying, as we say in my country.

There was a State Visit by some national leader on at the time, and my friend had an urgent appointment. He had heard that the main streets were closed to ordinary traffic. As Elector of London, however, he was given a police outrider escort, with sirens, along the tabooed processional route.

He was thus delivered, in state, to the sandwich bar where he was due to demonstrate a new gadget to the owner, who was much impressed – whether by his arrival or by his product was unclear. The German had told him on the telephone only the day before: 'On no account be late. In Germany we do things properly.' He wasn't lying, either.

When the Elector got back to his hotel, his sale completed, the manager was waiting for him. It's all up now, he thought, but at least I have unloaded my sandwich machine. Ushered into the regal office from which the manager seldom emerged, my friend was introduced to a high-ranking police officer, who came smartly to attention.

'High-Born Herr,' the man said, 'I have to inform you that we have unmasked an impostor. Shortly after the arrival of Your High-Bornness, a man with a British passport (I regret to say he had a reservation here) appeared. When he saw your Elector-ship's name and rank in the register, he wrote 'Elector of Walth-amstow' as his own occupation.'

'How did you know that he wasn't a real Elector?' my friend asked, nervously.

The policeman pursed his lips. 'We looked at his passport,' he said. 'It gave his profession as "Sales Manager". A mere peas-ant. Besides, what is this Valtheimstow? I am here to assure you that we have ascertained that this is not a plot against you. The man merely sought preferential treatment by deception. All is therefore now in order.'

'Are you going to prefer charges?' My friend was trembling, but not with anger, as the others must have assumed.

'Not unless you wish to press them. After all, the deceiver was unmasked in time. Shall we institute impersonation proceedings?'

'No, I think I'll let the fellow go.'

'The Elector is most gracious.' The policeman clicked his heels, bent stiffly over the Elector's hand, and left the room.

But there was still a mystery. Why was the London Elector accepted as genuine and the Walthamstow one so easily un-masked? Might as well be hung for a sheep as a lamb, thought my friend – so he asked the Manager to explain.

'The Herr Elector will understand that we are not such fools as to take people at face value, begging Your Electorship's pardon', smirked the functionary.

'How do you mean?'

'Well, we had taken the liberty of looking at your own pass-port, when you handed it in. The part reserved for "occupation" is *absolutely blank*.'

In England, foreigners may not know, people are allowed to

fill in their own profession for passports – or to leave this part of their description blank. 'Director' and 'Consultant' are popular choices.

The English have a saying, 'Don't push your luck'. The Afghans have not, and so it was that the sandwich-machine man – Haji Abdul-Ghani Khan, former Afghan, now British Subject and Elector of London – felt he absolutely had to ask a further question.

'It is only, Herr Manager, that I thought you might wonder about my name, surely unusual in an English Elector.'

The Manager bowed. 'Your own English Royal Family is German, no? And they have had a great empire? Then they can appoint whomever they wish as one of their Electors. Now, if His Electorship has any desires . . .'

His only desire, soon gratified, was to get back to his own constituency with his sandwich-machine order. After all, the poltroon, the mere sales manager, who had been caught in the act of impersonation, might be tougher than he was.

And, as he put it to me later, 'If I can be confused with a hound or a quilt, why not with an Elector?'

So an Afghan, under certain circumstances, can be indistinguishable (by some) from an English person. One of the requirements, naturally, is that he must not be faint-hearted. And not only in Germany: later I shall tell of my own experiences in this connection.

On this subject of boldness, we have the important tradition of Sir Walter Raleigh, who is said to have scratched on a window:

Fain would I climb but that I fear to fall

and Queen Elizabeth, they say, wrote underneath:

If thy heart fail thee, do not climb at all.

You couldn't get more English than that, surely? Only, perhaps equal it, as did our own poet Saadi, who put it thus in his classical poem, written four hundred years before Elizabeth and Raleigh:

> In the vast sea are riches beyond compare:
> But if you seek safety, it is on the shore.

They have aplomb, most of these English. And those who

haven't are working on it. You can't tell who has it and who hasn't just by looking at them: 'A cow's milk-yield is not known by the length of her tail,' says our proverb.

It makes one wonder as to which English people are being described in all those books by their overseas critics. Karel Çapek, for instance, in his *Letters from England*, written after spending years here, described the people thus:

> They are hard as flint, incapable of adapting themselves, conservative, loyal, rather shallow and always uncommunicative; they cannot get out of their skin, but it is a solid, and in every respect excellent, skin.

Sounds clever, Mr Çapek: but I think it's as fallacious as the old English assessment of the Afghan.

7

I Never Give Them

Decision

The Income Tax authorities have abandoned a battle to compel William of Arethyn to pay tax on the first £100,000 of his stock market profits. William is an English sheepdog: the legal position is that a dog may own property in England, but only humans are liable for tax.

The Times, 5 February 1985

I was intrigued by what I read in the letter from an English dealer in autographs. Typed on the thick paper believed by psychologists to denote an inadequate personality, it said, among other things, that the dealer handled some of the most distinguished public figures in the land, and that he proposed to do the same for me – for profit and with 'appropriate discretion'.

All I had to do was to write down the two words which form my name, and he would sell the piece of paper with or without a photograph but with a 'certificate of authenticity and provenance' for £10: which we would then split fifty-fifty.

Ten pounds meant five pounds for me; two pounds and fifty pence a word. Now, if I write, as I often do, a book of about 90,000 words, some people grumble when asked to pay £10 for the whole book. But, I thought, the manuscript alone is worth no less than £225,000 at the autograph rate. And I'm only on ten to fifteen per cent of the cover price, usually; twenty per cent if I have a really big seller. I rang the man up. He had a smooth and reassuring voice, speaking like a Harley Street psychiatrist with a difficult patient. 'We couldn't get anything like nearly a quarter of a million pounds for one of your MSS, of course – not at the moment. But your image is growing, otherwise I wouldn't

have invited you to join our stable. But it *would* be a good idea
to keep all your written materials. They are worth more, by the
way, if they have corrections on them. Such pieces are going to
go up in value, because of the increasing use of word-processors.
There's less and less handmade hard-copy about.'

'Worth more if originally badly written than if perfect?'

'That's about the size of it.'

'Who on earth collects such things?'

'You'd be surprised. We've got some very important people on
our books, millionaires and so forth. The Highest in the Land have
good collections. You get bitten by the bug. Even *you* might
become a collector one day; stranger things have happened. Quite
a lot of people we have autograph arrangements with get so interested that they start to collect on their own account.'

Autograph arrangements. I had had an inkling of the demand
some years ago when more and more people wrote asking for an
autographed book, even for two or three. Indeed, only last year,
one man sent a bundle of some fifty identical sheets of gummed
paper, asking me to sign them all, and I had wondered if he
wanted to sell them; for one crazy moment, that is.

The dealer was still on the line. 'How about autographed
copies of my published books?' I asked.

'Yes, of course. How many copies are in circulation?'

'All told, about five million copies of thirty different books.' I
could not help adding, 'That would ring up about fifty million
pounds, twenty-five million for each of us.'

'Now look here,' he said, sententiously, 'we are talking about
a serious matter. As an autographer, you would be in the
company of Napoleon, of George Washington, of Winston
Churchill. They all command good prices.'

I suppressed a desire to answer, '*And* in the company of Hitler
and Mussolini, and Attila the Hun, for all I know'. Instead I
said, 'Sorry. What were you saying about my past output?'

'Well, old copies are really the best. I buy up secondhand
books, and get their authors to sign them – sometimes by the
crateload. Even when they live abroad, with high freight costs,
it's worth it. Nice little sideline. People like to think that they
have a book which has been autographed, and perhaps dated as
well, back to a time when the author was unknown.'

'How ingenious,' I said, instead of 'that sounds immoral to me.'

'Yes, isn't it? Then there's another wheeze. If you look in at any of W. H. Smith's branches, you'll see they always have a bargain table, full of books at knockdown prices. They're what the trade calls remainders, which can sometimes be bought from publishers at waste paper rates. I've done that before now. Some are by famous authors.'

'Famous authors don't get remaindered, surely?'

'Oh but they do. It happens every day. That's because the book has gone into paperback, and the expensive hardback stops selling. Or when the publisher has printed too many copies. They call them overstocks.'

I said that this must be like having your own mint.

'Mint? A goldmine's more like it. I once bought three thousand copies of one title by a famous authoress from a pulping-mill for five pence each. That's £150 laid out. She signed two hundred books for a lump sum of £500, so I'd spent £650 in all. I sold the 200 autographed copies for £30 each, which brought in £6000.'

'Six *thousand*?' I gasped.

'Yes, tidy little profit of £5350 there.'

'What happened to the remaining 2800 copies?' I asked.

'Oh, I sold them as waste paper, for re-pulping, at one penny each, to another paper mill. Got £28 for them. No point in saturating the market. I cleared about £5000 after paying postage and overheads.'

I wished he hadn't told me about the back-dating of signatures on old books, because that smelt rancid. Besides, it might even be dangerous. Our proverb has it: 'The night may be dark, but the apples in the orchard have been counted.' Pity, I thought. I told him I'd think it over, and regretfully hung up.

Then I remembered Witherspoon; was *that* what he had been up to? He first contacted me in the 1970s. A devoted fan, he has kept in close touch ever since, taking my old letters, press clippings about my work and copies of interviews. Then, of course, there were the swarms of students, always working on degree theses, who 'simply must have unpublished materials, preferably in your own hand, to give freshness to my work. Both for posterity and for the success of my PhD research . . .'

And there was that circular which came through the post, apparently because I am listed in a biographical dictionary or two, offering a 'Memento Kit of Miscellaneous Items by and about a well-know Author.'

I had once signed a contract for a magazine article, in no less than twenty copies. The signatures, at autograph rates, were worth £200. For writing the article itself I was to receive only £150. I wrote this to my Agent: who, showing no surprise, undertook to mention it to the editor of the magazine. I heard no more about it, though.

Then there was that lady, only last month, who had written a long letter full of questions, all of which had already been answered in my books. When I rebuked her for slovenly reading habits, she had a ready answer. 'I can't afford to buy books, I don't like public libraries (they are full of smelly tramps) and, besides, I wanted your autograph.'

Now, she informed me, she was sending my signature to a graphologist, to find out what I was really like. I hadn't the heart to tell her, after all that ingenuity, that the letter had been signed by my secretary. So, though tempted, I cannot decently write again, asking whether the graphologist has got my secretary's character, aspirations and potential right.

It might give away undesirable facets of my own character, but I have to confess that I am torn, in disliking them, between two autograph collectors, writing recently from opposite ends of England. One says, 'I have not read any of your books, but I *would* like your autograph for my little girl's collection.' The other is a man who seeks my signature 'because I so enjoyed your novel, *The Little Green Mouse*.' I haven't written any such book. Since some of my books have been brought out by Penguins, I have first-hand evidence of which paperback imprint autograph-collectors favour in their efforts.

Some collectors go so far as to enclose exhaustive lists of all my books, to prove that they have read them. The only flaw in this is that such listings often include the misprints in the titles which appear only in various reference books . . .

What are all these people like, anyway, this community of English acquirers of other people's scribblings? Sometimes they send me impossible poems: more often they offer the Great English Novel, which they have been working on for twenty years, for me to get published. And more. If I'd kept them, I would by now have a roomful of greeting cards, pressed ferns, dead insects, balloons, testimonials from Sunday schools, foreign banknotes, stocks and bonds of no value (for me to give an opinion on) and dubious offers of every kind.

So I don't really know much about these correspondents. But I do know that they have been around for a long time. Why not arrange to meet some of them? I once wondered. But then, faithful to my research into Englishry, I did some reading and tracked down a cautionary description of them in Ko-Ko's song from *The Mikado*:

> There's the pestilential nuisances
> who write for autographs –
> All those people who have flabby hands
> and irritating laughs.

And decided to do nothing. I have stood by this even in the face of one of the most English letters I have ever received: 'My Dear Sir, Please send me your autograph . . . P S – Who are you?'

I have, though, had one face-to-face autographical encounter: and it provided one of my most equivocal memories, a truly English-type experience. One day I was walking along Abbey Road, in London, deep in thought. I lived only a minute away and was going to make a note of something, so I had a pen and notebook in my hand. Suddenly I saw a knot of people standing on the pavement. A figure loomed from a sudden turbulence in the group and said to me, with a pleasant smile, 'Autograph?'

I brushed him aside, and just registered that he did look alarmed, or something, when I snarled, 'I never give them.' It was only some yards further on that I realised I had been outside the Abbey Road recording studios, and had passed up my chance of starting a collection with the signature of my interceptor, the Beatle John Lennon. Ms Noella Anton, of Phillips the auctioneers, says 'a good John Lennon autograph is worth about £50.'

Today I have to reach for my English aplomb once again as I read my mail. Here is a letter from a university don. He had asked for my 'sign-manual' and got my autograph back by the next post, as I was feeling in an expansive mood. Now, by first-class and registered mail, comes another letter, very formal: his name is typed at the bottom, and the paper is not signed. The entire text reads:

'The Anglicised version of your name as received this morning is not satisfactory or adequate. Please be so good as to sign again, this time with your full style and titles, as given in *Who's Who in the Arab World* (Beirut, third edition, 1972).'

I am not going to be so good. Let him go to Beirut for it. In happier times I was walking through a market there, the day after being interviewed for a Lebanese paper. A stallholder, I noticed, had pinned up a clipping of this article on a board beside his stock of ribbons, picture postcards and empty bottles. A notice above it indicated that for a trifling sum – the equivalent of about twenty pence, in local currency – 'An Idries Shah signature' could be obtained from him. When I asked for one, the man concentrated for a moment, and then inscribed my name on crimson paper in gold ink, with many a flourish. It looked far more impressive than the real thing. Why, I asked him as I pocketed it, did he not sell originals? It seemed that they were 'difficult to get, he is a busy man, you see.' Was a copy as good? '*Ya Sidi*, O Sir! Most people here cannot even write . . .'

Would the man whose signature he was forging, this Idries Shah, I asked, not object to such a trade?

'Such a man, Sidi, written about in the newspapers, and a man of learning, undoubtedly a man of generous habits, surely would not grudge me a living?'

No, I supposed not. Besides, I reflected, next time I felt like being a bit reckless, I could write my name down a few times on a piece of paper – and throw it away. Even twenty pence is money.

Yet England is a mysterious place. If you know where to look, you can find even Beirut prices being undercut: in an English village, for instance.

Someone came to the house to ask for gifts to be sold at a charity bazaar in the local village hall. She said that 'books would be especially welcome'.

I looked out the complimentary copies of books of mine which I had received, from time to time, from publishers. Then I signed my name, large, on the fly-leaf of each book, I gave them to the kind lady. At the sale, I opened a volume, curious to know the price a signed one might fetch. Under my autograph I saw the words, scribbled in pencil: 'Published at £8.50. Defaced by signature. Offered at 10 pence.'

8

Awfully near Tibet

Britain

Britain, an island in the ocean, formerly called Albion, is situated between the north and west . . . This island at present . . . contains five nations, the English, Britons, Scots, Picts and Latins, each in its own particular dialect cultivating the sublime study of Divine truth. The Latin tongue is, by the study of the Scriptures, become common to all the rest.

The Venerable Bede

The English are no dottier than anyone else: you can find oddness anywhere. With them, unlike other peoples, the characteristic tends to be strongly purposeful. They not only have a great pool of eccentric talent to call upon, but they make more use of it than most of us do.

Sometimes the unorthodoxy is distinctly useful, while the English people who use it don't seem to notice. The best explanation for that is that a group-mind is at work.

When living in London, I was visited by a lady who had read several of my books. She was a nice, middle-aged person of broad culture, who spent much time on good works and had travelled widely. We talked for an hour, though I did not find out why she had come to see me. That is not too unusual in England. One is often approached, for instance, by people who have something urgent to discuss, to 'have lunch'. Finding time for these critical meetings from a full schedule, I began to notice after about the tenth such meal that nothing even remotely urgent was ever broached.

I put this down to the English tradition that self-indulgence is sinful and things should only be done for a purpose, even if it is an imaginary one. English children are made to eat their porridge or shepherd's pie by being adjured to think of the starving children in Africa. (My children, though born here, would never wear that at all. 'It'll go bad before it gets there', they used to lisp; 'better send money instead'.)

I am not alone in finding this lunching question perplexing. 'Lunch is my biggest problem', Sir Shridath Ramphal, Secretary-General of the Commonwealth says. 'It's a way of life here. But I find it very disruptive.'

I did not have luncheon with the lady visitor, however, and did not think of her again after seeing her out.

The house next door happened to be vacant. Two weeks later the lady – I shall call her Mrs Smith – moved into it. Now letters for her started to be delivered to me, and she regularly rang the doorbell and asked if there was any mail. Assuming that she had given my address instead of hers for some technical reason connected with delays in the Post Office delivery system, I did not regard as sinister the fact that they were addressed to 'Mrs Smith, Care of Shah'.

It was only after a month of this that I found out that Mrs Smith was my biographer. She had sold the idea of a book on me to a publisher: I suppose at least partly on the strength of the fact that she knew me well. Her mail, after all, came to my address. I got out of that one by sending her intending publisher two books which already seemed to cover my life exhaustively enough.

She bore me no ill-will for this, merely trying to sell me, second hand, a collection of my own books which she had bought as source material on my life and thought. 'Now they're rather surplus to requirements, do you see', she said.

Knave or fool? Neither, probably just purposefully dotty. We say, in Afghanistan, *Divana ba kari-khud hushyar*, 'the madman knows what he's doing,' which I believe to be well in line with current English psychiatric thinking.

On the other hand, I did not give Mrs Smith the chance to explain, and there may be a perfectly simple explanation. If this seems far-fetched to you, perhaps you will consider another experience with English neighbours. If this had not run its full course, I would probably have been baffled by the strange English custom of putting rancid butter in one's tea . . .

It was like this. I got into conversation with two sweet old ladies at a bus stop not far from the house where Mrs Smith visited me. They were interested to hear that I was an Afghan, and invited me to tea at their home, a couple of hundred yards away. I was to be there at four o'clock, two days later.

When I arrived and had been settled in the front room near a table covered with plates of tiny sandwiches, toasted crumpets, cakes and so forth, one of the ladies wheeled in a dumb waiter bearing an enormous teapot – and a butter dish.

With a serene smile, she took the top off the pot and dumped about a quarter of a pound of old-looking, runny butter into it. A rare English custom? An unusual taste cultivated in secret, a sort of arsenic-and-old-lace situation? Was I supposed to react and, if so, how? My head swam, I felt myself fast losing my grip on reality. They both looked at me, and I tried not to look at them, or at the teapot.

Then, murmuring 'I hope that's the right mixture . . .' the presiding old lady stirred the concoction and poured three cups full.

I took mine and tried to sip it, while the two old dears bent looks of gentle hospitality upon me. When I had managed to get down a couple of gulps of the terrible stuff – it was strong, stewed Indian tea and the butter was really rancid – the expectant silence was broken.

'Was that all right?' the first lady enquired.

'Yes, indeed, quite all right', I lied.

She clasped her tiny hands together and said, 'Oh, I'm *so* glad. We were afraid, you see . . .'

Afraid of what? I couldn't trust myself to say anything, but assumed a posture of intelligent interest, trying not to think what they might do to me next.

'Yes,' fluttered the other old lady, 'we were afraid that you would find it – different.'

She had a large cake-knife in her hand.

'Oh, I don't know,' I said, now convinced that they were insane, and determined to humour them. If I got up, I thought – quietly – and backed to the door . . .

'Yes,' said the other one, 'you see, we only have a small school atlas.' That clinched it. They *were* absolutely crazy, both of them. Not for the first or last time in England, in London even, I was aware that my simple Afghan brain was just not equipped for this kind of thing. Only a small school atlas! Perhaps they had torn it up and baked it into the cakes.

'And', she was saying, 'we looked up Afghanistan. It's awfully near Tibet. It is on the world map, anyway.' She paused, head cocked on one side.

About the same distance as England was from Morocco, I thought, even on a map like that. But she was talking again.

'In the local library there is nothing about Afghanistan, but they have got an interesting book which describes how they make tea in Tibet. With powdered leaves and rancid butter. So we thought we'd make you feel at home if we made some for you. Is it rancid enough?'

My brain was working again, I noted with relief.

'Ah, yes', I found myself saying, 'Tea with rancid butter is something that I'm trying to give up, you see. I mean, I've been here long enough to have developed rather a taste for the way you serve tea in England.' As I burbled on, I realised that I had misjudged them, and had allowed myself, to my shame, to forget the Pashtu proverb: 'The eyes of a friend do not dwell upon the warts.'

The two old ladies, I saw, had not ventured to touch their own Tibetan tea. Now they exchanged delighted smiles. One tiptoed into the kitchen and came back with a pot of Lapsang Souchong.

Regaining my confidence somewhat, I launched into an anecdote, partly prompted by the sight of a framed and faded sepia photograph, of a British officer on a camel, which stood among the assortment of objects on the mantelshelf.

'My friend Colonel Baines-Hewett,' I said, 'once told me a story of great resourcefulness. Somewhere in Jordan, he came across an old man who was looking after a private library of hundreds of manuscripts. Many were very rare. He asked the ancient, "Have you ever lost any of these priceless books?" The librarian said, "Only once. A pilgrim, on his way south to Mecca, borrowed an unique volume, promising to bring it back on his return journey. Unfortunately he died in the Holy City, and was buried there, together with the book. The leader of his caravan reported it, when they returned."

'The Colonel said, "What a tragic loss. What did you do?"

'"There was only one thing to do", answered the ancient. "I sat down and wrote out another copy, from memory."'

The two ladies looked at one another in dismay. 'Oh dear, I don't think *we* could manage that' said one of them.

So perhaps the motivation of Mrs Smith, my would-be biographer, in using my address, is rooted in innocence. I wouldn't be surprised to hear that she was as blameless as the two old dears in St John's Wood. Whatever its basis, their hospitality has touched me so deeply that I think of it often, when I need reminding of human kindness. And even sometimes when I see butter.

And I still haven't solved the mystery of how the two old ladies got hold of rancid butter at only two days' notice, at most.

English people, though, vary in their reactions to these two tales. Some feel that the first may show rather too much – shall we say – sophistication, and the second too little. My own belief is that it is the English secret mind, something between an instinct and an intelligence, feeling its way, not always successfully, towards a solution of a problem.

But, in England, we have to beware of excessive emotion; the Englishman knows that it can be a terrible trap. When I related the Tibetan Tea story to my occasional technical adviser on Englishry, Henry Hope Edwards, he hastened to redress the balance, obviously to halt any slide into sentimentality.

'You were lucky', he said, 'that the old girls had not looked up that Tibetan Buddhist book about the usefulness of killing people. It says that murder can be a good way of helping to halt the reincarnation process and bring nirvana that much closer. Run out of people and you stop reincarnation and therefore misery. That's their solution.'

To clinch that, and because he had connexions with eminent Scandinavians, he later sent me a news item cut from *The Observer*. It was a quotation from the Norwegian Halvard Lange:

We do not regard Englishmen as foreigners. We look on them only as rather mad Norwegians.

Although an Englishman, Henry did not sympathise with my feelings of gratitude towards the two old dames. When I put this down to his Anglean sterness, he denied it; referring me to an earnest student of his country, the famous Emile Cammaerts, Professor of Belgian Literature at London University.

'Cammaerts', he said, 'pointed out that the English seek out what they think to be oddnesses, to give themselves a thrill.' The Belgian (in his *Discoveries in England*) put it, in fact, a little more delicately:

> Remote things take on a slightly solemn or grotesque aspect for which the English show a peculiar appreciation.

He quotes the stewardship of the Chiltern Hundreds, which a member of Parliament may be granted, but which hardly, if at all, exists; the Beefeaters (who used to be buffet waiters), Guy Fawkes Day (the celebration of which was once compulsory) and contracts in English law which stipulate that you shall not keep such things as cows on the third floor of a leasehold apartment.

All I can add is the powerful English word 'Quite'.

If unfamiliar with it, look up the definition in a good dictionary. You will not be surprised to learn that it can stand for either 'completely' or 'not completely'.

9

Jungle of the Holy Yahya

Chivalry

[Professor] Nicholson believes that the chivalry of the Middle Ages is, perhaps, traceable to heathen Arabia. Two other highly regarded orientalists, Lady Ann and Mr Wilfred Blunt, come to much the same conclusion. 'Knight-errantry, the riding forth on horseback in search of adventures, the rescue of captive maidens, the succour rendered everywhere to women in adversity – all these were essentially Arabian ideas, as was the name of *chivalry*, the connection of honourable conduct with the horse-rider, the man of noble blood, the cavalier.'

John Laffin: *The Arab Mind*

The English tend to pronounce foreign words as if they were English ones. The Afghans do something quite as baffling: they translate foreign names into their own language – and then forget the original form.

'I seek, in London, the hovel of the Swiss, which has two characteristics', my friend Professor Puladi confided to an Indian scholar in the next seat, on a flight from Bombay to Heathrow. Puladi, who had taught himself English (mainly from books, the radio and Littlewoods' mail-order catalogues) referred to his notes. He had made them when we last met and I told him that I lived near Swiss Cottage. 'Swiss hovel' was his translation. After all, English dictionaries give one meaning of 'hovel' as 'a small dwelling, a cottage'.

'Indeed', said the Indian.

'The two main characteristics, according to my friend Shah, are these', the Professor said. 'First, the hovel is a caravanserai, an inn called a *chalet*, not unlike the gigantic wooden houses, with carved beams, which cling to the slopes of the mountains of Nuristan. Secondly, it is located less than a *parsang* – the distance a horse can cover in an hour – to the east of my friend's house. Perhaps you know it?'

'Know it?' said the Indian, not for nothing a Sanskrit scholar, trained in debate at Banaras. 'But why should I know it? And why, for that matter, should the Swiss, who have a perfectly good country in Central Europe, maintain a hovel in London?'

He knew little of the north-western reaches of the capital, having spent most of his time in academia. This, for him, meant Bloomsbury.

'Someone must know, however', pressed the Afghan.

The Indian agreed. 'That is true. But I am thinking that you must be having more detailed directions, such as an address?'

Puladi consulted his notes. 'Yes. It is in the Jungle of the Holy Yahya, the number is twenty-four, and the location is the street of the Tapa of Kliftoun.'

'Who is this Holy Yahya?' asked the Hindu.

'Only unbelievers and idolaters do not know' said my friend, 'that the Holy Yahya was a prophet, and the teacher of the Prophet Jesus.'

If the Indian had heard of St John's Wood, Holy Yahya's Jungle, he did not recognise it from this version. Even less did he register that I lived in Clifton Hill. The Tapa of Kliftoun meant nothing to him, so, like a good academic, he referred Puladi to the School of Oriental and African Studies, in Malet Street, WC1.

'They should be able to understand you', he told the Professor. 'Although the place is something of a ghetto.'

Puladi thanked him and, after asking him to write it down, looked up the word in his pocket dictionary:

'GHETTO, the quarter where the Jews were strictly confined in an Italian city.' Quarter, what was that? He consulted the dictionary again: 'QUARTER, mercy or the fourth part of anything.'

He had not heard that scholars in England, where the Indian had picked up the phrase, loved to call one anothers' institutions, 'that ghetto'. Come to think of it, the information wouldn't have helped him much.

When the telephone rang, I recognised Puladi's voice, but as he spoke of the Indian, the Swiss, the Italian quarter and Palestinian prophet, I soon became as confused as he had been. 'Where are you speaking from?' I asked.

'The Writing-place of the Making Learned in the Tongues of the People of the East and of Africa. They call it SOAS. That's not the same as Swiss, is it? *Skul af Uryantal and Ofrikon Stodiz*, it's called in Inglizi.'

'No, Professor. But how did you get my number? I've only just had the phone put in. I'm not in the book yet.' What a feat of palaeography, or whatever it was called, on the part of SOAS, to track me down like that.

'The man here rang the Afghan Embassy. They had your number.'

So Professor Puladi got the spare room, and went out every day to the British Museum to pursue some arcane study, while working hard at his English. He liked to call it 'Inglis' because the Oxford dictionary shows that that's what the English actually called themselves until the sixteenth century.

Then, one Christmas, we heard the news: Russian troops had invaded Afghanistan, and women and children were already fleeing across the high mountains to Pakistan, through the snow blizzards.

Puladi said, 'I'm too old to fight, I'd only be a liability'. So he went out and got a job, as Heavy Washup Man, cleaning pots and pans, at a restaurant.

Every Friday he would bank most of his money for the refugees. He got free meals at work, and walked the three miles to and fro, so he had no fares to pay. He gave up smoking, and his clothes got shabbier and shabbier.

Life in England, as elsewhere, is not easy at the bottom of the pile. The Professor took most things in his stride, but sometimes it was hard.

One day he arrived home, as usual, at about three in the

morning, and knocked on my bedroom door. I had not seen him for almost a week, since his hours and mine did not coincide. He was unutterably dishevelled, and there was a strange look on his face. I took him down to the kitchen, and we sat drinking green tea and chewing Afghan nuts and raisins.

'I am now promoted', he said, 'for five days I have been a short-order chef.'

'Well done, Professor!' I said; 'Congratulations.'

'Thank you. It means more money. But I have also been disgraced.'

'How do you mean?'

'The work involves a great deal of deep-fat frying, and my work-clothes, which I keep there, are saturated with cooking oil. So are my shoes.'

I nodded.

'Being a chef is tiring, especially when you do not know how to cook.'

I asked him how he managed it at all.

'The old woman who does the washing-up shows me, and I give her a small gift each night.'

'Well,' I said, 'that does not disgrace you.'

He shook his head. 'Not that. What happened was this. I had an order for scrambled egg on toast. The woman was not there, to tell me the recipe, so I made thick custard and sent that up.'

'Well, these things happen', I told him.

'Listen first, talk later', said the Professor. 'The next thing I knew, the proprietor had called me up from my basement: the customer wanted to see me. I explained that my clothes were unsuitable, but he said that this was their best customer, and I must go to him at once. I walked through the restaurant, past all those well-dressed people, very ashamed. Then the waiter pointed out the man to me.

'He looked quite angry at first, but when he saw my miserable oil-drenched form, ragged and distraught, he changed. Remarkable, these English. He reached into his pocket and gave me a £10 note. Then he said, "Thank you, Chef. That was very good. Now you can go." And I found myself downstairs again.'

'That', I said, 'was a gentleman. No need to feel unhappy, you are not dishonoured.'

'It wasn't only that', said my friend. 'I was soon hit by another blow, and a terrible one it was, too.'

I asked him to explain.

'Well, there is a service hoist, a platform which can go up and down from my underground kitchen to the street. It is for bringing down stores and taking up dustbins. It is so hot below that I sometimes stand on it and go up to get a little fresh air. Just for a minute or two, you know.'

He mimed the movement of the hoist with his hands, and breathed in and out several times.

'After the affair of the custard the kitchen was quiet, so I went up on the platform. It was lovely. I was standing there, in my dirty clothes, feeling like a king as the cool air caressed me, when it happened.

'A tall, elegantly-dressed Englishman walking along the pavement walked right into me. He stepped back, was going to say something, and then stopped and stared at me. As we stood there I realised who he was: the vice-chancellor of one of the most important English universities. He had been chairman at more than one meeting when I had lectured before world scholars.

'He had recognised me. I was paralysed with shame. Should I acknowledge him and try to explain what had happened to me? Should I run away, or go down again on the hoist, or pretend that I was someone else?

'While I was wondering what to do, I could see that he had made up his own mind. He started to speak.

'"Awfully sorry to run into you like that," he said. Then he tapped me on the shoulder and went on, "Do you know, a thought comes to me. Ever occurred to you? Here it is: 'Nothing goes on for ever.'"

'Then he twirled his umbrella, wished me goodnight, and went on his way.' The Professor paused. 'Now what is that if it is not a really civilised man? He knew me, he knew I wouldn't take charity and didn't want to be recognised. But he wanted to encourage me, to make me feel better.

'"Nothing goes on for ever" was the title of my last lecture under his chairmanship. It was, actually, "*Miguzarad*" – the Afghan slogan – which stands for "This, Too, Will Pass".

'Yes', said Professor Puladi, 'these English are Easterners, in the very best sense of that word.'

It it amazing what the right word at the right time will do for a human being. Professor Puladi and I looked, at the same moment, at the old map of Afghanistan pinned to the kitchen wall: and I somehow felt fresh hope for our ragged, desperate people, fighting a superpower with negligible weaponry: that they would yet come out of misery and oppression into freedom.

Puladi stood, faced the map and began to quote from Hariri's *Assemblies*, and I joined him in the recitation: '*Ma 'in yadhuru aladhba . . .* '

> It hurts not the sword if its sheath be worn,
>   Nor the hawk if its nest be poor.

The English are not an over-sentimental people. But I believe that any two of them in our position (which God forbid they should ever be) would have felt the three things that we felt that early morning: gratitude for a kindness, hope of deliverance, and a little pride.

10

Dave

The Teaching of Life

The trivial and immoral works of Shakespeare
and his imitators, aiming merely at the recre-
ation and amusement of the spectators,
cannot possibly represent the teaching of life.
The sooner people free themselves from the
false glorification of Shakespeare, the better it
will be.

Count Leo Tolstoy:
Shakespeare and the Drama

Professor Aziz Puladi knew that anyone visiting England must,
at least once, see Stratfurd Anawan, home of the Imurtal Bord
Shakspir. Not only that, but there were things to do beyond
accomplishing the Ziarat, the pious pilgrimage. One should see
a play at the Tiatur and the Hut of Hatwi Khanum, Ann Hatha-
way's cottage.

The former kitchen-hand, five years on, now owned his own
business, a chain of fast-food outlets. Almost all his profits went
to help the three million Afghan refugees in Pakistan, and he
worked as hard as ever. But he was still a man of letters at heart.

We sat planning the expedition in St John's Wood: or, rather,
we sat while he planned and I listened. In the course of our
discussions, the Professor told me that there was a special
reason why Shakspir was important to him. There were many
Eastern tales in Shakespeare's works. Why, the Bard had even
taken a story from the *Arabian Nights*, about Abu Hasan of
Baghdad. Puladi, moreover, had met the research student in

74

Baghdad whose doctoral thesis maintained that Shakespeare himself originated in the Middle East.

'Oh, Professor, come on . . . ' I said. He took out a notebook.

'Have you a copy of the famous English work, Brewer's *Dictionary of Phrase and Fable?*'

'No, Professor, but I know it well: there is one in the reference library at the top of the road.'

'Very well.' He marched me out of the house, across the Finchley Road, up the steps to the reference section and demanded the book. There was his evidence, on page two. Referring to an *Arabian Nights* tale, Brewer said 'The same story, localised in Shakespeare's Warwickshire, forms the Introduction to *The Taming of the Shrew* . . . '

'And there are many other such correspondences' Puladi told me, sternly.

I finally got him back to the planning session, pleased with my English-type stoicism. I had successfully resisted the temptation to compete with Puladi on the matter of derivative literature. Scholars, I knew, had found an Eastern prototype of Robinson Crusoe, of Cinderella, even of Chaucerean tales and parts of Dante. But I wasn't going to wander all over Europe on an extended Puladi literary pilgrimage. Stratford would be quite enough.

It was the middle of summer, and our compartment was blisteringly hot as the train rattled along, towards the birthplace of the man whom Puladi called the Swun ow Awun, and I nearly fell asleep several times as my guest expatiated upon the meaning of such important phrases as 'but me no buts'. Suddenly a stocky, swarthy hook-nosed man in a very neat blue turban sitting opposite us leant forward and tapped the Kabul genius on the knee.

'Although I speak only Punjabi and English, I am making out some of your words, and I can tell that you are man of culture' he said.

Puladi nodded.

'May I introduce myself? I am Arwal Singh – making pilgrimage to greatest shrine of English letters, isn't it? What do you think of my name?'

'Very nice'. The Professor wasn't encouraging him. He preferred talking to listening.

'*Only* very nice? How about its literary relevance: association with contemporary letters in fullest sense?'

Aziz took no notice. The Sikh now looked at me with eyebrows raised. 'Well?'

'I don't know much about contemporary Indian letters', I managed.

'Indian letters, *Indian* letters? What are you talking about? Unlike your friend, you are not one man of education at all, I can see that!'

I was dying for a cup of tea, not for literature, but I muttered, 'No, I am afraid I am not'.

'Well, then, I shall explain. You are very ignorant man if you have not heard my name, Arwal, before. Yes. Arwal is name of famous English writer, George Arwal. I am named after him. He wrote *One Farm of Animals*, and also *One Thousand, Nine Hundred and Eight-Four*, very famous books.'

'Orwell?' I said.

'Yes, Arwal. Remember his name, now, and look at those books sometime.'

'Yes, I will', I promised.

For the rest of the journey, Professor Puladi, getting his wind back, lectured Arwal on Shakspir, while the Sikh listened politely. Having established himself as a figure in the world of literature, he was in no need of further advertisement. He did say, though, that he admired both Orwell and William Shakespeare as Fellow British Subjects.

As we tottered off the train, Puladi said, 'Now that is one of the things I came here for: a full discussion with an English man of letters. People of culture always recognise one another. There aren't many Sikhs in Kabul, of course, and those are mostly grocers. But here we have a man of wide reading, and one named after an illustrious Frankish man of the spirit.'

I dragged Puladi into the station buffet. 'Let's have a cold drink', I suggested. He agreed. The day was so hot that the chocolate bars had melted in the machines on the platforms.

What would he have?

'A glass of water.'

I asked the Spanish lady behind the bar for a cola and a glass of water. She stared. 'Sorry, we don't do water.'

I offered Puladi cola, orange, lemon, anything, but he refused them all. 'Why can't I have water?' he wanted to know.

'We don't do water' the woman said.

'I don't want you to *do* it, woman', thundered the Professor, 'I want you to give it to me, to drink.'

'We don't give it to you to drink.'

'What, do you sell it?'

'We do not sell it.'

At that moment the manager, a tall, thin perspiring youth with the name 'Dave' on a badge pinned to his coat, came forward.

'Sorry, Sir, it's B.R. policy. We don't *do* water. That's me instructions.'

'But I am from Afghanistan', Puladi said. It was true, I reflected, trying to drag him away at the same time, that this statement would have worked in various countries of the East, where mothers and nurses put children to sleep with the threat that if they don't shut up the Afghans will get them. Stratford was not such a place.

'Be that as it may' said the Manager, invoking my favourite English phrase, 'You can't have water.'

'Oh *Kafir* – Unbeliever!' roared my compatriot, taking my head in his hands and twisting my face so that it was thrust straight at that of the surprised youth; 'son of a noseless mother! Have you not heard that those who give water to the descendants of the Holy Prophet, such as this man here, will go direct to Paradise?'

'But *he* doesn't want the water' said the youth, with praiseworthy logic, given the unfamiliarity of the argument; '*you* do.'

'That's beside the point.' Puladi, though from Kabul, was of Pashtun stock, and such people can be dangerous, as everyone for hundreds of miles around has known, often to their cost, for more years than history records. I noted the beetling brows and braced myself. Puladi took a deep breath, and I could see that he was restraining his fury in a manner fully worthy of a man of culture.

Even so, I feared that at any moment he would shout the Afghan warcry, 'Unbeliever! It is time to be afraid!'

Instead, to my amazement, he started to speak, in a low but compelling voice, as though beginning a ritual.

'Dave, I command you, in the Name of the Great King Suleiman, son of David, upon whom the Salute – give us water this instant!'

My mouth fell open.

'Oh well, if you put it that way' said Dave, and slid two tumblers of water across the counter. There was even ice in the glasses, and we gulped gratefully.

As we walked away, Professor Puladi chuckled. 'There was no need to get really angry with him; I realised that as soon as I saw his name-label, Dave.'

'What do you mean?' I spluttered. 'Did you *know* him?'

'O Aga Idries, you have been away from us for far too long. Do you not recall what a Dayv is? Is it not a demon, and are they not intractable and disobedient until compelled to servitude by authoritative commands, in the great name of King Solomon, son of David, on whom Peace? They spell it differently here, that's all.'

Well, perhaps he was a Deyv . . . I gave up trying to work it out. English logic and Eastern legends were too strong a mixture for me.

After all our difficulties – and I have reported only a tithe of them, in the interests of brevity – Puladi slept through the entire play which we saw at the Shakespeare Memorial Theatre. Perhaps it was just as well, for Shakespeare was not on. The play was *The Alchemist*, by Ben (Son of the Right Hand) Jonson.

On the way back to London, I could not help asking the learned Professor how he had known that the Dayvs of England were exactly like those in Eastern fable: or he had been playing a hunch?

'No hunch about it', he said, rather grumpily. 'Your trouble is that you spend years here and you don't study English literature. There are *Jinni*, genies, here, so why not Dayvs?'

'*Jinni*, in England!' I simply could not make the connection. Pantomimes was as far as I got.

'Jinni, in England,' repeated Puladi firmly. 'Not only that, but the great Fakrash-el-Aamash is here.' From a briefcase he produced a tattered copy of a Penguin book: F. Anstey's Edwardian classic, *The Brass Bottle*; about an Arabian spirit who ends up in London.

'Oh, that', I said. 'Anstey lived from 1856 to 1934. A barrister-turned-novelist. His real name was Anstey Guthrie, and he wrote the sensationally successful *Vice Versa*.'

Puladi looked at me sorrowfully. I could see that he thought I was making up every word.

'Yes, that. Furthermore, when I nearly got angry, with the Dayv, I followed the wise saying actually quoted by the Genie Fakrash – here, read:' I took the book. The passage he indicated was marked:

Be disregardful of thine affairs, and commit them to the course of Fate. For often a thing that enrages thee may eventually be to thy pleasing.

The Professor continued, 'You see, out of his own mouth the spirit has told us what to do: be annoyed and you will be pleased afterwards. The book explains how he reached England.'

How oriental the English are, I thought: here, again, was nothing less than the great Dryden's promise of pleasure after pain, put by an Englishman into a Genie's mouth. But must one create the pain to earn the pleasure?

As the train lulled me towards sleep, I thought of the legend of the Englishman who stormed the office of the Obituaries Editor of *The Times*.

'You've printed a death notice of me, and I'm still alive: I demand a retraction!' he cried.

'We never apologise, of course' said the Editor, 'but we can make amends. Tomorrow we'll run an announcement that you've just been born, and that'll give you a fresh start.'

Offering pleasure after pain, he was, undoubtedly. And – two birds with one stone – carrying on the tradition of never explaining. Puladi and I still have much to learn from these resourceful people.

This reflection made me realise the horror of our situation. We two Afghans, Professor Puladi and I, would never make proper tourists, we just didn't have the genius for it that the Anglo-Saxons do.

Many years before, I recalled, I had been in an antiques shop in Jerusalem. The owner was over-selling some garish metal plaques to an American tourist lady:

'You buy, very cheap, beaten copper picture of the Last Supper . . . '

She gave a scornful laugh. 'What would I do with a picture of the Last Supper? Now, if you had one of the *First* Supper, that would be something. Anyway, when's the next Supper?'

Brilliantly Anglo-Saxon, though the Atlantic has diluted the subtlety. An English person would have said something like

'And the last shall be the first and the first last, eh?' And beaten an orderly retreat. Either that or 'Supper? You don't mean "dinner", do you?' Or even, 'Oh, innit lovely? But we've got a picksha in the lounge already'.

Like tourism, the world of letters here is not without hazards. But we have all been warned: those of us who have done enough homework. An Englishman, John, Viscount Morley of Blackburn, recorded it for us over a century ago. His stricture is unequivocal:

Literature – the most seductive, the most deceiving, the most dangerous of professions.

11

On the Telly

Legal Rights in England

Hares may not be killed on Christmas Day or
Sundays, but rabbits may be hunted.
Reader's Digest: You and Your Rights

I do not for a moment claim that, when the English put you on
television, they try to brainwash you. But the searing lights, the
signing of contracts undertaking to do this and not to do that, the
abrupt changes of plan, the looking into a mirror and seeing a
stranger grimacing back . . .

I had signed the document, giving the BBC all kinds of
Rights. I had been invited to lunch (of course) and offered great
quantities of food and alcohol. I was told of dire consequences if
I failed to turn up on the day. I was introduced to important
people: and then shown a studio where sweating technicians,
masters of the moment, aimed instruments at the jittery cel-
ebrities. I recognised more famous faces, people who always
looked so carefree on the screen: but who, here, were little more
than bundles of nerves . . .

Was it by accident or design that, in conformity with brain-
washing tradition, something nice was always followed by something nasty? 'Twenty million people watch the show, you'll be
famous next week . . . of course, you'll be in the hot seat, won't
you?' someone said; 'but don't worry.'

I hadn't met any actors before. Not realising how many of
them suffer terrible stage-fright whatever the circumstances, it
seemed obvious to me that they had been brought to this pathetic state by TV and its acolytes.

Even the overheard, informal, chat followed the patterns of hot-and-cold treatment: 'Yes, she's getting a fee of seventeen thousand. Did you know that old Harry collapsed and died on the set just *seconds* before the cameras started rolling?'

I was to be interviewed by Richard Attenborough.

Even the driver of the long, black limousine which took me to rehearsals played his part, gossiping about royalty and heads of state, bringing that whiff of the unreal which always lingers near the seats of power.

A week later, another huge car, a different driver, another monologue about stars and statespersons, once more sweeping through the gates guarded by men in uniform. Report to Studio B.

Down the long, concrete tunnels, stark corridors with doors on either side. A little grey man popped out from somewhere and drew me into a room, whispering gently in my ear, 'We'll soon have you right, never fear.' Right? What was wrong? The last time I'd heard that phrase was in a hospital . . .

He stood in the middle of the tiny room with blazing lights and rigged me up in Arab robes over my perfectly good three-piece suit. Inside the collar of the camelhair *mishla* was a label: BERMANS THEATRICAL COSTUMIERS. I fished in my pocket and drew out my sunglasses. When I had them on, the sight in the mirror was of – 'An Arab sheek to the life, dearie, even to the shades!' The little man was giggling.

'Now get all the gear off, pet, and you can have it back when you've been done. I said we'd get you right, didn't I?'

An amazingly self-confident young woman with a stopwatch suspended by a leather thong around her neck grabbed my sleeve as I relinquished the sheikhly robes, and pushed me into the room next door. Here a languid, lacquered beauty dumped me into a chair, again dazzled by lights, and fussed with sprays on my hair, something for the cheeks, a reassuring pat on the arm. 'Now then, that wasn't so bad, was it?' Makeup.

'No, thank you. Not bad at all.'

'Back to your dresser, dear.'

Again the little man. 'Now the Sheek's uniform, soon have you sorted out. Let's see you standing straight. My, you *do* look like Lawrence of Arabia!' He tittered and stood back as I obediently stiffened my neck with appropriate aristocratic insolence.

Now I was padding, in my bedouin sandals, towards a little knot of people huddled around the table of the hospitality (locally called the 'hostility') suite.

'Just a snifter old boy' – then the portly, horn-rimmed functionary looked up and saw me – 'O Gawd, look what the cat's brought in.'

I explained, to the falsely interested faces set with uncaring eyes, that none of this was my own idea. 'You see, everybody in the West seems to think that everyone from the East is some kind of Arab. So they've done this to me. It's rather as if *we* imagined that *you* were all crusading Franks, and so on.'

'Well, never mind, sport: have a double brandy. Those lights out there will kill you, otherwise.'

He turned away, giggling to someone else, 'He's not real, speaks English too well – he's an actor!' I asked for a glass of water, but didn't get it. 'Bad as that, eh?' someone called out.

Now I was being led straight onto the stage: or so I thought. It was, in fact a large and opulently furnished room, and I was faced by a prosperous-looking man with Important written all over him. He had the smoothness I always associate with psychiatrists. Shaking my hand too warmly, he smiled and then rubbed his hands together. No, not a psychiatrist. More like a superior kind of social worker.

'I hope you won't take this amiss, after all your trouble and all that.'

'No, of course not.' With any luck the transmission had been cancelled.

'You see, we feel that that rigout of yours is a bit much. What have you got underneath? I see. A lounge suit. Well, so has Dickie. It'll look better, you see. Lounge suits. I suppose they didn't tell you not to dress up.' He smoothed the lapels of his own, immaculate suit.

'Jolly good. Knew you'd understand.'

A run back to the dressing-room, herded by the haughty beauty. Off with the motley. 'What a *crying shame*, Duckie; just when I was getting used to you like that.' The dresser looked downcast.

I was feeling quite paranoid by now. This was a technique right from the textbook. Put someone in inappropriate clothes, to make him feel uneasy. Then accuse him of being behind it all himself. But do it in the nicest possible way.

A classic manipulative procedure. I almost knew the page and paragraph of one of those paperbacks on mind-bending. Depersonalisation/repersonalisation, the KGB called it.

Or were they filming it all for *Candid Camera*?

I swayed as someone took my arm and noted, for the first time, that I had only the bedouin sandals between my feet and nakedness. 'The sandals don't go with the suit,' I muttered.

'Feeling bad? Oh, sandals.' The man blinked his eyes rapidly, thinking. 'Never mind, we'll make sure that the cameras show just the upper part of your body. They're quite used to that.' He was telling me about how news announcers used to wear only the jacket of their dinner suits before the fixed cameras in the old days when a harsh, metallic voice grated from a loudspeaker on the wall. '*Two minutes to transmission – good luck, everybody!*' Someone pointed at my feet. 'Lose the sandals, for Heaven's sake.'

'Can't do that', someone else answered, authoritatively, 'He'd get in a bate – it's part of his native costume. Remember that fellow a fortnight ago, the one with the . . . '

I was propelled into the great hanger of a studio, a tiny corner of it mocked up as a study. I was looking wildly around when I was captured by the reassuring smile of Attenborough guiding me towards his outstretched hand and then a deep armchair, framed by a wall of imitation books.

I do not remember much about the interview, apart from a man wearing earphones who crawled along the floor making wind-up signals which I assumed meant 'keep talking', and was only afterwards told meant 'hurry up'. And the sticky sensation of the sweat oozing through the makeup on my face while a more rapid flow, uninhibited by pancake, caressed my bare feet. Yes, the lights were hot: and someone had snatched off my shades as I was making my entry.

The strangest thoughts were going through my head: about yoghurt, mint-sauce, saffron. I had recently been looking into their history. I suddenly realised why English people became fractious when in foreign parts, and caused bewilderment among the natives. Discomfort, the impossibility of handling one's situation, being robbed of the ability to make decisions: these all brought miscellaneous thoughts to the surface . . .

Yoghurt: the English, absurdly, had first started to use it, in the nineteenth century, as a crank food. It was supposed to keep one young. Mint sauce, imported from Saracen Spain the books said, was really a salad dressing. Here they used it only on roast lamb. As for saffron: in England it was baked into cakes, for heaven's sake.

And my clothes. Three-piece suit, no socks, and sandals. Just in time, just before I cracked, the words of the classic book of conduct, the *Akhlaq-i-Mohsini* ran through my head: I must keep calm: 'The garment which never wears out is – patience.' And then the Afghan saying *From Patience, Victory*! Hold fast, Shah. Nothing lasts for ever.

'Well, thank you for appearing on the programme.'

I think I replied, 'Saffron and yoghurt, with mint sauce, any time.'

As we were faded out, someone from the huge glass-fronted control room which brooded over us crooned effusive thanks over the intercom. The Director of Something had telephoned. He was pleased.

My sister Amina had watched the interview at home. 'You looked all right', was all she said about it, and I did not like to ask for more. It was an English-type remark, and therefore might have concealed terrible truths.

My cleaning lady, who had also seen the programme, was polite enough to volunteer nothing at all about how I had looked or sounded. All she said was 'Inee a lurverly man, Richard A'enbra? Seen all 'is flicks I 'ave . . . Ooh, inne 'annsum? And just fancy YOU meetin' 'im'.

Now, I like and respect Sir Richard Attenborough, too. So it was reassuring to know that this feeling had not been induced by any Machiavellian technique practised in the dreaded depths of the Television Centre.

The distinction of being presented to the viewers in such august company may have played its part. It is sometimes said that, pretty soon, everyone in the country will have been seen on TV. I don't think so at all. Say, if you like, that I have a vested interest in holding this opinion: but experience teaches that it is not easy to have the English take any notice of you. Often they don't even bother about natural disasters, such as their climate. You may care to read Maria Edgeworth's *Essays*. In them she makes the matter clear, when alluding to the earthquake 'which had the honour to be noticed by the English Royal Society.'

12

Going to a Mortimer

Liverpool

In Liverpool . . . 'Why bother calling it
England?' demanded a taxi-driver bitterly,
'why not just call it London?' The south-east
would be happy to saw off the rest of England
and let it float away into the Atlantic.
Graham Turner, in *The Daily Telegraph*

'Shan't see thee tomorrow, I'm going to a mortimer.'

A mortimer? I had heard of John Mortimer, and enjoyed his
marvellous autobiography, *Clinging to the Wreckage*. I knew Sir
Mortimer Wheeler, the archaeologist. I knew about thee and
thou, and even shan't and won't, which are elusive problems in
English, but 'mortimer' as a common noun?

I was in the street of a medium-sized Northern town, and the
scrap of conversation was between two strapping wenches, red-
cheeked and dressed in blue jeans, fussing with perambulator
blankets and in no way different from the millions of other
English mothers to be found in such places.

I memorised the word, because I felt that I could hardly go
right up to the two and ask, straight out, 'Excuse me, what's a
mortimer?' That wouldn't be English.

But this was not the effete South and, besides, the women
knew one another, luckily for me, well enough for the second
one to shrill, 'What's a mortimer, then?'

I edged closer, trying to attune my ear to the cadences of
upper England.

'A mortimer's what they've got on at Town Hall, that's what.'

She glanced at me, and I decided that I had done enough edging
for the day, and I strode away with my scrap of information.

There was no notice about the mortimer up outside the Town
Hall, so I walked straight in, to find a small, shrivelled-looking
girl sitting behind a desk in a marble hall evidently modelled on
St Pancras Railway Station and designed to overwhelm anyone,
by its Victorian, incarnate civic pride. The girl had the name
LORRAINE spelt out in large gold letters suspended from a
thin chain about her neck. Lorraine? I searched my memory.
The phrase, from a history book, came up: 'Part of Germany in
1871 . . . ' That seemed little use.

'I've come about the mortimer', I said, not being able to think
of anything more circumlocutory yet direct enough to be acceptable north of Watford.

'Tisn't till tomorrow, love. It's going to be a big one, though.
Haven't had a mortimer like it since July.'

'A big one, eh, that's good.' But was it? Are mortimers good
or bad? After all, the sum total of my information to date was
that it was tomorrow, it was here, and it was going to be big.

'Where actually is it to be held?' She might say Ballroom,
Conference Hall, Sauna Bath . . .

'Through that door over there.'

I tried again. I had come from the south. I did not know this
young lady at all, and could not therefore be so direct as to ask
fundamental questions straight out. So, 'What time will it be?'

'Ten-thirty in the morning,' Lorraine said.

A big mortimer at ten-thirty. Now she was going to say
something else, was bound to add to my information.

'Make sure you're prompt, though. It's going to be a big one.'

'Right.' That didn't help very much.

Still I lingered. Lorraine turned her head away and combed
her long, bleached hair into her typewriter, glancing sidelong
towards me at the same time. I tried to divine the meaning of
that look. It might tell me whether a mortimer was good or bad,
was a celebration or a memorial service, a protest rally, perhaps.
No, nothing to be gained from her expression: professional,
calm, slightly modified by the tugging of the comb through the
hair . . .

Lorraine's nerve wasn't going to break, but of course she was
English, and she was protected by the official nature of her desk,

typewriter, wastebasket, sheaves of papers; by her comb. Well, my Afghan nerve wouldn't break, either. I stood my ground, even though, in anthropological terms, I was not really entitled to any territory here. As our saying has it, 'Leave home, but take your battle-flag.'

'I've come from the south', I said, almost adding, 'south of Watford', which was, I knew, acceptedly a pretty terrible region, London and all that. I suppose I did it to ingratiate myself with her, just as some beasts in combat will suddenly offer the jugular vein in token of submission, or at any rate, to seek an end to hostilities.

'The south. You a friend of Nora Pertaw?'

Nora Pertaw. It sounded familiar, but yet it did not, quite. I mumbled something unintelligible. The south, evidently, meant Nora Pertaw to her. But, I suddenly realised, I had missed an opportunity by not at least catching the edge of the offering and expanding the context, as all good books on social intercourse advised.

Perhaps there was yet time.

'Do you know her well?' I enquired.

'No.'

Maybe Nora was famous, a pop-star perhaps, that one saw singing on the television. Or it could have been just a remark, on the lines of 'You from America? Then you must know my Uncle Jack.'

'Is she in the south?'

'No, she's here, in town.' Lorraine was frowning slightly. Nora Pertaw *here*! 'How interesting. Here. I see.' She gave me a funny look.

'Now I'm rather busy', she said, taking out a bottle of nail-varnish and using the tone of a mother losing interest in the endless questions of a tiresome child.

'Yes, of course, I'm so sorry.' I backed away.

She gave me, suddenly, a pleasant, fixed smile, the kind you get with 'have a nice day' in the United States. 'Well, come to the mortimer. Then you'll be able to see Nora.'

Had Lorraine decided that I really did want to see Nora Pertaw? I think so. And this would be her small contribution, giving me the information that Nora would be there, and I would be able to see her.

Still backing as I went down the grand flight of steps leading to the street outside, I collided with a large group of Pakistanis, all beards and turbans, furry hats and smiles. They picked me up, dusted me down, laughing and chatting.

'You all right? Good. Sorry we bumped into you. We were not looking where we were going, isn't it? You see, we're so excited about Mortimer. Coming in to make final arrangements.' Each of them spoke one line, like people in a stage act.

I could not stand it any longer. 'Brothers', I gasped, 'What's a mortimer?'

The long-bearded leader of the Pakistanis looked at me with disbelief. 'Do you not know what it is?'

'It is one meeting' said the second most-bearded Pakistani.

'*One* meeting? Oh, I see. But what kind of meeting?' I asked.

'Any kind of a meeting,' said a third Pakistani.

'It is a proper Eastern word for a meeting, a *Mu'atima*, meeting, meeting, *Mu'atima*,' said a fourth.

'That is vy ve use the vord at all' said another. 'Don't you understand English langvidge?'

'I suppose that you are one Cypriot' said the most bearded Pakistani, not unkindly. 'And so I shall explain. You are welcome to come to Mu'atima. It is a meeting, of a kind which we regularly have, with English natives of this town where we are settled, generally in connection with matters associated with trade, industry and commerce. And shops' he added helpfully.

I knew what a Mu'atima was, I'd known it for most of my life; but how did so many of the English natives know it? And know it to the extent that they used the word like one of their own?

'Do they like mortimers?' I asked.

'Tremendously. We serve them jelabies, Indian – I mean Pakistani – sweetmeats, and we have discussions.'

Then the head man introduced himself: 'I am Mr Pertaw, and my wife, Nora, has taken initiative in planning, as she is a native-born here, and from the South. Attend our Mu'atima tomorrow. Come, I'll arrange it with the reception desk inside, so that you get a good place on platform, there's one lady there who does this thing, this arranging. She is Miss Lorraine.'

Suddenly I sensed danger. Supposing I went back into the Town Hall and Lorraine informed Mr Pertaw that I had been enquiring about his wife? Mr Pertaw was much bigger than me;

in fact he was massive. I suddenly remembered that I had
another pressing mortimer to attend, gabbled apologies to my
Pakistanis, and fled.

As my train started to move southwards, with no sign of a
Pertaw-Mortimer pursuit party, I relaxed. One day, I was sure,
there would not be a city, town, village even, in England without
its regular mortimer. The English had absorbed, almost without
trace, the brutish Normans who had actually conquered them:
already many of them had accepted Mortimers as perfectly
normal occasions. The time would come, I was pretty sure,
when only benighted foreigners would have to ask 'What's a
mortimer?'

I have chosen the tale of the Mortimer to represent a certain
tendency of orientalisation which one sees on every hand in
England these days. Some people (not me) seem to see it even
where it may not exist. On second thoughts, though, they may
be right: they are English and I am not, and they ought to know.
Perhaps some hidden hand *is* at work.

There is no space to go deeper into this matter, but I note one
striking coincidence in passing. An English newspaper columnist commented that the BBC was styling Welsh Television
programmes TELEDU, supposedly a Welsh word.

But, when he looked it up (in the *Oxford English Dictionary*,
naturally) what did he find but this: '*Teledu*: The Stinking
Badger of Java and Sumatra, or Stinkard.'

Is Asia penetrating into Wales as well?

When I referred this, for comment, to my Welsh expert,
Judge Huw Ifor Lloyd, he said, 'we may have been paranoid to
begin with, *bach*, but they certainly do help to keep it going,
don't they?' And he should know, as his first language is
English.

13

Mr Verloren Hoop

Historical Talent

The English are the world's masters of the most useful historical talent, the talent for forgetting anything that interferes with the gratifying pictures of their national past . . . The Englishman sticks to the dogmatic, false and immensely valuable view of his own history.

D. W. Brogan: *The English People*

He was introduced to me as Mr Vernon Hope, but soon confided that he was really called Verloren Hoop, 'from The Netherlands, which everyone in England calls Holland, though of course they have a Holland of their own, in Lincolnshire'. Like many Dutchmen, he spoke excellent English. I noted only two unusual points: he left the second 'l' in when saying 'Lincolnshire'. And for him the word 'sugar' was *syougar*, just the way it is written, but never said, in English.

Mr Hope was a highly cultured man. In fact he was so cultured that he told me so again and again. His interest in mysterious England had begun when, knowing that the Dutch and English respected one another, he had been mystified to find that 'the Englishman Butler' in his *Description of Holland*, had written something which seemed to indicate, as he put it, meretriciousness:

> A land that rides at anchor and is moored
> In which they do not live, but go aboard.

'At first', Mr Hope informed me, as we sat having tea in the Waldorf's palm court, 'I asked an Englishman, and he said Butler must have been drunk, Holland seemed to him to sway like a ship. Then', he took the sliver of cucumber from his tiny sandwich and laid it aside, swallowing the buttered bread at one gulp, 'then I thought, "perhaps he is making fun of me. A funny joke." So I decided to embark upon a voyage of discovery, as you might say.'

His pale eyes fixed me through his rimless glasses and he wagged a bony finger. 'Naturally, I am cognisant of the fact that when you say, in English, "As you might say", you really mean to say, "As *I* might say". 'Indeed', he continued, '"As *I* might say" in England really means "As I am actually saying"!' He sat back with a look of quiet satisfaction, such as one might expect on the face of a teacher who had just explained something to a backward child.

Then he surveyed the tea-table. 'Sugar', he muttered (he actually said 'syougar'), 'is an eastern import. The word was originally *shakar*. Another word for it, *qand*, is, of course, our "candy". Comes from the Middle East, what the Americans called The Near East.'

'Mr Hoop', I ventured, 'is it possible that we might collaborate in this investigation, to any extent?' Mr Hoop instantly proved the truth of our old Afghan observation, 'One straw can set fire to a whole barn'.

'That's an interesting construction', he rejoined, 'because in English, "To any extent" can mean either "To the limit", or else "Not to the limit".' Again the self-satisfied pursing of the lips. He was a very scholarly kind of man.

For some reason, I prevented him answering my first question – although I realised that his last remark had been parenthetic – by asking, 'What is the English definition of a pedant?'

Hoop looked, with approval, at the wrought-iron of the Waldorf's gracious stairway, at the pastel decor and nineteen-twenties lamps. Then he placed his palms together and smiled.

'A pedant', he answered obligingly, 'is, in English, "One who is learned without being judicious, whose learning is undigested, or allowed to appear unseasonably: one who attaches too much importance to merely formal matters in scholarship".'

Well, *he* had said it, as we say in England. Then, 'You say collaborate. Collaborate is a word I do not like. This is, of course, only a technical question, if attentively examined. The aetiology may be adequately established if mention is made of the central factor: to wit, that the German occupation authorities during the Second World War employed this word to denote the work of those nationals of an occupied country or other territory who were disposed, or could be induced, by whatever method, to work together (and that is the meaning of the word, from the Latin, not English) with the aforesaid Teutonic military or, quite usually, civilian, apparatus, sometimes, or rather, specifically, established for the purpose of what they were pleased to term "Collaboration". Naturally, those days are gone, and we are all one, a part, or, more accurately, our countries are parts, of the European Economic Community, which it pleases some to term "The Common Market".'

'Thank you', I said.

'I have not yet finished. The choice of words notwithstanding, I am disposed to accept your proposal. I shall now repair to the House of Lords.'

When he returned from wherever it was (leaving me struggling with subordinate clauses, which may have occasioned the style in which I am, not unnaturally, attempting to couch this passage) he explained, again with a smile.

'You have been the victim, or should I say, in seeking to put the matter more concisely, the subject, the object, even, of a jest. In Den Haag, the Netherlands' capital city, there is a certain bar where alcohol may be obtained. It is called The House of Lords. I therefore styled the bar of this hotel, analogically, in this fashion. Were you persuaded that, shunning your company and hieing forth upon some egregious errand, I was indeed proceeding towards the English Chamber of the Nobility?'

'Only for a moment' I said. 'Let's get on.'

I spoke for a few minutes about my experiences, but he was anxious to relate his own, and simply waited for me to pause. 'You will note that I am wearing a certain garment. What is its English name?'

'A Norfolk Jacket', I said, feeling like a contestant in a television quiz.

'Wrong', he said, 'or, rather, right in the sense that it is in fact widely known as such. Wrong in the sense that it was originally a Bavarian, a German, coat, and is called that by those few people still alive who remember the occasion of its introduction among the English.'

'How interesting.'

'Yes, but depressing too.'

'Why should that be?'

'Because so much that is customarily considered typically English turns out to have come from somewhere else. Did you know that whisky could not have been made in Scotland unless the Saracens had introduced distillation to the Continent in the Middle Ages?'

'But Scotland is not England.'

'It's the principle. Besides, the English love whisky. So do I.'

I told him that there must be a lot of things about England that could not be considered foreign, and he immediately asked me which.

'Roast beef and Yorkshire pudding, for example.'

'Roast beef is the translation of a French phrase, brought by the Normans. "Pudding" is merely the French "Boudin".' He looked at me with an expression of gloom. It was obvious that this kind of thing mattered very much to him. To jolly him out of it, I said, 'Well, how about "*Suet* Pudding"?'

'Pudding you already know. "Suet" is from the Latin *sebum*, fat. All etymological dictionaries feature it.'

I could not help asking him, 'Mr Hoop, how do you know so much about language?'

He gave me a knowing, or it may have been a modest, smile and narrowed his eyes. 'Through a discipline invented by an Englishman. It is called The Study of Culture at a Distance. It rapidly gained academic respectability.'

'You mean that you don't have to go to a country to investigate its ideas and ways?'

'That is so. But continue.'

'Well, now . . . Richard the Lionhearted?'

'Spoke only French: *Coeur de Lion*, of course, originally. And I have worse news for you, since you have obviously not investigated the sources regarding this English King who despised the English.'

I gagged a little on my Darjeeling. 'Mr Hoop, I wonder whether I have heard you aright?'

'Then I shall give you the very words from Esme Wingfield's *The History of English Patriotism.*' He took a sheaf of papers from a bulging briefcase. 'Volume I, London 1913, page nine. She reminds her readers that King Richard Coeur de Lion, of England, hero of a hundred English tales of the Crusades, so disliked the English that one of his favourite oaths was "Do you take me for an *Englishman*?"' My senses reeled, but I persevered. 'Boadicea?' I offered.

'Boudicca, pre-English. There were no English people on these islands when she was alive.'

'They were still in Schleswig?'

'Perhaps farther afield still. They originated from Scythia, in the region of the Jaxartes River, also called the Syr Daria, in the Ilaq of Ferghana as it was to the ancients, north-east of Bokhara and Khorasan. The caravan route from there extends to Beijing.'

'The Battle of Waterloo, Wellington and all that?' Something nearer home would, I hoped, interest him, though his knowledge of North and Central Asian geography was impressive.

'Unfortunately,' he declaimed, 'we cannot say much about that, if we are to be fair, unless we allow the determining contribution of Marshal Blücher, who was a German.'

He paused for breath, but only for a moment. Then he continued, relentlessly.

'In case you are thinking of the English gentleman's monocle, about which your military allusion reminds me, I have to say that it is from the French, and – earlier – from the Greek and Latin *monos, oculis.*' He screwed up his face, as if accommodating an eyeglass, and intoned, 'Robin Hood was a Norman, and even Churchill, Churchill was half American, and part Red Indian on his mother's side.'

I took up a biscuit and started to nibble it to cover my ignorance. 'Ahah!' he cried, 'I see that you have in your hand one of those shortbread confections called, in English, "Petticoat Tails"!'

'Yes.'

'French!' The word was delivered with almost Gallic verve. 'The name is but a mispronunciation of the French: *Petits Couteilles.*'

He brightened a little when, reaching into my store of recently-acquired knowledge, I said, 'But you must admit that the French say "Higgie-Liffey" for "High Life"; and I often heard, when in Latin America, *Hora Inglesa*, 'English time', meaning punctuality . . . '

The gloom lifted only temporarily. He went on:

'On the other hand (derived from a foreign phrase and in fact meaningless in England) "check" is Arabic and "lilac" is Persian, "verandah" is Indian and "ottoman" is Turkish. Did you know that syrup, zircon, jasmine, filly and tariff are all oriental words? Would you have contracted to eat your hat if anyone had offered to dissolve away almost all English words and phrases which you could have thought of in an afternoon, and if he had been successful?'

'I suppose so', I ventured.

'Then I am delighted to be able to inform you', said the indomitable specialist, 'that you might have so agreed without fear of penalty.'

'How can that be?'

'Because "hat" – or "hatte" – is in fact a sour milk preparation which English children used to reject when offered it by their nurses with the adjuration to consume it in order to grow big and strong. Eating their "hat" was entirely possible, though a revolting prospect. Hence the ejaculation, "I'll eat my hat if . . . "'

A man with miniature compasses as a charm on a watch-chain across his fat stomach weaved past, and I had an idea. Only a few days before Lord ('Bill') Astor, a big shot in Masonry, had tried to enrol me, with feverish indirectness, in the society. I said, 'Well, everyone knows that Freemasonry started in England: or Scotland, at any rate.'

Mr Hoop shot me a glance of deep sympathy, such as one might in the case of a singularly ignorant child.

'One reference book among many distinctly states', he intoned, as if quoting holy writ, 'that Freemasonry was brought into Spain by the Saracens in the ninth century, whence it reached England.'

For some reason, I was starting to feel a sensation akin to surfeit (from the French, *surfait*), and – perhaps also because my knowledge had been shown to be so very inferior to his – Mr Verloren Hoop said no more about collaboration, and so we parted.

Not long after this, as is often the way of things, I came across a familiar sequence of words in a book when looking up something else: 'Verloren Hoop = Forlorn Hope'. It turns out that Forlorn Hope, so redolent of English gallantry and derring-do, is not English at all. There, in black and white, was the documentation. This most English of terms is nothing more than a mispronunciation of the Dutch. It comes from *verloren hoop*, literally a Lost Troop.

As we know, in England, nothing matters too much. So, when confiding my latest discovery to English friends, I was surprised to find that some would not believe me, and others were positively annoyed that this splendid phrase could be anything but English.

Even Mrs Coggins said, 'Werl, them Dutch, they speaks English, doan they?'

My theory is that all this is bound up with the provable fact that the Empire (upon which the Sun never sets) has not been dissolved at all. That, in turn, explains why a lot of English people chuckled when they heard it alleged that they had lost an empire and not yet found a world role. It was in October 1984 that Mr S. M. Gordon Clark, writing from the Carlton Club, broke security on the unsetting sun, in a letter to *The Daily Telegraph*.

The 'network of dependent territories', he explained, still existed. The Sun would continue to rise above some part of the British possessions until 1997, when Hong Kong was scheduled to return to Chinese control.

Fair enough, I thought; but surely this was simply postponing the inevitable, giving the Empire only another thirteen years at most? There must be an Englishman with an answer to that one.

It was the kind of thought that would first have cheered Mr Hoop (with Mr Gordon Clark's letter), and then dashed his hopes with the realisation that only a dozen years then remained until the end of the sundrenched imperium.

Unlike Verloren Hoop, I had spent a lot of time in England, and had therefore learned not to jump to conclusions, even about the demise of the Empire. The English, as I knew from experience and observations, are a veritable embodiment of Newton's Third Law of Motion: To Every Action There Is An Equal and Opposite Reaction. They would deal with 1997 all right. Wait and see. Sure enough, no more than three days had passed when *The Times* came out with the leading article which I had been more than half expecting.

The Royal Observatory, it announced, had determined that 'there is an overlap of some forty minutes' daylight between Pitcairn and Chagos, even under the most unfavourable astronomical circumstances.' So, the Sun would continue to shine over the Empire, even if there is no longer the Empire we'd been used to.

But, I wondered, what if Pitcairn, or even Chagos, were to go? Or might the link not perhaps be broken in some other place? The map is always changing. *The Times* came up with the answer. It suggested, on 6 October 1984, that a British satellite could be placed in stationary orbit wherever a gap might present itself: 'perhaps containing a small quantity of British soil and a flag.'

But satellites are expensive. It would cost millions to put up one, let alone the several which might eventually be needed. After all, the United Nations wants to decolonise even peoples (like the Gibraltarians) who like things as they are. So, in the spirit of English amateurism, I decided to make my own Anglean-type contribution to the problem. How, I asked myself, can I prevent the Sun setting on the British Empire?

It came to me in a flash. If the Union Flag, tea-drinking, fish and chips, roast beef and the rest can be dismissed as innovations, how about the sunlit Empire itself? I looked up the source of the phrase 'The Empire upon which the Sun never sets'. Sure enough, I found that it was used, long before there ever was a British Empire, by Claudian. It really means the *Roman* Empire. There you are – vanished it.

Given time, one can think oneself out of anything, in England.

I am aware that many people, especially foreigners, are under the impression that whatever *The Times* says is official, the voice of the Government, and therefore represents accepted policy. Does this, you may well ask, not mean that my solution may not be adopted, since the powers-that-be will have settled the matter in favour of satellites?

I'll admit that that did give me a moment's thought. Then something else came to my aid. It was the lavishly-produced

magazine issued by *The Times* to celebrate its bicentenary. As I
realised, perusing page 33 of this inspiring document, those who
think the paper reflects Government policy could not be more
wrong. Thus Mr Gladstone (Prime Minister): 'The insolence of
The Times becomes more and more a national evil'. Then the
words of Lord John Russell (another Prime Minister): 'If
England is ever to be England again, this vile tyranny of *The
Times* must be cut off.'

An unEnglish tyranny it may be, but foreigners may be for-
given for not knowing it. After all, page 50 of the same magazine
distinctly states that King Edward (Rich Guard) VIII asked his
Prime Minister, Mr Baldwin, to stop publication of an article in
The Times. He had to be told that the Government had no such
power. If the King of England did not know how the paper stood
officially, what hope is there for foreigners?

The Times has more power than the Government. It could
easily put up a satellite, or look up Claudian.

This matter did not come up in my discussions with Mr Verloren Hoop, which is probably just as well. He had tried to delve
into the past, believing that legends and scholarship must pro-
vide useful information; as we say, *Man talaba, wajada*, who
seeks, finds. The English do not seem to be so sure. In his
Assessments and Anticipations, W. R. Inge, the redoubtable
Dean of St Paul's is quite clear on the matter:

> What we know of the past is mostly not worth knowing.
> What is worth knowing is mostly uncertain. Events in the
> past may roughly be divided into those which probably never
> happened and those which do not matter.

As Mrs Coggins said, when I mentioned the matter to her,
'That don't leave you a lot to put in your book, do it?'

14

Ark Not Found as Recluse
Leaves Thousands

Funny

The only funny thing about England is the
English, and they don't know it.

Constance Wagner:
The Major Has Seven Guests

'People in England lead a dull life', said the Italian anthropologist whom I met at the Notting Hill Carnival. Ten thousand or more people were jumping up and down, and playing such loud music, that he could hardly make himself heard. 'That', he shouted, 'is why they exaggerate. Look at the media.' He had recognised my face from one of those international conferences, which scholars have to attend to impress one another with their wisdom or to arouse jealousy at the size of their research grants. So he was less easy to shake off than most people.

He went on to illustrate his point with two telling examples. First, he had been terrified by the headline ENGLAND COLLAPSES, only to discover that it referred to a game of cricket. Then he had watched, on television, what seemed to be a Government health warning, saying that you'd be a monkey if you drank tea, only to find that it was tea that the chimps were advertising.

Infected as I was by English attitudes, I found at least a part of me automatically rejecting the idea as preposterous. Surely it was the *Italian* media which were known, worldwide (well, in

England, anyway), for exaggeration and intemperate reporting?

I demurred: 'Look', I said, 'it hasn't been like that with me. A reporter once came to the house. I looked something up on a map of the tenth century, and he didn't think it at all odd.'

'*Tenth century?* There weren't any maps in those days', he said.

'Oh yes, there were,' I told him. 'Still extant, excellent maps, by my compatriot Al Biruni of Ghazna. Amazing detail, wonder of the world.'

'And is the map still accurate?'

'Still accurate.'

'So that you can use it?'

'Yes, of course.'

'That only shows you are *almost* a real eccentric. A true one would use a map that was *not* of any use. But you are strange enough. The English would not find you odd at all.'

'But I had no other map in the house.'

'That's all the more eccentric, in the twentieth century. Now, if you have stopped talking irrelevancies, I shall tell you a tale about the English.' Like a good anthropologist, he had 'collected' it; and here it is.

An Englishman died, and found himself in a garden, a perfectly symmetrical one, without a plant, a blade of grass, even, out of place. 'This,' he told himself, 'this must be Heaven.'

He walked through the maze and along the paths bounded by painted ceramic gnomes, until he came to a place where people in funny paper hats were sitting at tables, eating eel pie, faggots, tripe and onions or cow's foot jelly. An orchestra played, again and again, the haunting air *Greensleeves*, which, some say, was composed by Henry VIII.

In a large building nearby were paintings by Stubbs and Landseer, and books such as *Beowulf* and the *Ecclesiastical History* of the Venerable Bede. The Englishman was pleased to find that it was carpeted in Wilton. Tea and warm beer were served free, on demand.

There was even a bus queue to join, without the disadvantage of having to go anywhere, because the buses were on strike. There were rainy days as well as hot ones, when thick anoraks, bedsocks and hot-water bottles were free to all. One could watch cricket, darts and championship snooker . . .

'Yes,' continued the anthropologist, 'there was all this and much, much more, and the Englishman felt, if not in the seventh heaven, at least in the first or second one.

'One day he came across a miserable-looking foreigner, the first he had seen during the million or so years since he had arrived. The foreigner was struggling to open one of those packets of potato crisps which are designed to afford the necessary exercise before your high-carbohydrate intake. He was, at the same time, trying to understand what was happening in a television serial in which, one after another, people took part in long shouting-matches.

'The Englishman wasted no time. "And what" he demanded of the interloper, "what are you doing in an *English* heaven?"

'The other man said nothing, but merely pointed, despondently, at a sign which the Englishman had not noticed before.

'It said: "This Hell is reserved for NON-ENGLISH consignees."'

The Italian grinned, and what with the carnival, which was very ethnic, and the heat, which was, uncharacteristically for London in August, at 80 degrees (Fahrenheit), I thought I would get out of town. I even felt like saying to the Italian scholar, 'I don't think I'd mind a cup of tea and a blast or two of *Greensleeves* myself, at the moment.' But, mindful of the need to be objective, I gave him my telephone number, smiled my *pregos* and *grazies*, and sought the cool heights of Hampstead Heath.

I needed a rest, some air. It would be nice to go to the seaside; after all, nowhere in England is more than seventy miles from the sea. But, I remembered, in England seventy miles is a very long distance. And anyway, Mel Calman in his Diary in *The Times*, had written that 'the English like to sit in their cars and stare at the sea'. I didn't feel that I could face that.

As my car nosed intrepidly ever upwards, through the areas now known to immigrants as British West Hampstead and Belsize Pakistan, I realised that the Heath, though cooler and more inviting than the throbbing flatlands of the W11 postal district, was but an empty space. As a man of words, I felt that need for a readaholic fix, as my esteemed friend Professor Dr Robert E.

Ornstein (Institute for the Study of Human Knowledge), the twin-brain theory exponent, englishes the message of the neurones, or it may be supracortical phenomones. You get the idea: the message from within.

'An Englishman never enjoys himself without a purpose', was the dictum of the great A. P. Herbert; so I bought three newspapers, to do some work as I relaxed. In England, of course, the guilt of the Puritan or nonconformist conscience is still very strong. It was not a foreigner who wrote the music-hall song which begins 'This is so nice, it must be illegal.' Thus it was that, within two or three minutes of buying the papers, I realised that I was in fact, engaged upon essential research: in an ideal position to investigate whether the Italian academic's opinion about the exaggerating Press of London really had any basis.

Not that I could give the idea much credence: the Press was, in my experience, a model of sobriety. One of today's headlines was TRAINS BREAK DOWN BECAUSE OF HEAT, SAYS BRITISH RAIL. Quite so: the words had a comforting ring, they were calm and direct. Only a few months before, I recalled, the headline had been equally placid and appropriate: TRAINS BREAK DOWN BECAUSE OF COLD, SAYS BRITISH RAIL. Anyone who had been to an English school knows that one is carefully instructed there that 'Britain has no extremes of climate: it is therefore said to be in the Temperate Zone.'

'Not made for this weather' they say, quite truly, when the telephones don't work, the car doesn't start, or the pipes all freeze.

Temperate: that was the English image.

On Hampstead Heath I settled down on a bench, only partly vandalised and not entirely covered with toffee-papers, and opened the *Express* at random. The words almost leapt off the page; a reader – admittedly from Scotland – was asking 'if we live in Britain by choice, why can't we be content with British ways?'

I was thankful that the English press had changed so much for the better since Willian Cowper's time. Two centuries before, the Italian's criticisms would have been borne out by their content. 'What a medley are our public prints,' cries Cowper, 'half the page filled with the ruin of the country, and the other half filled with the vices and pleasures of it.'

There was no point in reading too much about the perennial preoccupations: sport, industrial matters, international affairs, show-business; people always seized on what the papers said about such matters to analyse the English mind, and I was trying to break fresh ground. Skimming all that, I came to the nitty-gritty.

A search was on for a replacement for the kidnapped cat, Proudfoot, which had been earning £100 a day; Bob Wilson, of Somerset, was claiming a reward of a thousand pounds for breeding the first pink canary . . . A little too mercenary, perhaps, to be typically English: Love of animals taking second place to material considerations. But perhaps the items were there because they showed unusual behaviour, on the man-bites-dog principle. Yes, two other stories clearly underlined this. In one, two uniformed policemen had been thrown out of a festival by people from a Peace Convoy where drugs were openly on sale at Wakefield, West Yorkshire. And a newly ordained Catholic priest, a member of a celibate vocation, was married, and with children. He'd been a Church of England vicar.

I turned to the *Daily Mail*. Smash-grab raiders fail to break newsagent's window in two attempts in Hampshire. In Harrogate, Lord Charles Spencer-Churchill's ankle is better. In Oxfordshire, Judo Star Weds Beauty Expert, and Airline Pilot is Robbed by Bee Rustlers. Plenty happening in Oxfordshire, then: but nothing too sensational.

Cheltenham seemed pretty active, too: there was a mock shoot-out at a Wild West Type Wedding there. The *Mail* provides plenty of international and celebrity context to its reportage. A British deserter (from the Foreign Legion) has been held following a murder 'near Buckingham Palace'. The *Foreign Legion*, of course . . . A Charity Olympics had been cancelled when no spectators turned up. Perhaps they had gone the wrong way: the events included running backwards.

The *Mail* is worried about the prospects of another patriotic newspaper, the *Daily Express*. Its future, we are told, seems to be under the influence of an 'odd trio'. These are given as Dr Marwan, President Nasser's former son-in-law, plus Czech-born Robert Maxwell, and *Observer* owner Tiny Rowland ('German-born'). Nothing about that in the *Express*, but I read my horoscope prediction there ('You are in a hurry to get through what you're doing') and fulfilled the prediction by hurriedly turning to the *Telegraph*.

Here I found a story to match the Foreign Legion/Buckingham Palace piece. A Moroccan professional footballer (from Casablanca) was accused of trying to murder a woman barrister 'near Mrs Thatcher's home'. Foreign again. The paper also notes that Noah's Ark has not been discovered on Mount Ararat, and mentioned that a half-million-pound picture in the National Gallery is probably a fake.

There was quite a splash of the story about a lady who lived as a recluse and died of tetanus after being 'apparently' bitten by rats in her house. She surprised her neighbours by leaving the sum of £260,000. Her perplexing them in this way proved to me that the people of this country are not as eccentric as everyone else says. If they had been, this item would not have been used. Such things would surely have been seen as quite normal.

I went back to my flat to think it all over. Could it be that English reporters were irresponsible? I pulled out my notebooks and found a letter on the subject, from Professor Sir Hamilton Gibb: H. A. R. Gibb, of Oxford. He had quoted Humbert ('probably means Giant-Bright') Wolfe thus:

> You cannot hope to bribe or twist
> Thank God! the British journalist.
> But, seeing what the man will do unbribed –
> There's no occasion to.

Interesting, but not specific enough to form a judgment as to whether the British Journalist was hysterical. He might, on this showing, even be unbribably phlegmatic . . .

I now immersed myself in books which referred to the English Press and – presto! soon found what I was looking for. It was the – typically English – complete answer to the Italian's fury: the Press was something which one should *ignore completely*. I had it on no less authority than that of the Marquis of Salisbury, who said in 1861:

> Can it be maintained that a person of any education can learn anything worth knowing from a penny paper?

The English had won again, leading the foreigner to imagine

that something was of significance when it was really worth nothing.

During my studies, the red light of my telephone answering machine had started to flash. I played back the tape, and found that there was a message from the Italian, inviting himself to dinner: he wanted to compare notes. He was on the way. I laid in some Kentucky Fried Chicken and waited.

When he arrived, he was in a dreadful state: clothes torn, one shoe off, his numerous gold rings, his stylish chain and Cartier watch, all of them gone.

'Mugged at the carnival?' I asked him.

'No, just outside the door', he gasped.

He refused to ring the police, or even to bathe his black eyes, shouting instead that he wanted to use my typewriter. He had made a great new discovery, which would be the high point of his doctorate thesis.

Impressed by such dedication to the cause of learning, I looked over his shoulder as he typed, in Italian, the equivalent of the following:

'In virtually all ages and countries, travellers have been encouraged to carry, and to use if necessary, some means of self-protection. In England, however, this is absolutely forbidden.'

I said, 'Well, if everyone was armed, you wouldn't know the crooks from the others, would you?'

He shot me a hate-filled look, and continued hammering on the machine:

'Theft, assaults, rape are common there. Why do the police, we ask ourselves, fail to catch the majority of the criminals?'

'They'll get it under control sooner or later', I said, in his ear. But he was not listening:

'The reason is clear. If the police can't handle the problem, this would question the wisdom of having a police force. In England, it is already fallaciously established as wise. *Ergo*, the desperadoes flourish.'

I said, 'I say, that's putting it a bit high, isn't it?'

'Institutions', he said, 'are sacrosanct among the English. They don't want to abolish the police.'

I asked him whether they had got rid of them yet in Italy. 'We are discussing England, *Signor*', he reminded me, with impeccable logic.

'Oh, I'm sure the English can organise things as well as anyone', was all I could think of saying.

He turned a stern, anthropological gaze upon me, and waved away my fried chicken. 'My friend, the English are masters of what they do. The problem is whether they *do* it. Look at the gorgeous ceremonials like the opening of parliament. The Earl Marshal is acknowledged throughout the world as a perfect organiser. What I want to know is, why organise some things perfectly and others not at all?'

I was starting to reply, but the question was obviously rhetorical, for the next moment he thrust a copy of a London evening newspaper into my hand. Wondering how he had managed to hold onto it through his recent trauma, I looked at the marked pasages: ' . . . generations of national confusion of purpose . . . we are essentially a very soft and flabby people today, so accustomed to perpetual compromise that we are utterly at a loss when confronted by an adversary willing to yield nothing.'

'That's your answer, then', I said, 'just don't yield to muggers.'

His face was a mask of fury. 'That is a typical *English* remark!'

Yes, perhaps it was a bit strong, I thought; so I said, 'Well, the English are clever. Perhaps they are just working on the problem. Suddenly, *presto*! they'll come up with an answer.'

'Typical English remark!' was all he would say.

Then I remembered his first words to me: people in England live such a dull life . . . the Press of London exaggerate . . .

Full circle, like most things English. And very oriental; I like ceremonials put on by the Earl Marshal, I like to think that all will be solved when the Anglekins get around to it. But then, I am from the East, not from Italy: I have never, so far, been mugged. And unlike the anthropologist, I don't wear masses of gold ornaments.

Still, I couldn't say any of those things, from politeness; and also because he would only give me the catch-all, 'Typical English remark!' that I didn't know how to answer. The only hope was to take the initiative.

'Now, Signor', I said, 'just a moment. If you lot don't like the way things are done here, why did you let it all happen?'

'*We* let it happen?'

'*You* let it happen.'

'We would *never* have let it happen. In any case, what do you mean, "let it happen"?'

'What I say', I told him calmly, now that he had fallen into my trap. 'It's in plenty of history books. If you would read more history and less anthropology, you'd know what I mean.'

Then I told him:

'You see, the British appealed to Rome, to their former colonial masters, for help against the Saxon invaders. Rome said no, too busy fighting the Huns, Attila and that lot. So the Angles and Saxons won, and the England you see today came into being. If you'd helped the British, you might have had a kind of Italian Albion . . . '

He looked so flabbergasted by this that I refrained from adding several other equally telling remarks, and contented myself with a gnomic oriental utterance. 'The mystic Saadi', I said, 'wrote

> "When you set fire to the scrub,
> Be wise enough to avoid the tigers".'

Now, though I have no idea why, the Italian is studying me. He writes down everything I say, so I have started him on my notes on England, with Cotgrave's dictum (of 1611):

> Let reasons rudder steere thy prow
> Least thou make wrecke on woes enow.

That should keep him busy for a bit, while I get on with my study of the English.

15

Istabrandt

Difficult to Determine

'I concluded that there was no sure way to ascertain if an Englishman was intelligent or stupid . . . it was practically impossible to separate the dull from the stupid, the Sherlock Holmses from the Doctor Watsons, as they all behaved and spoke alike.'

Luigi Barzini: *The Europeans*

'Tell me, men', said the huge, hulking figure on my doorstep at three in the morning, 'where could a fellow stay for the night?'

He was all of six foot four inches, and in his mid-thirties. He grinned at me through a black walrus moustache as he hunched off his heavy backpack.

I knew that he couldn't be English, even before I heard his gutteral pronunciation. No Englishman would wake you in the middle of the night with such nonchalance, even if your house was on fire. Invasion of privacy is not only central to the people's thinking: it is an Anglean idea. One of the very few uniquely Angle principles, according to the country's historians, is the inviolability of the home: apparently the Saxons, Jutes and others did not have this feeling.

Mind you, the actual phrase 'An Englishman's home is his castle', is not recorded anywhere until 1581, according to the *Oxford Dictionary of Proverbs*. That was more than a thousand years after the Angles got here; but the idea was there. It may have flagged again in Charles Dickens's time, as he called it 'gammon', but it picked up again later, as things tend to do in

England. It was an Englishman who had once said to me, 'Absolute rotters, those Gestapo blokes. Wake a fellow up at two or three in the morning.' It had happened to him, then a Germanophile, in the Third Reich just before the Second World War.

He went on 'I know I thought a lot of the Nazis at the time, soon realised my mistake. When I got back to England, I was grilled by the Special Branch. I really warmed to them: different type of thing altogether, came round to the house and asked the servants when they could make an appointment to interview me, don't you know . . .'

And there was something faintly Teutonic about my visitor. I looked at him, noted that he was clean and neat, invited him in. Mind you, my vitality was low. Only an hour or so before I had pushed out the last of the revellers who had arrived, uninvited, to celebrate my election to the Fellowship of the Royal Society of Arts. I had had to let them in. Celebrations, in England, are among the very few occasions when friends can invade your house.

That is how I acquired Dirk van Buren as a very long-staying house guest.

He was travelling to gain experience of the English way of life. South Africa had given him everything it could, and he needed new horizons, 'now thet I'm fully bilingual, men'. He showed me a South African certificate, in Afrikaans and English, as proof of his full bilinguality. His reason for choosing my flat was almost as eccentric as an Englishman's might be: he liked the front door. 'We don't get thet kind of wood in Sath Efrika, men; shows up the grain even under the street lights.'

I handed him a bedroll and showed him the sitting-room floor: it was only a small flat. 'This bundle,' I said, 'is what we call – in my language – a *bistar-band*. Use it, and sleep here.'

'Thenks, boy, I'll remember thet. *Istabrandt*, thet's a new word to me.' Dirk stayed for months, and everyone came to call him Istabrandt. He used to spread his bedroll any time he felt tired, pulling it out of the sideboard cupboard no matter who was in the room. His goodnight was confined to 'Well, I'll jest get into my *istabrandt*, men.'

Now and again, singing for his supper I supposed – he ate like a horse – he would start a conversation. Buttonholing me (sometimes when I was on the telephone, or rushing out of the house for an urgent appointment) he would always begin with 'How are things in Ethiopia, men?'

'About the same, I think. Now, if you'll excuse me . . . '

'I'm truly glad to hear thet, for your sake, men.'

'Thank you, Istabrandt.'

'Don't mention it, boy, old fellow, I mean, men.'

Still, at least he didn't give me that old, familiar speech, the automatic English association with the word 'Afghanistan', especially from older people:

'From Afghanistan? Ah, I remember so well your dear, brave little Emperor Haile Selassie, how he stood up to those beastly Italians, pleading for his country at the League of Nations Assembly in Geneva, it was in all the papers and on the Movie-tone News. He said, "Abyssinia", er, "Afghanistan" . . . er, sorry!'

I knew a terrible bore who spent his time buying, selling, collecting or talking about paintings. He used to telephone about once a month and ask me to dinner, and I almost always found an excuse to get out of it. One day, not long after Istabrandt's appearance, he did it again. It was late evening, and I had climbed over Dirk, already cosy in his Istabrandt, to answer the phone. 'No, sorry, I can't come to dinner tomorrow,' I told Hector; 'I'm busy.' Casting around for a reason, I noted Dirk lying there and added, 'I've got a house-guest, you see.'

'Marvellous!' said Hector, 'man or woman?'

'Man.'

'Even more marvellous! You'll be sure to bring him along? I'm two men short and I have some new Mendoza-Scarlattis to show you. Make it six-thirty for seven will you?'

I was caught. 'Oh, all right, thanks' I said.

Dirk, who was working the eight to three-thirty day shift as a waiter at a big hotel, was delighted at the invitation. 'I cen meet some real English people et lest, men. All the staff at the restaurant are Filipinos and the customers are mostly Erebs and things. I want to go to a *blanks alleen*, all whites, affair.'

'But what about a dinner-jacket, Dirk? This is a very posh house we're going to. Black tie.'

'No problem, men. It's what I wear every day at the restaurant.'

I had discovered that Filipinos and Arabs were not the only ones who failed to understand Dirk: English people didn't follow his fully-bilingual English any too well, either. He was looking for 'high people' to speak it with: his teachers in Sath Efrika had told him that that was what they were imparting. 'A posh house? I cen prectis my high English, men.'

'Just don't tell them you're a waiter, that's all.'

'Wouldn't dhream of itt, men. I'll not let you down. A pal's a pal, Trekker. Alleen for one and one for alleen, like the musketeers. Going alone to these posh houses can be risky.'

I had my doubts but, as we say in my country, the shoe was stronger than the foot.

At the Chelsea house, Dirk grabbed the butler first. 'Jest announce Colonel Eddie Shaw and Count Graaf Dirk van Buren, Trekker', he said, before I could get a word out. Istabrandt nudged me.

'Thet's how they do et in the movies, boy', he whispered.

'This isn't the movies!' I hissed.

'Make up your mind, men, you said all these people were in pictures.'

I was beginning to think that the evening would turn into the kind of farce which English people love (to watch on the stage, that is) and end with us being chased out of the house as impostors. It would not be as funny in real life as it might be on the stage.

But things turned out differently. In the first place, Dirk made no further mistakes. In fact, he said almost nothing. Everyone talked about pictures and collecting, about auctions and painting, and Istabrandt's opinion was frequently asked.

All he did, whenever anyone said something like 'Tell me, Count, do you not think that Rembrandt was not just a touch *too* realistic?' was to screw up his eyes and assume a look of great concentration. With this simple stratagem, he had ten people, dealers and collectors, some of them wily millionaires, eating out of his hand. My neighbour whispered, once, 'Your Dutch friend is a shrewd one, all right. Deep, you know, these Amsterdam collectors.'

Dirk, as he told me later, had hardly understood a word of the conversation. Upper-class English (or what my host and his friends imagined it to be) was altogether too much.

Yet he learnt a lot about the art-lovers from their body-language and the tone of voice. He quoted an Afghan proverb he had heard from one of my friends. 'Ef the camel could only see its own hump, boy, et would die laughing.'

One art-dealer had been trying to impress a collector by saying that he had actually met a certain tycoon, and I was wondering how the collector would trump that one, when he was so quick that I almost missed the reply: 'Yes, he's one of my best men; done a lot of work for me, actually.'

In one-upmanship a certain Mr Enroughty scored even higher – you could see it in the eyes of the company – when he answered an attempted put-down concerning whether his name was North Country. I knew that, in the south of England, North country is distinctly down-market. How would he fudge that one? I wondered. He did better.

'Yes, I believe so, originally. That reminds me of a rather amusing fact. It seems that in our family we always used to spell our name "Enroughty", – from the French Crusaders, "En route", you know, but pronounced it *Derby*. That was because a forebear of mine, at Court, was always referred to by Queen Victoria as "Mr Derby". Sort of a distinction, you see . . . '

The evening, even though the conversation was as wide-ranging as I have related, was a great success. When we got home, however, Dirk was depressed. 'I've simply got to get me tongue round this High English, men. Hardly understand a *verdamdt* word.'

So I decided to help him.

I had got hold of a dictionary, and prepared myself to coach Istabrandt from it. High English was to have much in common with Dutch. He told me, first of all, that he wanted to buy a tripod for his camera. 'I need a standt, a sort of support, for my picture-box, men. Where do I go to get thet?'

'I can not only tell you where, I can tell you how', I said. 'The Top People's photographic shop is the best. They speak High English there and you'll be able to prektis it as well as buying what you wandt, Trekker.'

I felt I really must have some compensation for all those days and nights of free board and lodging and my forfeiture of the sitting-room floor.

So I went out of the room to look it up. When I came back, I had memorised a couple of words.

'Now, what High English do you need, Dirk?'

'I want a standt for my picture-box, men.'

'That will never do. In High English that is "An drievoet for mine kiektoestel."'

His eyes were round with delight. 'But it's almost egzakly the same in Ofrikons, men!'

'Of course it is;' I told him: 'that's because English is a Germanic language, and its *really* High words are the pure, Teutonic ones. Using high words and pronunciation is what we, in England, call Talking Proper.'

I coached him carefully, making sure that he used High Gestures as well as words. Finally he was word-perfect:

'I *sall* hev a drievoet for mine kiekjemachine instantly, boy! An order is an order, Trekker.' He was quite accomplished, too, at banging his fist on the table in time to the words.

The next day was his day off. Dirk set out in his black jacket and trousers and bow tie, with a borrowed bowler hat and beautifully furled umbrella. I had to admonish him for using a phrase which he had picked up in the restaurant kitchen ('I feel like a poof at a picnic, boy') but that was all. Actually, I thought, he looked more like a strong-arm man dressed to look inconspicuous at a select smash-and-grab raid in Bond Street.

He was also wearing a pair of furlined boots which I had lent him. To help explain the rigout, I had injected a little culture into the affair. 'Head and feet must be well looked after, Istabrandt', I had told him; 'because it is an old English custom.' I referred him to the *Oxford Dictionary of English Proverbs*, where the protection of the extremities and the necessary haughty manner of the True Englishman are both encapsulated in a memorable phrase:

'Keep your feet dry and your head hot; and for the rest live like a beast.'

'Be warm and tough, Trekker', I said at the final briefing. 'That's groot English wisdom, passed down the ages. Comes from an *Oxford book*.' Those were magic words to him.

As he walked down the stairs of the house at two o'clock in the afternoon, I heard him declaiming the introductory phrase, 'You will definitely hev observed, boy, thet I am a true witman, a gentlemen, end will brook no disobedience, men'. I had explained that shopkeepers, though they might use High

English, were nevertheless only in Trade: something which true gentlemen did not rate highly, and should generally treat with scorn.

It was teatime before he returned.

'You were wrong, men' he said.

I had, of course, prepared a perfect English excuse to cover my deception. Dirk was fully bilingual, as he'd assured me so many times. Therefore he'd have to accept the ruling of the English Lord Byron, which was to explain my hoax:

> And, after all, what is a lie?
> 'Tis but the truth in masquerade.

I had the poet's collected works open at the right page, for proof. In the event, I didn't need it.

'Et Wallace Heaton's photographic emporium in Bond Street they may speak High English', Istabrandt told me; 'but, probably because they are common fellows, *smeerlaps*, they don't understand et. Then they hev counters of glass, so you can't even beng on them like a gentleman. I went to several other shops, too. At one of them they were so low down thet the *dwaases* said they'd call the police if I didn't leave.'

'Incredible,' I said.

'Yes, reely, truly, men. Et one place they were so ignorandt they reely thought I was *gedrunk*, sozzled, men.'

We drank some tea in silence. Then Dirk said, 'I'd like to go end hev a full overall washup, boy. I've been swettin like a Kaffir. But thet thing in the bathroom is behavin erathick. What do you call it in English?'

I made a rapid excuse and left the room, to consult my dictionary.

'What was that you were saying, Dirk?' I asked when I returned.

'I want to know the name of thet thing in the bathroom, thet the water comes out of. They come on the end of water-pipes.'

'Oh, that. You must mean the kraan', I told him.

'Yes, men. We have the same word, kraan. I think I'll jest pop out and findt a men to mendt the kraan.'

I was telling some of this to Mr Coggins, when he said, 'Wel, guv, that beats the Dutch.' Just an English idiom, for 'hardly credible'.

After that Dirk emigrated to Australia, so he had yet another language to learn, men.

He must have got the use of someone's telephone out there, for after a few weeks he rang me up, hoping that things were still OK in Ethiopia, boy.

'Fine, I think, Istabrandt. What's it like down under?'

'You're not going to believe this, men, but they've got sorta dirty groot rebits, all over the place: hopping ones, men. They call them kengeroos.'

'You've been away from England too long already, boy,' I said, 'shooting a line like that isn't done over here, you know, Trekker.'

'Sorry, men.' I couldn't get him off the line. He went on about Australia until, from sheer boredom, I started to read from a Chaucer that I had before me, reciting from the master English poet in ringing tones, imagining them bouncing off the satellite link:

'For though the best harpour upon lyve Wolde
 on the beste sowned joly harp . . . Touche ay o streng . . .
 It sholde maken every wight to dulle.'

'Gosh, Cobber', said Istabrandt, 'I reely like that. I didn't realise you were such a good poyt. Far better than all thet Pommie chundering thet the Ukkies call poyms. Jest groot. Keep it up. Somebody might publish it. Make you famous.'

'What's an Ukkie, Istabrandt?'

'Don't you know, sport? It's them people from the U.K., the Brits. Everyone calls them thet over here.'

'It doesn't sound a very nice word to me, Dirk . . .'

'Sorry, men: I didn't mean to cause offence. I didn't mean *you*, you know.' You're a witman: pommies are niksnuts.'

But the word Ukkie, somehow, rattled me. I felt that, as a United Kingdom Citizen, I was in danger of being labelled as such, even if only by foreigners. I knew that I would have to do some Angle-ish weaving to avoid the epithet.

The First Baron Colyton (of Farway and of Taunton: PC, CMG), albeit all unawares, came to my rescue. In a forthright letter to *The Times* he asked whether we could 'get away from the perpetual "UK"'. He releases me from feeling an ukkie because it was only King James I (of England and VI of Scotland) who renamed the country 'without the authority of Parliment'. And Baron Colyton is not only a very distinguished former diplomat, but he authenticates his letter with the immemorially significant code-word 'Be that as it may'.

16

Treasure beyond Belief

Coveting

As thorough an Englishmen as ever coveted
his neighbour's goods.
> Charles Kingsley: *Water Babies*

The smell of fresh coriander leaves burning on the charcoal of
the kabob grills mingled with the heavy compounds of musk and
amber, jasmine and rosewater wafting from shops hung with
saris and kaftans. A pair of Arabs in flowing robes climbed out
of a customised Mercedes and tripped, hand in hand, into an
emporium from which blared the amplified voice of Umm
Kulthum, the great singer of the East. A newsvendor thrust
copies of *Al-Ahram, The Gulf Times* and *Afkar* towards me. A
heavily-veiled woman paused to read the Arabic and Persian
graffiti, in dayglo aerosol, denouncing national leaders, on the
railway bridge.

I bought an apple for twenty-five pence, for this was London,
and I was on my way to catch the night express for Penzance, to
be given the clue to the greatest riches in the world – the
Treasure of the Dolmabaghche Palace of Istanbul, by a dying
man. Strange things had happened to me in the mysterious East;
but here, in England, I felt that I was moving towards one of the
strangest of all.

Yet I had learnt to be cautious in my ancestral glens. Why,
after all, should *I* be getting the fortune? At the whim of one of
those inscrutable Englishmen: that should be enough for any
sane foreigner. But perhaps I had been in the country too long to
believe that things were always what they seemed. And the

English, people of other nations say, are so mad that they think
they are not mad at all.

I, too, could have contracted this malady: believing that
nobody could be so crazy as to choose me to become the richest
man in the entire world. But . . . 'You're my pal, and I'll give it to
you, one day.' That's what he had said.

I turned the matter over in my mind as I sat aboard the
Cornish Express, gliding through dark England, going West.

My friend Charlie was an adventurer. One of the last great
rambler-gamblers, he had sought gold in the Yukon, had
gambled on the stock-market, winning and losing fortunes
before the Great Crash of '29. He had written poetry and fought
Circassian bandits. He had, if his tales were true, been loved by
princesses and hated by district commissioners all over the old
British Empire. All that, and a hundred other things as well.
When a millionaire, he'd been a buddy of Jack London – and of
J. P. Morgan, the great American tycoon.

Now he lived in a tiny cottage on the coast, with steps inside it
leading down to the water's edge, once used by brandy smug-
glers from France. He was well over eighty years old. I had met
Charlie in London when he was trying to sell the cottage with the
proviso that he should be allowed to live there until he died. I
wanted to move in earlier than that, so we came to no agreement: but we became friends.

I used to spend time in the British Museum library, and I had
checked – so far as possible – Charlie's stories against dates,
places, names. He may have exaggerated, but in matters of
detail I was never able to catch him out in a lie. So, although I
had a feeling that the hoard would somehow not benefit me
personally, I was sure that if Charlie said he had a document
about a treasure, he was telling the truth. And he needed the
money.

He had told me about the Dolmabaghche Hoard several
times, as we sat in London coffee bars on his visits to Town,
talking the night away.

Some years before the First World War, Charlie had been in
Istanbul, then the capital of the mighty Turkish Empire. There
he met a minor member of the diplomatic staff of the British
Embassy: together they went on a drinking spree in the Arme-
nian Quarter, the only part of the city where liquor was freely

sold. After some hours the diplomat, maudlin from the effects of *raki*, pulled a large wallet from his pocket.

This man, Charlie told me, had once accompanied the British Ambassador to the Dolmabaghche Palace where an audience had been arranged with the Sultan-Khalifa, Emperor of the Ottoman Realm. Since only people of the highest rank were admitted to the High Presence, the junior diplomat was left to wait in an anteroom. Here, peeping from beneath a cushion, he saw a wine-red leather wallet which, on impulse, he seized and concealed inside his shirt.

When he got it home he found that the object was in fact a slim book, full of writing in the Ottoman script. It was of no interest to him as he could not make out a word of Turkish. He had intended to return it to the Palace, but had not been able to think of a way of doing this without the risk of being traced. He was still carrying it with him when the alcohol did its work – and he pressed it on Charlie, relieved to get rid of it.

Charlie went back to his suite in the sumptuous Pera Palas Hotel and, the next day, showed the book to his dragoman, a Levantine Christian whom he had engaged to show him the sights of Istanbul. The man read out the first page, headed by the Imperial Cypher:

In the Name of Allah, All-Beneficent, All-Merciful!
KNOW that this is the detail of the greatest treasure the world has ever seen, the patrimony of the Elevated House of Osman, the all-conquering Khan of all Khans, passed down to the family of the Sultans-Khalifa, Shadows of God on earth . . . follow these instructions and you will be possessed of the great and ancient riches of the Empire, concealed yet accessible, hidden yet awaiting discovery, kept in trust for a time of need. Reveal this to none but the purified . . .

Charlie had then stopped the Levantine from reading any more, and sent him home. He wanted time to think. But, in the early hours of the morning, he woke with the dragoman's dagger at his throat, as he hissed: 'Where is the book of the treasure?'

Charlie was not a seasoned adventurer for nothing. As he summarised it for me, 'I broke his neck and showed the Ottoman Empire a clean pair of heels.'

Within a year the First World War broke out. For the next

fifty years Charlie carried the book in his breast pocket, never able to work out exactly what to do about the treasure. It went with him through the horrors of the battles of the Somme, into and out of a Paraguayan jail, into the South African gold mines – even aboard a pirate sampan in the China Seas.

Now, regarding me as a friend, and because I knew something of the East, Charlie was going to hand it over.

He would give it to me when he felt that the time was right, he kept saying. But, since the book had been lifted by the diplomat, there had been two world wars, the Turkish republican revolution, and goodness knew what changes to the map of Istanbul, or wherever the treasure was hidden. Still, who would not follow up such a matter?

Charlie's telegram (COME GET WALLET) was in my hand as I knocked on the cottage door. A moment later he was there: thinner, much older looking in the three years since I had last seen him, his worn face smiling, hand outstretched.

There was a rabbit stew on the hob, and tea was brewing in a large tomato purée can. Re-used teabags. He was as poor as a mouse in a mosque. Charlie was not well, either; he coughed continually as he motioned me to sit down and rummaged behind a row of books stacked against the bare stone wall.

'Here you are, pal.' It was about the size and shape of an old-fashioned wallet, several flimsy pieces of yellowed paper bound in ancient pinky-red morocco leather, very scuffed and dirty.

I took it from him. Such an insubstantial thing, I thought, to be so important. Inside, the first page did indeed carry the handwritten *Tughra*, the imperial sign-manual of the House of Osman. The writing was stylised, elegant, flowing and very large. I know little of the language of the Turks: but, like other Middle Eastern tongues, classical Turkish is full of Persian and Arabic words. Perhaps I might be able to make out some of it . . .

Yes, I could recognise single words: Osmanli, Ottoman; Padishah, king – then: *Hazine dairasi*! That could only mean Chief Treasury. Charlie was telling the truth, the Levantine dragoman had been right, hadn't brought out his dagger and lost his life for nothing. I closed the book.

Taking the next train back to London, I went straight to the British Museum to find a Turkish scholar. He emerged, old, thin, bespectacled and bent, from behind a frosted glass partition, and took the wallet.

'Hmm, Ottoman, about a hundred years old. Leather perhaps from Tunis. The Bey there was nominally under Turkish suzerainty, you know. The first page is the usual thing, promising the great treasure . . . Then comes the rest.'

'What *is* the rest?' I heard myself asking.

'The rest? Oh, that's the text of the obligatory Islamic prayers, in Arabic of course. *They* are the "great Treasure".'

I snatched the wallet from his hand: for I can read the Arabic prayers. I hadn't look at it carefully enough the first time, and the Levantine would not have been able to make them out. I now saw that it was a book intended to teach Moslem lore to the young princes and princesses. I'd even had one quite like it myself when I was six or seven years old, in Persian and Arabic.

Back in my flat I opened, at random, a volume of Dryden's poems. Suddenly a passage in it showed me where, in English terms, I had gone wrong. I had expected too much for too little. Greed had struck the three of us. You have to suffer before you can enjoy: the English experience reinforces this teaching, again and again. So, as Dryden says:

> Rich the treasure
> Sweet the pleasure –
> Sweet the pleasure after pain.

I hadn't suffered enough, obviously, to merit an Ottoman hoard. Maybe Charlie hadn't, either. But what was I to tell him, waiting alone, unwell and penniless in the tiny Penzance cottage? He was my friend, and I wanted to help him. I racked my brains for hours.

The telephone rang, to tell me that fate had decided for me. 'I'm Charlie's neighbour: found your number on his table. Sorry to have to tell you that he passed away last night.'

But I am sure that Charlie died happy. After all, he was an adventurer – and he was right in the middle of an adventure.

17

The Mortgaged Castle

English clothes

the men would not think of wearing a new suit
until it had spent one or two nights in the
garden, making it look at least a year old.

Nancy Mitford: *The Water Bottle*

He was small and neat. His tiny hands were folded trimly upon
his lap; the hooded North African *burnous*, of the finest brown
wool, was draped over his spotlessly clean white gown: and a red
tarbush decorated his small head, perched above the eager
features set with piercing dark eyes.

I bowed, and he placed his hand on his heart in reply as I
stepped into the battered Rolls-Royce which took us up a steep
incline towards the battlemented castle.

We did not speak until, in the library of the great building, he
pulled out a long scroll. 'This is what I want you to look at,' said
the Duke, 'since we've got this Moroccan chappie I mentioned
coming to take over the castle. He seems to have the right to it,
do you see. Sort of an option. Rather awkward I mean, where
could a fellow go?'

I had not realised until that moment that this little dark figure
in flowing robes wasn't the Arab of the Duke's confused telephone call, wasn't the Moroccan Chappie himself. He'd rung
me up with 'Understand you're good at Middle Eastern matters.
Be grateful if you'd pop down and have a talk. Meet you at the
station, don't you know. Can only say it's to do with an Arab
fella. One would be awfully obliged.'

The scroll might help to clarify things. Lots of English people

123

The Natives are Restless

start discussions somewhere in the middle and work outwards, as it were . . . 'Let's have a look at the document, your Grace' I said.

The butler came in with coffee and, without turning a hair at sight of the costume, bowed to my host. Perhaps the Duke often wore clothes like that.

The Duke caught me eyeing his Moroccan outfit.

'Thought I'd just put on these things, get into the skin of the part, dontcherknow, make the fellow feel at home', he said, unrolling the parchment. It was in English as well as Arabic. I started to read it out:

> Praise to God alone! This is a copy of the writing of the treaties of peace between the Lord of the Faithful: who is crowned Defender of the Law, by the Grace of God of the Universal world, that his prosperity may never be at an end; Muhammad Al Mahdi Al Yazid, whom God has crowned at the head of his troops, that his fame may be continued to be named in his dominions; and George the Third, *Jurji Ath-Thalith*, King of England, in forty-three Articles.

'That'll do. Stop there' said the Duke, tapping his foot in its bright yellow slipper on the floor. 'What d'you make of it so far?'

'So far', I said, 'it seems clear enough to me. Al-Yazid, you know, was a Filali Sharif, of the Hasanite Lineage, and ruled from 1789 to 1792 in terms of current Western chronology.'

'And what else?'

I continued with the genealogy. 'He was the father of Hisham, father of Suleiman, father of Abdur-Rahman, father of Mohammed II, father of Hasan . . .'

'No, I don't mean *that*. What else do you find from the preamble?'

'Nothing', I was forced to admit, after scanning it several times. The coffee didn't help: it was that powdered stuff, made with hot milk.

'I'll fill you in in a minute' said his Grace. 'But first you've got to have the history. This Moroccan Sheik, quite a decent fellow he seemed, was staying at the same hotel as me, in Tangier last summer. Speaks English, American rather, pretty well, too. We used to talk a lot. After a time he told me that he'd always wanted to meet me. Appears that he's got a paper from an ancestor of mine. Gives him the right to take over this castle, whenever he likes, for fifty camels or their equivalent value at the time of exercising the option. The contract is binding on whoever is the current incumbent. A sort of perpetual mortgage.'

'What ancestor?' was all I could think of at that point.

'Time of King John, actually, the Magna Carta feller. He sent an embassy to Morocco, offering his homage to the Sultan there. The mission got into financial difficulties, and one of the Sultan's kinsmen helped out. Got the castle option in return for some gold.'

I remembered something from my reading, about England nearly becoming an Islamic country because of John's desire to ally himself with the master of Spain and Morocco, then a kingdom full of centres of learning and what would now be called a superpower. In 1208, the year our own great poet Saadi was born, England had actually been put under a papal interdict because of King John's infidelity . . .

The Duke was now pushing a book into my hand. 'Look,' he said, 'I've managed to find a historical reference. Fella in a library came up with it, in London: there it is'. It was indeed; I read:

> John sent a secret mission to Mohammed al-Nassir, the very powerful Emir of Morocco (he uses the emir's name in its Latin form of Murmelius) with an offer of homage and tribute . . . The envoys were instructed by John to tell 'the great king of Africa, Morocco and Spain' that he would voluntarily give up to him himself and his kingdom, and if he pleased would hold it as tributary from him; and that he would also abandon the Christian faith, which he considered false, and would faithfully adhere to the law of Mohammed.

'"For Allah created the English mad – the maddest of all mankind!"' I muttered.

'Whatcha say?' growled the Duke,

'Kipling, in *Kitchener's School*', I explained.

'Oh, I see. Sorry,' he said.

'But what's this George III treaty got to do with the castle?' I asked. 'There's no mention here of any castle in England.'

'My dear fellow, you simply do not understand', said the Duke. I haven't got a copy of the *original* agreement with the Miramolin's man. But another forebear of mine was involved in the eighteenth-century treaty.'

I tried again. 'And the George III treaty does have some bearing on your problem?'

'Yes, intricately, but it does. Listen carefully. It is a matter of style and title, as understood in the usages between Courts.'

'I think I've taken that aboard, your Grace.'

'Very well. As you must know, such documents as treaties are only signed after going through several drafts, and after a deal of high-level bargaining.'

'I do know – I've been involved in some of that, myself.'

'Exactly why I asked you down here', said the Duke: 'now, part of the bargaining before the signing always deals with exactly how the respective rulers are to be styled in the document. It's a matter of prestige.'

I agreed. 'Very much so. It has been said that the names and dignities of the signatories are just as important as the body of the text.'

'Right. Now look at the treaty again. You will notice that the Moroccan king is styled far more extravagantly than the King of England.' The Duke smacked the paper with the back of his hand.

'Yes', I said, 'there is no doubt about that.' The Duke leant towards me. 'So we are agreed that, in the eighteenth century, the English king is, effectively, spoken of in an official document, in terms inferior to those employed for the Moroccan monarch?' I knew that the Duke had been involved in diplomatic work in his younger days, so that explained his meticulousness in setting the scene; but I wished he would get to the point. Perhaps I could speed things up a bit. 'So, what does that mean?' I asked.

'It means' said my host, 'that the Moors have established themselves as senior to us in protocol terms; it means that the treaty, of which the Moroccan doubtless still has a copy, will show the Miramolin with perhaps even greater prestige. It means, as a result, that I am obliged to yield the castle.'

I sat, stunned, unbelieving – and wondering what it had to do with me.

'It means,' the Duke repeated, 'that, unless you can bring some personal, family, pressure to bear – in some suitable form, of course – that I shall be obliged to yield up the castle.'

So that was it. The Duke stood up, made a gesture with both hands as if pushing the whole affair into my lap, and started to stride up and down the room.

Slowly, my head cleared. 'In the first place', I told him, 'that sounds ridiculous to me.'

'And in the second?'

'In the second,' I was compelled to say, 'you have got your genealogies mixed up. I have no clout in this matter.' 'Come, now,' said the Duke, 'you are a Sharif, and the King of Morocco is one too. That's in the books. Means you come from the same lineage. You can talk to the fellow.'

'It's not as simple as that,' I told him. 'You see, even if I talked to the King of Morocco, he would not be interested in what this predecessor of his, the Miramolin, did or didn't do.'

'Not interested? A member of his own family? I can't believe that.' The Duke, I could see, thought I was trying to get out of it.

'Just a moment. I said you'd got your genealogies mixed up. The great Miramolin was a Muwahid, no relation of the Sharif family. Mohammed Al-Nasir, Master of Spain and Morocco and ninth in succession, was a caliph, but he was not of the Sharifian lineage. A branch of the family re-established its sway in North Africa much later than the time of King John, so they have nothing to do with what the Muwahid caliphs did.'

'See what you mean,' said the Duke mournfully, 'so a treaty made by the Muwahids does not involve you at all?'

'Not in the slightest. It may bind the present King of Morocco as successor to the Muwahids, though I doubt it. That would be an international and constitutional matter. It would not bind the Moroccan King, Sharif or not, to me.'

'Even as a kinsman?'

'No. Sorry.'

'Then I am treed, do you see,' said the Duke.

'Well', I could not help saying, 'your predecessor should have been a little more careful. This is a priceless castle. Surely he could have offered something of less value?'

The Duke gave a hollow laugh. 'Not in the thirteenth century, when the transaction took place. It was just the ruin of a modest

Norman pile then. What we have now dates from the fortune we made in the eighteenth and nineteenth centuries, slaves from Africa, loot from India, that kind of thing . . .'

I felt like saying 'Well, you've had a good innings, then.' But that would have been hitting below the belt. After all, he'd got used to living in a castle.

'Look here,' I said, 'the law will protect you. There can't be a court in the country that would uphold that old contract. Statute of limitations, or something. And there is the European Court of Human Rights; the Duke of Westminster went to them after the British Government, as he believed, acted illegitimately. You are a human being too, as we say in our country. There must be a loophole or something.'

'Loophole', said the Duke; 'That's exactly the point. I refuse to look for loopholes. The motto of my family is "Word Given, Word Sacred".' Well, I thought, to some this might sound noble, and all that, but it also seemed positively medieval. Or even earlier, perhaps Schleswigian.

'Quite right,' I said diplomatically, still trying to grapple with the implications; 'We have a saying, "Lawyers' houses are built on the heads of fools".' But what could I do, even if I borrowed a spare burnous from my host, and put it on?

'Just give it a bit of thought, will you?' The Duke stroked the sleeve of his robe reflectively, and I could tell that he was truly worried. The change of clothing alone now told me a great deal. It recalled the story, widely current in his country, about the English aristocrat and his terrible old suit. His wife had said, 'Don't go up to London in those clothes, they are falling to pieces!' He had replied, 'Why not? *Nobody* knows me there.' When, shortly afterwards, she said, 'Don't go into the village dressed in that old suit', he'd replied, 'Why not? *Everyone* knows me there.'

For a duke to change his clothes . . .

The medieval associations of the Duke's dress and the tale of the nobleman's suit set me thinking about Middle Eastern reactions to the Franks at the time of the Crusades. Their negligent attitude towards clothes, I remembered, had been observed by the great Al-Qazwini, the 'Saracen Pliny' in the thirteenth century. Ancestors of the Duke had taken part in the Crusades, and Qazwini notes that these Franks were 'marvellously bold; they never think of flight in battle, and prefer death.'

He saw, too, that they had other preoccupations than elegance. Whatever the sanitised image of the Crusader projected by Victorian romantics, they had a ducal disregard for appearances:

> But their clothes they never wash at all from the day they put them on for the first time until they fall off in rags. They shave their beards, and after the shaving hideous stubble grows on their faces.

Of course, since they had been granted absolution for going on the Crusade, their motto was perhaps the English proverb, 'Better to Heaven in rags than to Hell in embroidery'. I resolved to discuss the matter of the Crusades with the Duke if ever the present crisis were resolved.

We had just finished luncheon, each absorbed in his own thoughts, when the Duke stood up and crossed the room to the window: a luxurious car had swept up the driveway. A few minutes later the butler appeared, preceding the occupant of the custom-built Cadillac with diplomatic number plates and crimson pennant.

The tall, unbearded figure (no stubble), with luminous black eyes and a wide grin, dressed immaculately by Savile Row, bounded shouting into the room, drowning the 'Sheik Ubba-dub' which was the flunkey's attempt at his name.

'Sammy, Sammy, just great to see you!' His American accent was of the eastern seaboard. The Duke stepped forward with tragic dignity and took his hand. Then he introduced the Sheikh to me.

'Great, just great! Well, gentlemen, you will understand that I am anxious to claim my patrimony, or, at least my rights. A debt of honour, eh, Dook? The camels will arrive at any moment. They are racing meharis. You can have you a ball with them. Milk-white, you know. Bred at my own ranch in Arizona.'

The Englishman and I looked at one another briefly. He raised his eyebrows in silent question. I answered, by shrugging my shoulders. He braced his own. I knew he would put a bold face on it, even if all were lost.

The Duke said, 'Milk-white? Excellent. Just the thing. Better show you around, then. First of all, remember that you'll have to keep parts of the place open to the public on certain days. There's a commercial contract or something. Now . . .'

Talk about Stiff Upper Lip.

'Okay, okay', interrupted the Sheikh, who turned out to be from the Gulf and not a Moroccan at all, 'you win, Sam. I tried to throw a scare into you with that story, that day at the Minzah Hotel in Tangier; but now you've called my bluff. I'm glad I don't play poker or you'd have cleaned me out.'

We all sat down: that is to say, I slumped into an armchair, the Duke perched delicately on a straight-backed one, and Sammy turned another around and sat astride it. 'Why, in Heaven's name, why did you do it?' I croaked.

'Steady, feller' said the Gulfian. 'The Dook was boring me stiff with all that King John stuff. And, besides, we have to keep these Limeys under some sort of control or there's no knowing what they might get up to.'

He roared with laughter, shoulders shaking.

The Duke still had his castle, but I could see that the hoax had hit him hard. So I used the phrase which I had been saving to soften the blow ever since I had heard his sad news.

I said, ' "We were not fairly beaten, my lord. No Englishman is ever fairly beaten." George Bernard Shaw, *Back to Methuselah*.'

'Thank you', said His Grace.

The Sheikh stayed to dinner, and I was able to do some interesting, though anecdotal, research on the English problem.

'It is a firm belief in many Middle Eastern countries,' I said, 'that the English are hostile to the people there because of the Crusades. Not only fighting them, but losing. What are the facts?'

'Bernard Shaw', said the Sheikh, 'whom you quoted earlier, once wrote, in *Man and Superman*, that an Englishman thinks he's moral when he is only uncomfortable.'

The Duke asked him what the devil he meant by that.

'No offence, Your Graceship. What I mean is that we can apply Harvard Business School methods to this statement: interrogate it. Now: what does your Englishman do if wants to feel moral? He has to make himself uncomfortable, or get someone else to do it. Hence the Crusades. The English were made uncomfortable by Peter the Hermit, who preached crusading, and they set off, via Marseilles, to fight the Saracens, so as to feel moral by actually seeing and killing infidels.'

He might have been educated in the USA, but, like many Middle Easteners, he knew a lot about the Crusades.

'Paynims, heathens, we used to call them then' mused the Duke in that familiar English far-away voice. For a moment I almost felt as if he was talking as an eyewitness. But, in fact, he had read a good deal about the history of the time. 'And my people were rather mixed up in it, dontcherknow. And *I* see what you mean about morality and discomfort.'

'They say that King Richard was French, anyway,' I remarked.

'That may be', said the Duke, 'but he was often on the right lines; he was in the process of becoming English, as it were. He was unEnglish enough to take part in the Crusades, I'll admit. But there was always the instinct of his men, who may not have been feeling as moral, or uncomfortable, as he was.'

The Sheikh said he understood that the Crusaders under Richard the Lionheart had fought very bravely indeed.

'Yes, bravely, bravely, when they finally got there. Wasn't much else they could do, d'you see. It's *before* that that their instinct went to work, no matter what Richard wanted.'

'How was that?' I had to ask. I had no idea what he was driving at.

'Well my dear fellow, it's all in the history books. Richard sent his men on ahead, to assemble and take ship with him from Marseilles. Now we all know what Marseilles is like. Richard's men use their own initiative when they got there. By the time the King arrived, they had spent all the treasure earmarked for the expedition to the Holy Land, on the local ladies. Matter of recorded history. Followed their instinct, dontcherknow. Often happens, that kind of thing. Brutal and licentious soldiery, knights included.'

'You mean they weren't feeling moral enough to look after the money?' asked the Sheikh.

'I mean they weren't feeling guilty enough to feel moral until they had' said the Duke, with inescapable logic.

I am not much better than many others in perceiving when the English are joking and when they are operating the English teaching system. At that time I hadn't read these words of Sir Francis Doyle's; but they are of a piece, I believe, with the description of the English fighting men whose comrades had a last fling at Marseilles:

Poor, reckless, rude, low-born, untaught,
Bewilder'd and alone, A heart with English
instinct fraught
He yet can call his own.

Of course, a lot has changed in England since those times:
there's far less class-distinction about, especially since every
writer, sociologist and visitor to the country has dissected it *ad
nauseam*.

As is the way of these things (the Pendulum Effect) scholars
first found that England was riddled with class-prejudice, then
that it did not go as deep as they had thought. The Angles, with
their disinclination to follow leaders, their penchant for commu-
nal decision, may be at the bottom of this.

The Afghan sociologist Siyaposh says, in an acute report on
his field-work here:

Traditionally, people of all cultures have thought their servants dishonest. Among the English, however, it is the servants who harbour deep suspicions of their employers.

And this was even before Thorstein Verblen (in *Imperial
Germany*) noted that 'the allegiance of the English might even
be called a mitigated insubordination rather than loyalty'.

Support for the view that the class-system is dead or dying,
comes in today's post, which tells how one can share in the booty
of the upper classes. The mail-order catalogue says that I can
buy a 'valuable watch' at the HIT PRICE of Only £21.88. Less than
the turn-out charge made by my plumber:

In times passed *[sic]* these impressive time-pieces were only
found in the upper classes. They were passed down from
generation to generation.

'Makes you think, you know,' I said, rousing myself from my
reverie, as Sammy asked, in the nursery lingo which people of
his type often lapse into, 'Cat gotya tongue, then?'

It seemed a safe enough, very English, phrase.

'Don't know about that at all.' The Duke was pursing his lips.
'Shakespeare knew a thing or two. Got his books in the library,
ya'know. How about this, from *Julius Caesar*? "He thinks too
much; such men are dangerous." Best thing he ever wrote, in
my opinion. Stop thinkin'. I'm going to have a large brandy.'

18

Sammy's Place

Home Life

In such a household, everything was strange and different, their self-reliance put me at ease, and I was fascinated by the feeling of continuity with the past.
> Wilfred Thesiger: *The Marsh Arabs*

A number of newspapers persist in referring to the Duke of Edinburgh as Prince Philip. This is not only contrary to normal usage, but is inaccurate in fact.
> Valentine Heywood: *British Titles*

I had gone down to Sammy's place at mid-morning on a Friday, and by two in the afternoon the Duke was Sammy to me because, he said, it would give the servants the wrong idea if I carried on calling him Duke much longer. I am still not sure what that meant, but no doubt I'll find out sooner or later. In England, there are times when one simply does not ask questions. At other times, it is all right. Knowing which is which needs experience.

The next morning, the Sheikh had to rush off, and the other guests began to arrive, as this was not one of those tiresome weekends when the castle had to be opened for busloads of workers anxious to see how the other half doesn't really live.

We were sitting waiting for the Prince when I decided to test English reactions to Eastern humour with a tale attributed to

Nasrudin, the Middle Eastern joker and reputed wise man, whose teachings are carried out through jokes.

I had read, in Hesketh Pearson's *The Smith of Smiths*, that the nineteenth-century clergyman and humorist Sydney Smith 'was perhaps the first to realise that one could only quicken an Englishman's intelligence by tickling his sense of humour'. This might be a promising basis for an experiment.

I decided, as an introduction, I would tell a story composed by an Englishman, the distinguished lawyer Michael Rubinstein, who had, with appropriate exactitude, enclosed written permission to reproduce it ('please use it as and if you wish') when he posted it to me.

'Sammy', I said, 'I'd like your reaction to a tale. The famous Mulla Nasrudin was in a new supermarket, having filled his shopping trolley, when he found that he had left his money behind. He tried to offer the items to various other shoppers, but there were no takers. When he left, he said, "I don't think that place will make much money. Why, nobody would even take the stuff free of charge!"'

I looked at Sammy expectantly.

'Interesting', he said, 'and why do you suppose they wouldn't?'

The Prince, a member of a great, if now dispossessed, Balkan family, had in the meantime joined us, and Sammy was so intrigued by the mysterious Nasrudin story that he had me repeat it for His Highness, who is known as Rory, 'from Ruritania, you know'.

No sooner had I finished the second recital than Rory said, 'Yes, he was right. I have had some experience of commerce, myself – it's a tricky business.' Placing his feet delicately so that one covered the hole in the sock of the other, he continued.

'When I left Gordonstoun and the old country had gone up in smoke – or, more accurately, had been smothered in borscht – I looked around for a means of support. No skills, really, except how to crew a boat in Scottish waters, and the Scots already knew how to do that. So I took my violin and tried my luck with gypsy airs outside Selfridge's. That's a shop in Oxford Street, you know. Bit like Harrods, but not quite.'

'Not a bad idea. Made a lot, I suppose', said Sammy. I couldn't make out (as is so often the case in England) whether he was being obtuse, since the Prince had said that it was tricky, or whether he was just acting as feed-man.

'Ah, no, unfortunately. Not at first. Plenty of people shopping, none of them generous. So I looked around to see why the other street musicians were getting so much.'

'Good idea, Rory, quite brilliant' said Sammy.

'Yes, I thought it was rather good' said Rory. 'Anyway, I found that each of them carried some sort of a sign, you know the kind of thing, "Ex-Service", "Blind", "Pensioner", that type of stuff.'

'So I prepared a placard, reading "Exiled Prince".'

'Yes, tricky, but still good' breathed Sammy.

'Wrong again' Rory informed him. 'Took a bit of time to hit my stride, you see. But I got it in the end. My mother, rallying round, came past and put a coin in my tin. All the money we had at the time, actually. She thought that that might serve to *encourager les autres*, if you see what I mean.'

'And people started to give you money?' I asked, since in the pause that followed nobody had said anything.

'No, old boy, no such thing. Someone said to someone else, "I wonder who that was?" – my mother is, after all, rather striking do you see. So I said, "Madam, that was a Princess!"'

'Suddenly, everyone was giving me money. So I repainted the sign to read UNDER ROYAL PATRONAGE – and I made quite a packet. Of course that was before some rotter labelled UNEMPLOYED CRICKETER pinched my pitch.'

'Darned tricky' said Sammy. 'Hard cheese.'

'Not to worry!' said Rory; 'lately I've been working on a better idea. I'll let you know if it pans out.'

At dinner, the talk turned to foreign travel, largely in honour of Rory, who hated it, having been born, educated and brought up in Britain. To cover someone's gaffe about Balkans people, said in a thoughtless moment, I told my experience on a Swiss train, and how an Englishman had said that some unruly Swiss conscripts had been 'no gentlemen'.

'I should hope not', said the Duke, 'I wouldn't want to be one meself.'

I thought that I had misheard, until my neighbour, luckily a competent amateur genealogist, noting my open mouth, hissed the explanation into my ear.

'Sammy is referring to the definition of a gentleman in England, the correct one, according to all the best authorities.'

'What ever is it?' I croaked.

He was word-perfect, as I subsequently confirmed:

'"A gentleman is a man entitled to bear arms, but who is *not* a nobleman." The Duke is not a gentleman: he is noble – he is a Duke.'

He continued to the table in general, 'Yes, I have always thought what a rotter that fellow must have been who wrote "When Adam delved and Eve span, who was then the gentleman?" Obviously, Adam and Eve were not gentry, but they must have been nobles. They couldn't bear arms, since there was nobody to arm against, except a snake, and that wouldn't have counted. They were not peasants, either, since there was nobody *over* them, except God. In fact, Adam and Eve must have actually started the nobility. These levellers are pretty ignorant if you get down to it. Never occurred to that idiot poet, I suppose. The man who started it, John Ball – a sort of Leveller – was executed in 1381, of course.'

'Of course', said the Duke, though I didn't think that he had been listening to a word. Dukes don't have to. I had just read Jon Akass's observation in the *Daily Express*:

Dukes are at the top of the social tree – more so, for some reason, than royalty – and they make up their own rules.

Sammy's rule at the moment seemed that he wasn't going to talk. There was another silence, so I tried to fill it. Perhaps I could get some useful information on England.

I said that, since almost all the gentlemen I had heard named as such, in the newspapers and so on, had now been eliminated by the genealogist's definition, what was the nature of this vanishing capacity of the English which extended beyond the ordinary?

Most of the guests sat silent, seemingly deep in thought. The Prince, however, said, 'Yes, I've read that the Druids could make themselves invisible, by producing magic mist. So could the early British saints.'

The Duke's youngest daughter, a girl of about twenty, took up the point.

'That's *ordinary* disappearance. We're talking about something more subtle: and I know just what you mean. Now look at me: I am known as Lady So-and-So. But, as the younger daughter of a Duke, I'm only able to use the title *by courtesy*. It isn't really mine. So the real me has vanished into a non-real title, though nobody knows this. Like hundreds of other guys and girls in this country, maybe thousands, I have no genuine title, not one of my own. But people are convinced that we are real lords and ladies, and so they're impressed. I suppose it's because they want to be, though.'

'Same with me, if you like to put it that way', said the Duke. 'Y'see, Duke comes from *Dux*, Leader, in Latin. Well, we've got rid of the Romans and Latin too, for that matter, and instead of being Bill Smith, I'm Duke of Blankshire. We've vanished the origins, and vanished ourselves. Nobody knows our real names. Except friends – or unless they look them up in Debrett and so forth.'

I mentioned that I thought the Angles had done much the same by merging with the Saxons. 'Are there any more titles which have worked in a similar way?' I asked.

'Plenty – in fact all of them' said the genealogist. 'Look at Marquis, the next title down, after Duke. It's French. You don't use a fellow's name, you call him "The Marquis of Such-and-Such-a-Place". Then you've got earls, Scandinavian title, no Scandinavians here now, but *we* still use the title. William the Conqueror actually tried to get rid of earls, but people weren't having any, too convenient. William wanted to convert them into counts, so there was an English compromise.'

'Which was?' the Prince was almost incredulous, in a well-bred sort of way.

'Which was, and still is, to call the earl "Earl", but make his wife "The Countess".'

'But there must surely be *one* really English title', I said.

The Duke shook his head 'Goin' down the list there is only Viscount, then Baron. Both foreign.'

'No more?'

'No. Oh, yes, there is that new one. Very English: called Baronet. Started in the seventeenth century, and officially cost only £1000 to acquire. Later it became an honour for services. They've stopped granting it since 1964. Last one was Sir Graeme Finlay.'

'But knights are surely something?' I remembered all the tales of chivalry . . .

'Certainly not. "Knight"' said the genealogist, 'is the Germanic word *knecht*, which means "lad". And it is not a part of the *nobility* of the United Kingdom. Knights *tried* to be chivalrous: nobles were that already.'

'The Angles', I said, for I had just remembered something, 'were noted for the fact that they had no discernible leaders. They worked and fought as teams, in combination, unlike most other fighting units.'

'There you are, then!' said the Duke, in delight, 'I always said that we're all common people at heart. What's all this nonsense about us puttin' on airs and graces, and all that rot? If you ask me, it's the reason why the Anglo-Saxon countries have this theory of decentralisation of powers as far as possible. It's the Angles' influence, still goin' strong.'

He fell silent. This was a very long speech for him, and he looked all in.

'Daddy is an earl as well as a duke' said his daughter, the Lady Eunice (Happy Victory) Smith, 'and you should see the faces of some of the Danish and Swedish tourists who come to see the castle. We're carrying the title, Earl, of some old Scandinavian ravers who terrified everyone in this country demanding *Danegeld*, blackmail money. If they were alive today they'd be put in an institution or prison or something by these good people. Instead, they lap it all up. It's called atavism. My boy friend, Sid, is the drummer with the Behemoth Pop Group, always uses that word. The Behemoths are atavists, too.'

She looked quite worn out with all the talk, just like her father.

'Eunice Smith is right, of course,' said the genealogist, 'to say that she's not entitled to be called Lady. Her three brothers – all known as Lord – haven't really got any such title. Doesn't stop them insisting on using it, though, and the papers love it, especially the gossip columnists. I suppose that you know that *you* are more entitled to be a Lord than any of them?'

'Me? I don't use foreign titles in this country . . .' I didn't quite follow him.

'No, not that, a lord because of an English entitlement.'

'First I've heard of it', I said.

'There you are, you see. Nobody in this country except for a few experts, really knows anything about it, but they're all fascinated.' He peered at me, proudly, through his pince-nez.

'Okay,' I said, 'tell me about it. How did I become an English Lord?'

'You *are*, in fact, Lord of the Manor of Newmarket?'

'Yes, I am,' I said.

'Well, the Manor, or feudal barony, of Newmarket is a legal title. You are entitled to be styled as having that lordship. On the other hand, the young lords who are sons of dukes or eldest son of a marquis, have no legal right to that style at all: they are plain Mister.'

'You mean because *I* have the documents which officially make me Lord of the Manor, Hlaf-Ward, Bread-Keeper, of Newmarket, and because the Duke's sons are not legally lords of anything?'

'That is correct. You see, the term "courtesy title" only means, in this context "a title used by someone who is not entitled to it, though his father is".'

'But', I said, 'since "Lord" only means Bread-Keeper, in any case, that doesn't amount to much, does it?'

'Well', said the genealogist, 'it is indisputably an ancient feudal barony, and therefore better than one to which you are not entitled.'

'But,' I reminded him, '"Baron", only means "man", which I have been for some time, anyway, without my lordship title-papers. And who wants to be a bread-keeper?'

'That's true', was all he replied; but I don't think that he liked my attitude to my documented, provable rights.

I felt that I'd tapped a garner of information, and, to give everyone time to return to normal, I said to the Duke, 'Do you have much trouble with your neighbours, trespassers and so on?' I'd recently been looking into footpaths and rights of way, another English obsession.

'Not a lot' he said, 'how about you?'

'Well' I told him, 'there was a strange incident when I moved into a house in Kent and planned rather a large party. A three-day one, in fact. The people who had some land and a house nearby heard about it, I suppose. The next thing I knew there was a uniformed chauffeur at the door. "Her Ladyship's compliments", he said, "and you seem to have forgotten to send her an invitation. I'll take it now."'

'Well, it's the kind of people they're givin' titles to nowadays, isn't it?' said the Duke. 'What ye do to the feller?'

'I told him,' I said, 'that he'd better be off right away as he was obviously an impostor. No lady would ask for an invitation from someone to whom she'd not been introduced. Although I wasn't too well up in Englishry, I took as my pattern what we'd have said among the Afghans.'

'That was the feller's lucky day, I'd have whipped him off without a word' said the Duke. 'Ye did the right thing. Your Afghans must be rather like the old berserkers and earls of the Danes, y'know.'

I remembered the day, when as a small boy, I had been in a London shop with my father, and I decided to tell the story to the company, to give them an idea of the short fuses of some of the Afghans.

'It was a shop in the Strand' I said, 'near our hotel. My father looked at some braces, and asked the assistant if they were really good. "Indeed, yes, Sir" he said; "the manager himself wears them."

'My father looked away and said, softly, "Are you deliberately trying to annoy me?"'

'Oh,' said the Duke's daughter, 'I don't think that he was angry. Daddy would have done the same, you know. He was probably just thinking aloud; thought it but didn't mean actually to say it, you see.'

You see, it's this benefit-of-the-doubt thing, among others, which makes the English seem so oriental to me. Say or do anything, and since there may always be some explanation (or no explanation needed) you always have plenty of options. Things are not what they seem.

Prince Rory, perhaps because he had been brought up in England, was able to rehabilitate himself through this precise mechanism. Unruffled by the cricketer's taking his place as a busker, he turned to clairvoyance. And that was not all.

I saw his picture soon afterwards, outside a meeting-hall, where he was billed as RORIYEV THE GREAT SEER, Amazing Readings: Every night at Seven-Thirty. Fair enough: but pasted across it was a slip of paper with the words: POST-

PONED UNTIL NEXT WEEK DUE TO UNFORSEEN
CIRCUMSTANCES.

Unforseen by a seer? That, I thought, must have put the
kybosh on his miraculous promised revelations. But no; next
time I drove past I saw that people were queuing at the box-
office to hear what the future held for them. The English always
give you the benefit of the doubt. What was unforseen by the
seer last week might well be foreseen adequately enough this
time.

Making allowances, that's one of their great strengths. I recalled something else which the Duke's daughter had said,
quoting a saying current in her circle 'Always be polite to young
women of no title; you never know whom they might marry.'

Or, as our Afghan sages have put it, 'wait a year, then praise
or condemn.'

19

The Dove of Peace

Example

It must be acknowledged that the English are the most disagreeable of all the nations of Europe – more surly and morose, with less disposition to please, to exert themselves for the good of society, to make small sacrifices and to put themselves out of their way . . . and they think that they are not bound to excel the rest of the world in small behaviour, if they are superior to them in great institutions.

Sydney Smith, in Hesketh Pearson's
The Smith of Smiths

Let not England forget her precedence in teaching the nations how to live.

John Milton:
Doctrine and Discipline of Divorce

I should have been warned, of course, when my new Middle Eastern friend confided some of his discoveries about the English to me. But I was not, and so I ended up with the dove problem.

'You see', he had said, speaking with great authority, 'they are not like us, not at all really. They have little idea of dignity.'

I asked him to give me an example. 'Well, there is this curious thing about shops. Instead of shopkeepers keeping in their place, they have things called "famous shops". Now, how can a shop be famous?'

I supposed it meant that the place was well known. 'Yes, known to all. But not, surely, a resort of all.'

'But isn't that what a bazaar or souk is?' I wanted to know.

But there was a real difference, as he soon explained. 'Famous, even distinguished, people, here in England, *actually visit shops*, and enter them.'

I was sitting at one of those rickety tables which they give you in London stores when you are put on show and expected to sign copies of your books. My new friend had plunged into this conversation without any introduction. Was he implying, I wondered, that I was little more than a peasant, for even being here? Or that he was one himself, or merely slumming? To gain time, I gave him an English-type, or equivocal, answer.

'Amazing,' I said.

'Yes', he continued, 'I thought that would surprise you. The point is, as I have discovered, that everything is back to front over here. Instead of the shopkeepers visiting their important customers, the customers, without dignity, go to the shops. Why, they are even photographed doing it. I have seen this in the newspapers!'

He shot me a glance of triumph. 'Hard to believe, but true, nevertheless. When I first saw that, at home in films, I thought that they were all comedians . . .'

Of course, I should have been warned when he asked me to go with him to a lecture on hydrotherapy. 'Bathing treatments are good for health. These British people may know something about the art. I understand that they have had some innovative natural philosophers' was how he put it. But, after all, you cannot be on your guard all the blessed time, even in England.

The hall, by the time we found it, was full of people, and the lecturer was a tall and impressive-looking clergyman, with, as it turned out, a particularly forthright way of expressing himself.

As we had arrived a few minutes late, I had not seen the title of the lecture in English. And when the speaker started to address us, his first words rather confused me.

'My dear friends', he began, 'we are here to consider that wonderful image, common to all men, the conception and the promise of The Dove of Peace.'

Trapped in the middle of a row, I suddenly realised that we were here through some error, and I could only hope that my companion could be converted to a belief in the sovereign power of doves as readily as he had been to the virtues of water.

The fact was that, seeing the notice of the lecture in a newspaper, he had looked up the word Dove in his English-Arabic dictionary and found it to mean *Hamam*. Sure enough, Hamam means Dove: but Hammam means bath. So 'The Dove of Peace' had meant for my friend, 'The Peaceful Bath'.

But these thoughts soon passed out of my mind as I settled down, in the manner customary with us Easterners, to attend as dutifully as possible to the words of our instructor.

He quoted holy scriptures (Matthew 8, 16), political and poetic usages, art works featuring doves, and even the employment of a dove as a trademark on a shock-absorber much esteemed in industry.

The dove was not only the Holy Ghost; the clergy of the Church of England are allegorised as doves in Dryden's *Hind and Panther* (part iii, 947, 998). Doves epitomised gentleness, peace, everything that we should be and were not. As if to emphasise this by example, he delivered his harangue with a fierceness and intensity which dazed us all.

Well, not quite all of us. Sitting near me was another formidable figure, equally towering in stature as the lecturer, grey-haired and neatly-dressed, who continually snorted and shuffled his feet. Once or twice he even went so far as to interject 'Rubbish', 'Poppycock', and so on.

Now people were starting to look at this egregious character; and some of them, who had earlier been smiling and nodding their heads in agreement with the lecturer's words, showing every indication that they responded appropriately to the need for gentleness being hammered into them, began to hiss and even to cry such things as 'throw him out!'. Indeed, I thought, it is just as well that we are in general an assembly of the converted, people dedicated to peace. Otherwise, such seemed to be the provocative character of this man's intervention, any normal audience would surely have been shouting 'Kill him!'

The speaker, evidently accustomed at this stage in his remarks to involving the audience in the subject, and well into his stride, suddenly pointed to the interrupter and demanded, 'Now, Sir, what do you think about doves?'

'That they are quarrelsome, aggressive and cruel, and an

excellent object-lesson in hypocrisy, because they manage to make people think that they are serene and pure, by their appearance, while their habits are most objectionable from the human point of view', he immediately replied. '"Harmless as doves" is nonsense.'

There was silence for a moment, while the audience, having listened to the booming voice of the grey-haired man, presumably tried to reconcile what he was saying with the general consensus that doves are the very emblem of love, gentleness and harmony.

The speaker gasped once or twice: the veins stood out on his peaceful forehead. After an obvious and, indeed, a noteworthy effort to control himself, he said, in a lower but still strongly carrying tone, 'And how, may I ask, are you able to stand there and say such blasphemous things?'

The other man glared back at him. 'I, Sir, happen to be Professor Mandrill, of the University of Wessex; I am, furthermore, recognised as a world authority on doves, and that is why I am here!'

'No, no!' said the speaker, 'we are not talking about *that* kind of dove . . .'

At that the Professor walked out, followed by my Middle Eastern friend, pulling me after him. As we left the hall, the Middle Easterner could not resist calling out, as a parting shot, 'He who has no shirt shows off his shoulders!' A well-dressed member of the audience bawled back, 'Marxist!' We had not left a moment too soon.

Sitting in a nearby cafe just afterwards, my friend explained that clerics in England were all mad. 'They do not know what they say, and believe that plunging into water is connected with religion.'

I tried to explain that 'dove' had nothing at all to do with bathing or even with water. 'Unless', I added, 'you connect it with Americans, for whom the word *dove* is the preterite of the verb "to dive".'

'And you claim to have a knowledge of the Frankish tongue?' he snarled: adding, quite gratuitously, that he wondered who it was that really wrote my books. 'Here it is, in black and white, here, in this dictionary.'

I looked at the book which he had fished out of his pocket.

Sure enough, the word Dove means 'a diver . . . Latin *columba* is the Greek *kolumbis* (a diver).'

And so I stood disgraced, exposed as no expert on the English tongue.

I only wished that my friend, instead of a dictionary, had had a copy of the *Notebooks* of that great English thinker, Samuel Butler. He, now, was able to deduce a penetrating lesson, applicable to almost every field, from the phenomenon of X-rays. 'Their moral', he wrote, 'is this – that a right way of looking at things will see through almost anything.'

I had to adopt a very sophisticated procedure to bring my Middle Eastern friend around to a proper understanding of what he had just been through. 'The English', I said, 'produce, now and then, people with strong and fixed ideas. You have just witnessed what they call the meeting of the irresistible force and the immovable object. They have many more words than lots of other languages, too, but since they often use the same term for several different things, as in, say, Chinese, confusion arises.'

Fortunately he was willing to learn: his interest had been aroused. 'But is it ever possible' he asked, 'to move any of them from their fixed position?'

'Indeed yes' I answered. 'You may not recall that there was a time when their currency was not decimalised. It worked by twelves and twenties, and even that is a simplification. Then they decided to change.'

'There was an outcry?'

'Tremendous. Why change it, people asked, from its immemorial twelve pence equal one shilling and twenty shillings to the pound? Why become so Continental? were the questions.'

'But', said my friend, 'how could such a clamour be silenced? What talisman did the English wise ones employ to silence the clamour of the masses?'

'They used a very simple procedure,' I told him; 'one which you find invoked again and again in England. It always works.'

'How can a simple method have such great results?'

'I cannot tell you that. All I can say is that I have succeeded in identifying it', I said.

'And you will impart this knowledge to me?' His eyes were pleading.

'I not only shall, but I must', I replied, 'for who can resist sharing the good things of life with his fellows, except such miscreants as we are constantly warned about in our Eastern classics of wisdom?'

I continued: 'You see, wherever there are fixed ideas in England, there is also, somewhere, the ancient Anglean voice, the one which says that things are not only other than they seem, but may be the exact opposite.

'Thus it was that representatives of this mysterious instinct, having gathered their forces and channelled them through the Press, radio and television, informed the protesting masses that there was another way, a right way, of looking at this question.

'The very word "pound", the main currency unit, which through some amnesia had been thought to be British, was in reality a heritage of the hated colonialist Romans, and brought here by them: it was the foul *pondus*. Then the shilling, far from being English, was shown to be a German coin. As for the penny, it was only a pfennig writ small.

'Now the pound being worth twenty shillings was proved by reference to ancient records to be an innovation. Indeed, it was originally worth three pounds, four shillings and seven pence: if you know what that means – or, indeed, whether you know or not.'

My friend's eyes were starting to cross, but he gallantly signalled to me to carry on. I said: 'You are wondering about the shilling no longer being valued at twelve pence, no doubt? Well, my dear brother, for a long period of English history it was valued at five pence, not twelve: and, as the reference books put is, was "later reduced to 4d".'

He took a deep breath, closed his eyes and then opened them again. 'Such a people', he said, 'are certainly capable of themselves frequenting the shops of merchants instead of being waited upon by them. They would undoubtedly find no difficulty in reconciling doves and baths. It is really satisfying to become the possessor of little-known wisdoms, as I now feel myself to be.'

I felt as if a great weight had been lifted from our friendship, and smiled modestly, as was clearly indicated.

I decided to add something else as a small bonus for his compliment. 'The English are currently showing,' I told him, 'little opposition to the introduction of the gramme and kilogramme instead of ounces and pounds. Perhaps this is as well, since the apparently English "ounce" is in fact the Latin *uncia*, which became the Old English *ynce*. Of course, with their customary originality, the English turned this measure of weight into the *inch*, a measure of length. See Sergeantson's *History of Foreign Words in English*, 1935.' I reckoned that he'd had enough by then, and honour was satisfied. I had regained my aplomb after the gaffe about doves.

Next time I saw him, he started where we'd left off.

'Now,' he said, 'tell me why people here put rugs intended for hanging on their floors, and hang up Eastern floor-coverings on their walls. Also I would like information about why the women uncover their legs in winter, getting them blue with cold, though their heads, already insulated by hair, are covered by hats. And wear trousers in summer. After that, there is the matter of why we have to eat up quickly and get out of restaurants; why the *Government's* statements are called the Queen's Speech – and where I can get a decent cup of coffee . . .'

I woke up at that point, finding that I had been dozing, in the library, over my reference books.

But what had got me onto the subject of doves in the first place? Dreams, of course, can cover enormous distances and great spans of time in seconds, so it might have been something which had happened just before I fell asleep.

I looked out of the window, onto the bleak Kentish country-side, covered with deep snow, flat all the way to the Urals, they say. A lady was standing in the garden, calling to me. I threw open the window and asked her to say it again.

'I said I'm feeding the poor birds, they're starving. But can't someone get onto the Royal Society for the Protection of Birds about the starlings?'

The starlings. Why did they, rather than the other birds, need protection? I asked her whether the turbulent doves were harassing them.

'No, of course not: it's the other way about. The starlings keep taking all the food away from my little birds. They ought to be protected, by getting the starlings to go away!'

As so often in England, I could see the perfect logic of this approach. But I have still not worked out the solution, and I doubt if the RSPB have, either.

Tell you what; find an English solution in some suitable phrase. Yes: shift it onto someone else's plate. I remembered that two bird-lovers – albeit different types of personality, have visited us recently. General Glubb, Glubb Pasha of the Arab Legion, and Robert Dougall, of the BBC. I'd talk to them.

They would surely know how birds could be protected, by bird-fanciers, from birds.

'Leave it to me', I called down, in my best command-and-control voice (such as we use here in the English countryside), 'we'll have the genwallahs sort it out. Why keep a dog and bark yourself, eh? Ump, ump, ump.'

Now, back to work: was I looking up doves, baths or X-rays?

Very intricate, this English business.

20

How to Become an Imperial Presence

Wogs

Your readers may care to know the etymology
of 'wogs'. The term was first used to denote
those Workers on Government Service engaged in the construction of the Suez Canal.
My 700,000 colleagues and I in the Civil Service are, of course, wogs.
Dr Geoffrey Diggle: *Letter to the Editor of
The Times*

He was short, fat, rather less than distinguished and a former
pedlar of black-market goods. He was the kind of man who was
so furtive that you over-compensated, tending to think that
nobody could be as crooked as he looked.

He was, however, listed in a reputable biographical dictionary, among men and women of consequence. The entry was
spattered with impressive letters, abbreviations which reminded
one of universities, research institutes, distinguished military
service, the lot.

Aching to find out how all this had happened to him, how he
had earned his honours, I wrote to the West End address which
the book gave, asking him, against my better judgment, to meet
and talk. After all, I told myself, anything in the cause of
learning. I simply had to know how a man, described in court as
a considerable ruffian, could rub shoulders with the great, even
be named as one of them.

I arranged to meet – let us call him George (Husbandman)

Fudge – after losing track of him for years. He had been out of circulation, as a Royal Guest in Dartmoor.

'Royal Guest' was how he put it, plunging straight into the subject. 'It all depends upon how you phrase it, old boy. I got into the reference book because of the letters: they hardly ever check such things.'

'You mean they're false?'

'Not at all. *They're all genuine.*'

With a flourish, he handed me a visiting-card. Although printed by thermography, imitation engraving, a dreadful mistake in the eyes of the English cognoscenti, it otherwise looked good.

GEORGE ARCHIBALD FUDGE
MC CE DDS

'I like it, Fudge' I said, 'but you have not won the Military Cross, you are not a chemical engineer, and if you are a doctor of dental surgery I'm a monkey's uncle. Don't you know that this is fraud?'

'No fraud about it, old man: look up any good English dictionary of abbreviations. All legitimate, recognised contractions: MC is Master of Ceremonies – which I am when called upon to officiate at social events; C.E. is Church of England member, and so on.'

'And what, may I ask, is "DDS"?'

'Bet you can't pronounce it. It's diaminodiphenylsulphone.'

'And how can you justify calling yourself that? Sounds like a poison to me.'

'Easily. Actually, it's the name of a valuable medicament which I am prepared to deal in; that is, if anyone wants some. All above board.'

I asked him why he had chosen these particular abbreviations.

'They straddle the spectrum, as it were. The first gives that dashing military air, the second is redolent of solid professionalism, the third is sort of medical. Of course, there are hundreds of others, all there for the taking.'

I handed him a photocopy of his entry from the book where I'd found his name. 'I see that you are an Oxford man and got your Bachelor of Medicine degree there.'

'Not at all. "Univ (Oxford) MB" means "universalist:" which

I am; and "Mark of the Beast". Got that last one at Oxford; I was passing through the town when some beast ran me over. In the High Street, it was.'

'Oxford men call it "The High", but never mind. Now, how about this LHD, which I suppose I am not to take as a doctorate?'

'No, not unless you're thinking of the alternative, *Litterarum Humaniorum Doctor*. In my case it means Left-Hand Drive. I used to have a Continental car, you see.'

Regius Professor, he continued, was not the significance – as an academic would have imagined – of the letters 'RP'. In Fudge's case, the abbreviation only referred to his confessional position: he was a Reformed Presbyterian. He could belong to the Church of England and also be a Presbyterian, he explained, on the same basis as the Monarch. 'Well, almost. You see, she's official head of two quite different churches, so why can't a loyal subject belong to both?'

'And Commanding Officer, Bournemouth, 1975?' I was sure that the man had never been in the Army.

'Listen, pal, you really must stop seeing things that aren't there. It says nothing about commanding or officer. "CO" stands for Criminal Offence. I was done for burglary.'

'And I suppose you were similarly convicted for a CO in respect of this entry, here, "CO (Aldershot) 1943", right in the middle of the war?'

'Wrong again. That's a perfectly true description of what happened, using the officially recognised contraction. "CO" here means Conscientious Objector.'

I said, tartly, that at least he couldn't claim to have the CB, to be a Companion of the Order of the Bath, since as a non-soldier he could never have been Confined to Barracks. Then, looking closer, I saw that his entry did indeed include the coveted letters, and of course, apologised.

'That's all right, chum. It did give me a bit of bother at first. But I got to Cape Breton in the end. Nineteen seventy-six it was, as you see.'

'And what happened in 1981 when you were not, I assume, Clerk of the Peace in London, which is what it looks like here?'

'Carriage paid London, of course. I took a train from Brighton, paid my fare, remember it distinctly.'

'This all reminds me', I said, 'of a maid I had once. I left her a note, asking her to get some food in, and marked "NB" – *nota bene*, note well. She did not buy the food, saying that she didn't understand it. Then one day she left me a note, marked "PN". Afterwards, when I asked her what she had meant, she said, "PN stands for 'Please Note', of course." Just made it up as she went along.'

'Listen Squire', said Fudge, 'that's sheer illiteracy, and I'm in a different league altogether. I insist on working with authorised initials only. The ones you find in reference books, and don't you forget it. Takes a lot of ingenuity to suit horses to courses, if you see what I mean.'

I was, indeed, beginning to see. This was undoubtedly a man to enrol in my select group of advisers, in the study of the mysteries of England.

'I find this country and its people', I told him, 'strangely oriental, and I'm thinking of doing a book about it.'

'No problem. Start with abbreviations. Now, if you look up this little book here, it's got some beauties. Oriental, you say? Let's look up "England" . . . Yes, here you are – the letter E stands for both "East" and "England". Got a connection right away.'

I said I thought that sounded a bit thin, but perhaps there was more.

'More? Certainly, I haven't even started. Under "Royal", we find Royal Asiatic Society. Well, now, you couldn't get a closer connection than a ROYAL Asiatic, could you? I bet there isn't another country in the world that has a society especially for Royal Asiatics.'

I appointed him RA on the spot. Not Royal Academician, of course, but Research Assistant.

He is a bit chauvinistic, though. 'Cor, the cheek of it!' he said, blazing fresh trails into the dictionary, 'AEIOU means "*Austria est imperare orbi universo*/Austria is to rule the entire globe," in Latin. You shouldn't be allowed to pinch abbreviations like that, not taking over every vowel in the language. Foreigners!'

I managed to console him, though, by pointing out that the French letters SM (Sa Majesté) might be a royal title over there – but in England it was listed as only equivalent to Sergeant-Major.

In return, he offered me the run of the *Dictionary of Abbreviations*, as his guest. Faced with such riches, I hesitated, but he soon helped me out.

'What is the highest ranking abbreviation in your own country?' he asked.

'Well', I said, 'I suppose it is the shortened form of *Ala-Hazrati Humayuni* – "High Imperial Presence", like "Majesty".'

'No sooner said than done', he answered cheerily. 'That would be, let's see, AH, would it not?'

'Correct', I breathed.

'Here you are then, AH, stands for *ad hoc*.'

With a thrill of discovery I realised that the Latin *ad hoc* means for 'For this Special Purpose'.

The trouble is that in England nobody seems to know that AH signifies Imperial Presence. For that matter, you need a dictionary of abbreviations to see that RP is Reformed Presbyterian, let alone Regius Professor. And how *did* Cape Breton get into it, anyway? It *is* there, I've seen it.

In case you are tempted to avail yourself of the quite legal use of abbreviations – in case, that is, I have started to lead you astray in this regard, let me warn you that there are certain problems in passing-off about which Mr Fudge failed to inform me. I found out the hard way, even if it was by accident.

I was invited to a house-party at an enormous English stately home, and took two Afghans who had attached themselves to me as retainers. I was given a suite of rooms, and the two were shown their own accommodation in the servants' quarters, which I inspected and found to be very good indeed.

Two days later, I realised that a great change had come over the assorted bishops, tycoons, ramblers and gamblers and unidentifiable jet-setters who were my fellow-guests. In a word, they all treated me with great respect, almost like an Imperial Presence, in fact. I couldn't account for it, until an American millionaire blurted it out:

'Say, that really is *something*! Having bodyguards who sleep across your threshold every night!' On checking, I found that my two men had used their rooms only during the day. At night they reverted to the traditional custom of lying on the floor in the passage in front of my rooms. I could not stop them, so I had allowed the matter to rest there.

That evening, however, the American, a true extrovert, started to talk about it during dinner, going on about how fantastic the whole thing was, how stunningly medieval – and so on. Everyone looked at me, and I was trying to compose a suitably witty reply when, from the end of the table, my noble host spoke up.

'I wouldn't place too much importance on that, Senator', he said, 'I'd rather look at the other implication.'

'Other implication?' asked the American.

'Yes. Hasn't it occurred to you that a really powerful man does not need bodyguards? People don't dare to attack him, you see . . . '

I smiled my thanks. After all, I suppose he was only trying, in his English way, to get me off the hook. The Afghans have it that 'The disgruntled man will fail to see the hovering angel'.

Who wants to be an Imperial Presence, anyway? If I were to become one, you might not be able to tell the difference between me and George Fudge.

21

My Stubborn Insensitivity

That Thing

That vain, ill-natured thing, an Englishman.
Daniel Defoe: *True-born Englishman*

The Countess was, as they say, no longer young; indeed, she must have been over seventy. But she was well preserved, a woman of the world, and something hungry about her expression was later amply borne out by my conversation with her.

She came from southern Europe, was sent to me in my London retreat by a friend who knew of our mutual current passion: the investigation of the English mystery. In the event, such perhaps is the effect of this bewitched land, we succeeded well enough in mystifying one another.

When I seated her, straight-backed and commanding, in the Athenaeum Ladies' Annexe, I adopted the posture, head on one side, which I hoped signalled deference to her age and a readiness to be of service.

'It was Sunday yesterday' she said, and handed me a small, exquisitely-bound book. She pointed to a page in whose margin she had marked a passage. I read:

'Were we to judge of what passes in the streets on all days but the Sunday' the writer was saying, 'we must conclude that the idea of a God is unknown in this country.'

'To which country is this person alluding?' I asked.

'*Inghilterra*. England.' She bade me read on.

'Here are no monks', the passage continued, 'in processions, richly clad, bearing crucifixes and relics; no host-carrying to the sick, to sweeten the moment of the soul's departure; the temples

156

are shut, and their God seems exiled from the place where he is most immediately supposed to dwell; not a priest in the streets to be seen . . . '

'Madam', I interrupted, 'anxious though I am to exercise to the full the arts and customs of hospitality, I beg of you to give me further clues as to the reason for this recital.'

She nodded gracefully. 'Very well, Signor. You have been reading a letter to the Reverend Father Stefano Lorenzini, at Rome.'

'I have not the honour of the gentleman's acquaintance', I said.

'The letter was written in the eighteenth century' she answered.

That explained it, of course; so far as it went. There was nothing to do but to wait for more. After dabbing her delicately tinted lips with a tiny handkerchief, the Countess continued:

'The writer was Father Batista Angeloni, a Jesuit missionary residing, for many years, in England.'

'But', I could not prevent myself saying, 'England must have changed a great deal since then. Is this a fitting starting-point for a reconnaissance in these times?'

She made a small gesture.

'I showed you the passage on purpose. Can you deny its validity today?'

'In what sense?'

'In the sense that we see no monks, crucifixes, priests, and so on, no processions . . . '

'Madam, I agree about that.'

'Then', she persisted, 'then I have made my point. This book has lain in our family library for over two hundred years. Some months ago I came across it, saw that passage and others and resolved to come here myself, to verify its content and conclusions.'

I inclined my head; there did not seem much else I could do. The club waiter brought our tea.

'Would you' she continued, 'perhaps care to go over some of the information which the Reverend Father has included, so that I may pursue my enquiries into those parts which have aroused the greatest interest in me?'

I immediately assented.

'Very well, *multo bene*. But first I should mention that the matter is one of some confidence, at least where my identity is concerned.' She took the book from me, turned to another marked passage, and indicated that I should read.

It said: 'I only desire that you would conceal these Letters . . . perhaps there may be greater freedom in them than the nature of our order allows . . . '

'You have read that?'

'Yes, Countess.'

'Well, of course, I am not a Jesuit, that would be impossible, since I am a woman. But it is the principle which I seek to impart. Confidentiality.'

'Say no more.'

'I shall say no more on that subject, but rather refer you to the Nineteenth Letter, written by the Reverend Father to a certain Countess in Rome . . . '

'Did such people, celibates and missionaries, write to countesses?' I could not help asking.

'That is what the book says: and since the lady was a predecessor of mine, and I share with Lorenzini a certain curiosity about similar matters, you will please assist me in my task.'

Again I signified my readiness to serve.

'Now', she continued, 'in any proper investigation you have to find the sort of people who represent the characteristics sought. Is it not so?'

'I suppose so.'

'Then please indicate, first, where one might go to seek the English who are described in the section here.' I read:

'It is the extinction of desire which is the object of every Englishman's pursuit.' I paused. 'I am not sure that I have met many like that', I said, 'except among foreign monks and the like.'

She made a small gesture of impatience. 'No, not that part. Begin at the next sentence.' Her eyes were gleaming a little now. I obeyed:

'Yet when they do love fiercely, no beings upon earth are so totally devoted to their passion as the natives of this isle; they hang, drown and shoot themselves if disappointed in their loves; nothing is restraint enough on their inclinations.'

I said, 'I have to interrupt the Reverend Father here, Countess. I have never come across this tendency quite to that extent, here in England.'

She glared at me. 'Perhaps it is because they have all hung, drowned or shot themselves' I added, lamely.

'Very well; I shall apply elsewhere for those. But continue reading. I should like to meet some of the infamous women who are at the head of society. So different from our own pure land.'

I looked down at the page again. The book continued, relentlessly, with its description of English manners:

'Men of the highest rank marry women of even infamy, not to say of extreme low birth, and ladies of noble birth wed their footmen, players and singers . . . that spirit which is ill understood for liberty, indulging them to think that all actions which are not directly criminal are not culpable . . . '

'I would have to make enquiries about that' I said, thinking wildly that a point of departure might be the gossip columns or even the court reports.

'Then you do not deny it?'

'Neither confirm nor deny.'

She gave what would have been a sniff in a less cultivated person.

'*Signor*, your studies in this country do not seem to have progressed far.'

'It may only be', I told her, reluctant to be bullied, 'that I have been concentrating on a different field. And, may I inform you, our master-poet Rumi reminds us that "Jesus went to heaven but his ass remained below."''

'Would you then not know' she asked, leaning towards me, 'whether here in England, rather than love . . . ' she pointed to an underscored line, "people are actuated by quite a different passion?"''

I forget what I mumbled, but I distinctly remember mumbling it.

The Countess sat up even more straight in her chair. There was a glow in her face, and she was breathing faster. 'My dear sir, I am convinced, through reading these letters from a Jesuit, especially this one to a lady on matters of "amours and dalliance," as he puts it, that there is something in the very air of this country which can transform even a man of faith and the greatest rectitude into one in whom the most tender sentiments boil and seethe.'

'I see.' I turned what I intended to be a quizzical gaze upon
her. Then I said 'And you feel that such . . . feelings might
animate a less restrained foreigner perhaps even more, once
landed upon these shores?'

'I am glad that we understand one another.'

Silently she indicated that I should continue with my reading.
In wonderment, my eyes met the following words from the pen
of that lonely man, the missionary to Darkest England, whom I
would have supposed to be beyond anything less than the
spiritual:

'Yes, such is the sensation of true love that I would renounce
all other enjoyments on earth to possess the object, and feel that
thrilling passion that I once knew; to see the emanations of
reciprocal delight darting from the eyes of her whom I adored;
our whole souls corresponding to each other's touch, like strings
in unison . . . the joy of being ever with her, and she impatient of
my absence, whether in the moment of exalted rapture, or in the
chilling hour which generally succeeds, alike ardently desiring
to be consubstantiated with her.'

Indeed, I thought, there are strange and powerful influences,
magics, in this land which the Romans styled bewitched, thus to
stir a man on a holy mission. I paused; the Countess, seemingly
also similarly affected, plucked at my elbow: 'Read on!'

I perforce obeyed, 'This, in spite of vows and prayers, possessed my soul entirely; this you knew and indulged the weak-
ness for the sake of the perfection in the object; this rapture you
will yet indulge . . . one thought of love and woman brings her
back in full power upon my bosom . . . '

'Really', I said, snapping back into my acquired role, the
English one which puts up a necessary barrier to the world, 'I
think that that will be enough.'

The Countess did not exactly shed a tear, but it was plain to
see that she saw right through me; or, rather, she saw only one
who has thickened his skin, like one of those who had given the
good Jesuit his impression of the English: 'the extinction of
desire which is the object of every Englishman's pursuit.'

I said as much to the Countess, and she at once agreed.

'Yes, young man. You are infected by the English disease of
stubborn insensitivity. But there *is* another influence at work
here, perhaps the very reason why these people are so careful

not to show their feelings. *That* must be the influence which so suffused the breast of the Reverend Father Angeloni , and I now know that I must seek it elsewhere.'

I see in the gossip columns that she has recently married a twenty-three-year-old stockbroker, so that must prove that the old magic is still at work.

Or is it? A seething and bubbling Englishman she may well have found, and I would not wish to call the learned Jesuit a liar. But his picture of the fiercely loving ones, devoted to their passions, is at variance with another account of these people.

A Frenchman, Dr Hippolyte Taine, wrote his own book, after years of residence among the English. It is called *Notes on England*, and he sees the people thus:

> My coachman, the other day, saw fit to rattle down a mews at full speed. He frightened two carriage horses which were being harnessed to the carriage. The groom advanced, took hold of the bits, and calmed the horses. No single word passed between these two men . . . these are people who have water mixed with their blood, exactly as their cattle are deficient in juice . . . That is why they are allowed to combine together, to brawl, to print what they please. They are primitive animals, cold-blooded, and with a sluggish circulation.

In spite of the Countess's remark that I had caught the English ailment, I feel I could hardly aspire to Dr Taine's detailed and daunting description. But his writing, presented in the usual convention as 'a letter from a friend', answers a lot of questions in a single sentence. Freedom of association, of expression, of the Press, are all due to a single cause, slow, thin blood, like that of reptiles. Now we know.

I admit they're cool. It is on record that, when the body and possessions of the great Dr Livingstone were brought back to Zanzibar by his faithful African porters, the British Consul sold the explorer's effects – for £3.

The Continentals seem even further from the English in expression than they once were. Virgil, in his *Eclogues*, written over 2000 years ago, has a more English ring than some recent writers:

penitus toto divisos orbe Britannos

where the Briton dwells, utterly estranged from all the
world!

So are the English cold or hot? A happy chance gave me the
opportunity to go further into this mystery. When she left, the
Countess dropped a piece of paper on which she had written,
evidently in preparation for our conversation, a short note in
English. It said, 'One seeks, you see, something in the nature of
a "cicisbeo".'

For a moment I was, as we say in England, stumped. This was
no English word, surely? I had never heard anything even
remotely like it. Better check, though; after all, I am a
foreigner. So I ascended to the first floor of the club and took
down a dictionary of the English language from the shelves.

There it was: CICISBEO, pronounced *cheecheezbay-o*. It
was a word in English use after all. And the definition, the
reason why an Englishman would want to know its significance?
It might well mean that the English were not, after all, as fishlike
in their feelings as some had said. The meaning of Cicisbeo is –
'A married woman's gallant in Italy.'

Perhaps the English *were* mercurial, after all. Look at a
football crowd. But no, careful students of the race insisted that
they were so dull as to be almost inert. I could not, as a compara-
tive newcomer, take issue with such respected and well-in-
formed authorities as Nathaniel Hawthorne. In *Our Old Home*,
he had been absolutely positive about their appearance and
character:

> John Bull . . . has grown bulbous, long-bodied, short-legged,
> heavy-witted, material, and, in a word, too intensely
> English. In a few more centuries, he will be the earthliest
> creature that ever the earth saw.

The whole thing seemed, for long, utterly unexplicable. Until
I made the breakthrough. I was looking wearily through my
notes when something suddenly leapt out at me. The inhabitants
of these islands, the Druids especially, were famed on the Continent as masters of magic and enchantment. They had obviously
passed this arcanum on to their conquerors, the Angles, who
had built it into the English temperament, so that, today (and
probably for centuries in the past) the English were able to

appear to others just as they wanted to appear, at any given moment.

Turning, with the relief of a man who has cracked an unusually difficult problem, to the day's newspaper for a little light relief, I saw that I needn't have cudgelled my brains after all. There, under a banner headline, they were giving the whole secret away, for those not too stupid to see:

BRITISH PR FIRMS WORLDS BEST . . . London public relations and advertising firms lead the world in image-building . . . Its object is the creation of a perception of an individual, firm or product, along desired lines . . . it is estimated that no less than thirty nations use U.K. image-builders to project the kind of picture of their countries and peoples they desire all over the world.

You must crack the shell before you can have the nut: that's what the English proverb says. As soon as I tumbled to the PR aspect, I could go back to the mystery of John Bull. What were the English really like, and were they fated to become ever more phlegmatic and heavy? I knew I had struck oil when I found that the earliest mention of John Bull was as late as 1791 in English writing. Less than 200 years. Like Canute, Alfred, Robin Hood and all the rest, he's time-bound and any Englishman worthy of the name may, when appropriate, shrug him off.

Silly me: it must be my stubborn insensitivity, as the Countess had said. And what is her English stockbroker *really* like? I hope he doesn't settle in her country; or, if he does, that he retains his Englishry unimpaired. After all, there is the old Italian saying, *Inglese italianato e un diavolo incarnato* – 'An Italianised Englishman is a devil incarnate.'

22

Detrigent

Folly

It is the folly of too many to mistake the echo
of a London Coffee-house for the voice of the
Kingdom.

           Jonathan Swift: *Conduct of the Allies*

'Are you a Cockney?' asked the earnest Turk who buttonholed
me near Fortnum's in Piccadilly. I thought I had misheard him,
but he pointed out the relevant entry in his dictionary, published
in Istanbul:

> COCKNEY: *bilhassa Londra shark mahallesinden olan ve kaba
> bir shive ile konushan.*

Difficult, but snappier, more sonorous, I felt, than the less
abbreviated English definitions I found when I dug behind the
one that most English people think is the true one: 'Born within
the sound of Bow Bells'.

You may not understand much Turkish, but I am not far
ahead of you in that. All I could make out of the above passage
was that it had something to do with the 'eastern district of
London'. It was when I took Hikmet Ozbeg to the nearby
Westminster Public Library (Reference Section) that my education in this direction started.

The whole thing is, of course, very English: 'Cockney' began
life as the opposite of what it is now. It started as a pejorative,
the epitome of a squeamish person and effete city-dweller
(Shakespeare, *King Lear*, ii, 4). Today it is a name proudly
boasted by many a towering docker whom I'd certainly not

invite to inspect the documentation. He would undoubtedly give me a bunch of fives for my trouble if I tried.

John Lyly, also of Shakespeare's time, treated cockney as meaning a 'foolish, spoilt, cokered child'. It was a term coined by countryfolk and much later restricted to, and then appropriated by, people born within the sound of Bow Bells in London.

But why cockney? For this, according to some, we can blame the French; London has been called the Land of cockaigne (though so was Paris), 'A land of idleness and luxury, famous in medieval story,' and the subject of poems, one of which, an early translation of a 13th-century French work, is given in Ellis's *Specimens of Early English Poets*. In this 'the houses were made of barley sugar and cakes, the streets were paved with pastry, and the shops supplied goods for nothing.' The word may come from 'a cock's egg'. Not much like the London we know and love.

Both the Turk and I had to admit, after due deliberation, that I could lay claim to few, if any, of the published possible qualifications in English books. An effete town-dweller, perhaps, and one 'possessing London peculiarities of speech:' but not one who is – or is supposed to be – 'wholly ignorant of country sports, country life, farm animals, plants and so on.' Even today, there is so much country lore given out on television that there are few Cockneys who don't know some of it, even if only from the pictures of beguiling countryfresh foods lavishly advertised in television commercials.

I didn't much mind not being a Cockney, but Mr Ozbeg was attracted by the thought that, as a citizen of Ankara, a completely new city built in the Republican Era by Kamal Atatürk, and knowing little about matters rural, he might assert his right to the description of the older, and therefore more genuine, type of Cockney. He didn't want to be a Pearly King, having discovered something I didn't know. Pearlyism is an innovation, too new to be called 'traditional'.

He was, as you will have guessed, a great Anglophile, and this it may have been which caused his attempted transfer of identity. He had come to London partly because he understood that it was the home of the Reverend Mr Garnett, inventor of the first English submarine boat, and subsequently a commander in the Imperial Turkish Navy. I had to explain that all this had happened a century ago; and that I, for one, no longer thought it surprising that an English clergyman should build submarines or become a Moslem Turk. Indeed, it seemed very much in character.

Ozbeg had read about the Londoner ('The Reverend Mevlevi Commander Garnett') and his reputed words that the Turks and the English were very much like one another, stimulated his interest even further. Then fortuitously, though he imagined, not purposelessly, Ozbeg had met, in Istanbul, an English member of the Turkish Spiritualist Association. If he could raise the shades of the departed, Ozbeg asked him, could the Englishman communicate with the English Moslem submarine commander and clergyman?

The spiritualist obligingly went into a trance and said – or some spirit said, through him – 'You are what I was; you shall become what I am.' Shortly afterwards the English medium collapsed and died, leaving the Turk pondering the gnomic utterance, whose deep meaning escaped him, and the unravelling of which became a passion, as well it might.

For years, Ozbeg asked everyone from England whom he could contrive to meet for possible clues. Ultimately a tourist, a Londoner, Heaven knows why, referred him to a passage in Thomas Cook's *Traveller's Handbook for Constantinople, Gallipoli and Asia Minor*, 1923 edition. Ozbeg showed me a photocopy of page 31, which was accompanied by a Turkish translation. According to this, the Turkish nature 'is probably not far removed from that which we ourselves possessed when physical battle was our almost daily portion'.

For Ozbeg, this bore out the idea behind the medium's words. The Turks, and hence Ozbeg, were what the English used to be like. This must mean, he reasoned, that a Turkish pioneer, visiting their land, would be able to find in the English the end-product: 'You shall become what I am' had been the words.

At first, this scenario seemed far-fetched to me. As I read further from the page, however, and infected by the Turk's powerful belief, I was struck by another sentence. The author, Roy Elston, in claiming affinities in the Turkish and English mentalities, may perhaps have had a point:

> Life was an accidental phase, a series of varying explosions which, to withhold, was to check the very purpose of life.

I had certainly, and often, had a similar feeling, that something like this lay behind the behaviour of at least some English people.

And Ozbek, pressing his tourist informant as to who the real English were, had been told, 'The Cockneys, of course'. They, in turn, were characterised, at least superficially, by their peculiar manner of speech. My new friend had accordingly decided to concentrate upon the English language 'as spoken, no doubt, by the Reverend Mevlevi, Commander Garnett.' I offered him various Cockney terms and tried to explain rhyming slang. He tried to follow, but at times his resolution to embrace his new persona wilted somewhat in the face of my attempts to instruct him in its language.

He kept testily asking questions like 'If "Apples and Pears" means stairs, how do you actually say "Apples" and what is the equivalent of "Pears"?' And, as a lover of Western classical music he refused to accept the alcoholic interpretation of 'Brahms and Liszt'. Totally excluding it, he inserted in his notebook instead: 'Drunken = *hunkan-munkan*', his own coinage, which I supposed to be Turkish, unless my English is even worse than I have been led to believe.

In spite of his reservations, I was not easily able to shake off the would-be Cockney Ozbeg. His forebears came from Konia, where a compatriot of mine, Jalaluddin Rumi, the poet and mystic, had seen to fit to settle in the thirteenth century. This, Ozbeg felt, linked us by an indissoluble bond. Since I, however, could read Rumi in the original, I was put in mind of one of his more graphic phrases about a visitor to embrace the nature of this bond. Rumi had said, 'He stuck to me like government soap.'

Ozbeg was, in fact, a government official, on holiday.

It was useless, indeed fatal, to try to explain that I had little free time because of my urgent research into life in England. Ozbeg, as a primitive Cockney, so to speak, was both anxious to explore the country and also felt spiritually part of London. We proceeded on the quest together.

He wasted little time as we moved from one incident to another, filling in with questions. 'Is it true that the king here is a woman? *And* the Lord Mayor of London?' I found these queries almost as hard to answer as 'What do they say in the

bazaars of England about our current Five-Year-Plan?' When I
responded to the first with 'Well, yes and no', he regarded the
answer as less than adequate. When, to the latter enquiry, I
said, 'It would take a long time to explain', he rejoined, calmly,
'No matter: I am in London for another thirty-five days. Take
your time. Let's now find a born Cockney.' We were to find one
sooner than we thought.

We were speaking, through necessity, in a mixture of English
and Persian, since Turkish has a fair vocabulary of English and
Persian words. Thus it was that, as we sat in a cafe drinking
espresso coffee, an Englishman with a lugubrious expression on
a ferrety face, taking us for tourists, noticed that we were
watching a machine which was automatically washing cups.

'You're foreign' he said, 'so you won't never have seen one of
them there, over there, would you?'

'What does he say?' asked Ozbeg, unable to penetrate the
Cockney dialect.

'*Yok maalum hazret, bir piyale aptest mashinsi*', I translated,
in abominable pidgin-Turkish. Not knowing the word for 'washing' (let alone the grammar) I had been forced to employ the
technical term for 'ritual ablutions'. So what it must have
sounded like to Ozbek was 'Not know you one cup ritual washing hands machine.'

He looked at me blankly, and then at the Cockney. 'Nar, I
fort not,' said our new friend. 'Well, you see, that gadget's full of
continnerus detrigent. You don' 'ave detrigent over there,
course. Detrigent's what cleans the cups. Sort of soap.'

'Thank you,' I said. I translated for the benefit of Ozbeg:
'*Detergent, yaani watery sabun, cup washsi.*' The Turk said
nothing.

'Nar', said the Cockney. 'You've got it all wrong. Just *tell* 'im,
will yer, like I said? *Not* 'dituujan, it's DETRIGENT.'

He confirmed my growing impression that he was something
of an amateur philologist, as well as a purist and friend of
tourists with a mission to inform, by his next words. 'Detrigent
comes from *detriment*. Wot it does is to the detriment of the dirt,
see?'

'No, we do not see,' snapped Ozbeg, looking at my puzzled
face and obviously annoyed at having to stay silent throughout
all the expositions and translations. Though his ear was getting
used to London English.

The Cockney squared his shoulders, so I thought that I might pour oil on troubled waters, and contribute to the discussion, with a reasonable question.

'Why,' I asked our Londoner, 'don't the makers call that liquid something *positive*? They could name it, say "Enhance", because it is intended to enhance the cleanliness of the article washed in it. Do you suppose' I continued, since he did not immediately take up my point, 'that it is a case of *Lucus non lucendo*? As you will recall, this phrase was adopted by Latinist natives here in England, from the Grammarian Honoratus Maurus Servius, at about the end of the fourth century AD.'

Even as I said these words, I inwardly asked myself what earthly reason I had for quoting Latin to a Cockney. Then I remembered: he looked uncannily like HBM's ambassador to Chile, whom I'd once met. British ambassadors, traditionally (though for no discernible reason) are classicists: they relish Greek and Latin tags. And, in England, unlike other countries, you can't tell a diplomat from a coal-heaver by his features, so my mistake was understandable: or so I consoled myself. Association of ideas is a powerful thing.

My interlocutor was looking at me levelly, as if making up his mind about something. This made him look even more like Our Man in Santiago de Chile.

'The reference,' I concluded, 'is, of course, to contradictions: "a grove from not being lucent".'

The Cockney tilted his head on one side and sucked one of his eye-teeth as the Turk and I looked at him, expectantly.

'Bleatin forners' he said, witheringly.

Ozbeg noticed, even across the linguistic-cultural divide, that the Cockney was not impressed by us. This made him pensive. After a silence, during which the Cockney had turned away, the Turk tugged at my sleeve.

'Perhaps he is a man of consequence, and does not follow your Afghan English', he suggested. 'Perhaps you do not understand him.' I said that I understood him perfectly, possibly better than he understood himself. But Ozbeg persisted. 'Ask him what he is, what work he does, and so on.'

'Do you work here?' I said to the Cockney.

'Yer, in the evenings, pearl-diver' he told me.

Oddly enough, this time the Turk followed every word. 'A diver for pearls! You must be a brave and monied man, *Bayim*.'

I tried, without success, to explain that this was slang for people who wash dishes for a living in London cafes, but Ozbeg was too impressed to listen. His eyes were shining as the washer-up spoke again.

'Yer. In the daytime I'm an Old Bailey Underwriter.'

This really set the Turk on fire. 'Underwriter, I know about that! I have been to Lloyd's of London, plenty of big merchants there, they are rich and insure ships. Difficult to become one. Old Bailey, I have seen that too, great criminal court, covers all city of London and Middlesex. You are rich and important man.' He took the Cockney's hand and shook it heartily.

It didn't add up. I knew that underwriters at Lloyd's were very reputable people. Whatever Old Bailey ones did, and it certainly sounded impressive, they did not, I would bet, wash dishes in the evening. Unless I had stumbled across yet another mystery of England.

I tackled the Cockney head-on. 'And what's that mean, then?'

'That', he told me, with a grin, 'is a bloke wot does a bit of forgin', alterin' motor tax discs, log books, that kin'v thing . . . '

He went on, as if the idea had just occurred to him, 'Ere, I've got some forners travellers cheques I want taken to the Old Tay Bridge I know . . . '

'Not likely', I said, hastily, 'but what's an Old Tay Bridge?'

'Werl, it's a middle aged lady bank clerk, like, innit? Anyway, there's nothing to it. I can change the name on yer passports, easy as kiss yer 'and . . . '

'Tay Bridge Disaster!' Ozbeg suddenly shouted. 'I like this man. Always wanted to see Tay Bridge. Twenty people killed in construction. Blown down by a gale. This man will take us there?'

'No, Ozbeg. It's near Dundee, and he's not talking about that kind of Tay Bridge at all.'

Desperate situations demand desperate remedies, and imagination came to my aid. 'This man is a . . . ' I said to Ozbeg. I was going to say criminal, but I did not know the Turkish word for it and could not trust him not to repeat the English one if I used that, with unpredictable effects on the Pearl-Diver. I was whispering into the Ozbeg ear, and, the moment I remembered it, I hissed the Turkish word *katil*, murderer.

That worked all right. Ozbeg leapt to his feet and pulled me away, across the floor of the cafe, out of the door and into the street.

'That was lucky escape', he gasped, as he shook my hand before running off into the evening shadows. And out of my life. The government soap had been washed away, if not by the detrigent, at least by a word whose significance has international currency. The great mystic Rumi, I thought, as I made my way homeward, would have approved. He also used shock tactics, in dealing with his more obtuse disciples.

23

Oil-Rich Prince and Man from Grim Fastness

Which side to be On

'It's always best on these occasions to do what
the mob do.'

'But suppose there are two mobs?' suggested Mr Snodgrass.

'Shout with the largest' replied Mr Pickwick.

Charles Dickens: *Pickwick Papers*

I had visited Saudi Arabia several times, had made the pilgrimage to Mecca, and had been the guest of the King, Abdul-Aziz
ibn al Saud. I got on well with his son, Emir Faisal, who succeeded to the throne. One day, when he was still Crown Prince,
I ran into him as we were both changing planes in Switzerland.
We passed an hour or two in private conversation, all unaware
that the eyes of England were upon us.

This is from an article which appeared in print a whole month
later, though presented as news:

> Prince Faisal, son of oil-rich King ibn Saud, held talks re-
> cently with the Sayed Idries, the international adviser and
> descendant of the Prophet, on the neutral ground of Geneva
> Airport. The Prince, who is Saudi Arabia's Foreign Minis-
> ter, is believed to be anxious to form a consortium with a
> view to developing some of Afghanistan's fabled ruby mines,
> which lie in the Sayed's territory.

In fact, the subject of rubies was never mentioned, and the mines are in Badakhshan, which is almost as far as you can get from our neck of the woods, Paghman, and still be in Afghanistan. And that 'is believed' – by whom?

I had, it was true, advised several Middle Eastern and other governments on various matters. Perhaps, as an International Adviser (what the paper called me) I even merited an article. The only difficulty was that Fleet Street had no idea what I was advising about: and usually not even whom.

A feature writer has few constraints upon his pen. There is the law, of course; but apart from that he has only to worry about his editor and whether he has access to a good cuttings library. There was plenty on me in such places. I had been written up as THE MAN BEHIND THE OIL SHEIKS (because I had advised some of them); THE MAN BEHIND THE MAN BEHIND THE INTERNATIONAL MONETARY FUND (I am not quite sure why), and even as THE MAN WHO TURNS DUNDERHEADS INTO EXPERTS. I got the last accolade because of the success of a psychological training system. And an English orientalist whom I'd annoyed had accused me of wanting to be Alfred Hitchcock. Evidently our intrepid journalist lacked access to a good cuttings library.

This handicap did not deter him: conjecture can always be used if facts are short. The man had tried to find out something, though: evidently first from the Saudis, who had refused to endorse his speculations:

> Saudi official circles deny that the move is intended as a hedge against a possible future oil glut, though the Arabs are known to be diversifying their investments worldwide.

The redoubtable and distinguished journalist Chapman Pincher, in his book *Inside Story*, did not exaggerate when he wrote that 'many newspaper stories are inaccurate when judged by those who know something about the issue being discussed.' Once in the cuttings library, of course, any article becomes 'research material' – which is English for 'something that can be paraphrased and presented as fact'.

I had not known that any such story was in the making, and so I was puzzled one day when someone rang me up, said that he was a writer in need of material, and asked about Saudi interest in Afghanistan. But my advisory work was not connected with

that country. I therefore said, truthfully, 'Can't tell you anything at all about any such thing. Sorry.' This is how to wring a
sentence out of such unpromising material:

> The Sayed refused to confirm or deny involvement in the
> matter.

The Saudi Embassy must have denied all knowledge, too,
when asked 'Are there any plans for a further meeting?' for:

> It is understood from official Saudi circles that no date has
> been set for the resumption of negotiations.

Just by annoying someone you can quarry something: plague
the Prince with questions and you get:

> The Prince was tight-lipped as he stepped aboard his private
> jetliner.

I would have been tight-lipped, too, if harassed – as prominent people often are – by importuning journalists.

The correspondent, having run out of both information and
imagination, now seems to have reached for the aviation reference books; for he continues:

> The aircraft, which reputedly cost more than £20 million, is
> believed to be equipped with the latest electronic communi-
> cations systems.

But *I* was not so equipped; so, even if there had been any
ongoing deal between us, Faisal wouldn't have got much joy out
of his gadgets if he had tried to use them to contact me. Still, the
implication was there, even if a moron might have guessed that
an aircraft costing £20 million would have more in the way of
instrumentation than sundials or semaphore flags.

The newshawk's editor may have asked for some meat in the
form of local colour, for the next paragraph supplied it:

> It winged its way [how else could it fly, I wondered] towards
> the desert kingdom which Prince Faisal's father has ruled
> since the day, as a youth of 19, when he and his bedouin
> warriors, the dreaded Wahabis, wrested control of the
> strategic fortress of Riyadh, in the arid northern region of
> Nejd . . .

No room there for me, I thought: Lawrence of Arabia had taken over. But no: our man had probably been reading a schoolboy thriller, and I was suddenly back in the act:

> The Sayed Idries, too, has a castle, the grim fastness of his ancestor, the mystic and warlord Jam Fishem . . .

Jam Fishem. Almost as Anglicised as Nert Blib, though I was not sure that I liked the name of my grandsire, Jan-Fishan Khan, treated quite like that. But I pressed on:

> His family palace and mosque and tombs, in the ancient Imperial style of the first resident Sayed and Nawab of this line, have recently been restored regardless of expense, to their ancient dignity, watched over by a Palace Guard, according to authoritative sources.

Authoritative indeed: he had been reading *Murray's Handbook*, 22nd edition, 1975, probably from his newspaper's library. It is almost a straight crib, though slightly jazzed up. But he gets full marks for presentation: I had no idea I was so exciting. How was he going to continue? I turned the page:

> The Shah's seat in England is in Kent, near Royal [that's all right, then] Tunbridge Wells. The family's connection with the United Kingdom dates from the First Anglo-Afghan War in the 1840s, when Jam Fishem . . .

Jam Fishem again. Sounds more like an experimental fish-paste than the name of the great warlord and mystic of the Hindu Kush. It's easy to write this kind of thing, I realised, dragging in all sorts of probably irrelevant detail: *mutatis mutandis*, as they say in Oxford. Our journalist would, I am sure, have added 'where King Charles once held his fabled Court.'

Such experiences cast useful light upon the English. Without such materials, it would be hard to lay bare a hitherto deeply concealed tendency and interest: one which might help to prise open one of the fastnesses of their thought.

The Press, in England, gives the people what they want. That is inevitable so long as people will buy papers, and pay money for them, to read what they desire. Very well. Now, what is the thirst, to assuage which these people are putting their money where their mouth usually isn't (for they never say it openly)?

In other countries it is usually conspiracy theory and a conviction of the demonic nature of others which keeps papers going. In England it is the desire to read extraordinary things, apparently for their own sake. I say apparently, because, if you remember, the characteristic of the English is to collect information for future use. A dose of the *Thousand and One Nights* is only part of it.

In today's papers there is a story, with picture, of a struggle between two unions as to which of them should enrol a mouse-catching cat. The dispute is about whether the cat is a management or a manual worker.

This may not appear to be as epoch-making as it is, since it has long been said that a dog biting a man is not news, whereas the reverse certainly is. That is where your typical English person will have erred on the side of modesty once again. How about this one? It is in a headline on 5 October 1984: SEPTEMBER WAS COOL AND RAINY.

Dog Bites Man? Surely, you say, this headline is even sloppier than that? You might not have been present at the biting, but must have had first-hand experience of the wet and rainy September.

Not necessarily. The astonishment and surprise occasioned by reading such a headline, the intense effort needed to understand why it is there at all, can fulfil the need for the extraordinary, and the inner striving, which the English crave.

Many English people make much of the Greek heritage in art and thought which they claim. But they write and talk a great deal about other Greek peculiarities. I believe that all those eccentric deities; philosophers living in barrels; orators speaking through stone-filled mouths, democracy sustained by slavery; Trojan horses and the rest, the weirdness of it all, are what fascinate them.

But, for all its efforts, there are still stories which never get into the Press; the upshot of part of my talk with Emir Faisal is one.

I had mentioned that a mutual friend, an Englishman, was soon to be married. 'In England,' I said, 'everyone gives something for the house-warming. It doesn't do to forget.'

The Prince did not forget. When I arrived at the party I learned that Faisal ibn Abdul-Aziz's gift was house-warming

indeed: a complete central heating system. I asked the bride-
groom whether I could take any message to the Crown Prince.

'Just ask him, would you,' the Englishman said, 'exactly how
he imagines I'm going to pay the fuel bill . . . '

Well, the house *has* got forty rooms.

When I next saw Faisal he had become King, and we spoke of
neither rubies nor central heating; nor did the substance of our
conversation reach the media. As Omar Khayyam puts it:

> To knaves thy secrets we must not confide,
> To comprehend it is to fools denied
> See then to what hard case thou doomest man,
> Our hopes from one and all perforce we hide.

24

Not Perfidious, but Lucky

Thinking

'They are ruled not so much by mendacious
Machiavellian and blundering Blimps as by
honourable and intelligent men whose ardent
desire to comfort themselves enabled them to
believe that they were stopping wars when
they were in fact joining in them, who could
say what they said and do what they did because they literally and honestly did not know
what they were thinking.'

J. H. Huizinga:
Confessions of a European in England

'We're lucky, so we don't have to be perfidious' were the exact
words of Field-Marshal Lord Wavell when I took up the matter
of Perfidious Albion with him. He also corrected me about the
attribution of the notorious phrase. It was not originated by
Napoleon, but he had derived it from Bossuet, who died sixty-
five years before Bonaparte was born. That's all right, then.

Lucky, yes, what with the oil-wells of the North Sea and so on,
but also inclined to take chances. 'He who Dares, Wins' has a
great attraction over here.

Habibullah Khan, King of Afghanistan, made a State Visit to
India in 1907. None of the British officials there knew what the
Afghan national anthem was. The Commander-in-Chief, Lord
Kitchener ('of Khartoum') was consulted. 'It does not matter',
he said.

178

The bandmasters therefore chose a tune from a heavy German march, and played it every time the King appeared.

The result? The English newspapers of Bombay, Calcutta, Madras and other cities visited by the Ameer printed columns about the 'weirdly beautiful Oriental strains of the Afghan national anthem'. As so often in their history, the English had dared and won: even the King of Afghanistan liked 'that catchy little Infidel tune'.

My father was among the Afghan pupils at Aligarh, an Islamic institution run on English public school lines, during the King's visit. He has written about it in one of his books; amplifying that account, he told me how alike the English and Afghans seemed to him, even as a boy. 'Both of them', he said, 'seemed inherently good at scoring prestige points.'

The Viceroy of India had invited the Afghan King: but, said Habibullah, protocol demanded that he receive a personal telegram of welcome, king to king, from King Edward in London, as soon as he crossed the border into infidel territory: and so he did. His great feudal chiefs, the Sirdars, mostly wanted to accompany the King to India, but, in an almost English way, nobody knew whether the ones he took with him were there as a distinction or because, if left at home, they might foment trouble.

To make an impression, thirty thousand British Rajite troops were marched past for the monarch to inspect. Since, however, his spies had earlier reported the intimidating size of this contingent, he was himself escorted by more than just a ceremonial guard or two. The King of Afghanistan's bodyguard numbered no less than eleven hundred Sirdars, Khans and miscellaneous trained attack troops, armed to the teeth.

Determined to show the northern barbarian real viceregal splendour and Anglean power, Lord Minto held a durbar at which dozens of Indian princelings, weighed down with jewels, fawned upon the great white chief. But, when introduced to the young Maharaja of 'one of the greatest fighting States of our Empire, your Majesty', Habibullah merely looked at the stripling and enquired, 'Is it a boy or a girl, your Excellency?'

Nothing daunted, though we may guess somewhat ruffled, the Viceroy had Kitchener take the King up in a balloon, at which His Majesty did not turn a hair, only remarking that he rather wanted to see the sea. Taken to Bombay and shown the limitless ocean, though, his sole comment was, 'yes, it is rather large, isn't it?'

When the Viceroy enquired whether the King did not find the Indians prosperous under the *Raj-i-Inglisi*, the ruler patted him on the arm reassuringly. 'Yes, Lord Minto, they seem fit enough. And if you haven't managed to get them into proper clothes after two hundred and fifty years, perhaps Nature never intended them to have any!'

But what most impressed my father, the schoolboy – apart from the bag of gold he got from the King for his recitation from the Koran – was what he said to the assembled School.

'"I have some advice for you, as to your best course in dealing with these English"' my father says the King told them, while 'the British officers in attendance gritted their teeth'. "And that is: *Learn from them, learn from them, learn from them.*"'

'We were quite surprised', my father added.

The interplay between the English and their Eastern visitors could form a study in itself; especially if you believe the newspapers. The Shah of Iran came to London and was told that he could not witness the execution of a sentence of death because there was nobody in the condemned cell at that time.

One columnist alleges that the Shah replied: 'That's all right – you can have one of my suite'.

I was with King Abdullah of Jordan one day, when an English journalist noticed the King stroking the head of a dog. He wrote:

> The King instructed a visitor in his special method of predicting greyhound race winners by the shape of their heads.

In fact, Abdullah and I had been conversing about the Sufi thought of Saadi, of whom the learned monarch was a great follower. The Hashemite Sharif's family, Saadi's and my own were all traceable to that of Ali ibn abi-Talib.

They are fascinated by people from the East, these English: it is almost as if they feel some ancient affinity. Indeed, when there are no Eastern potentates on hand, English people have been known to dress themselves up as such and – as in a famous instance – hoax the Fleet with a 'Royal Visit of the Sultan of Zanzibar' or something similar. And when a Burton, Lawrence or Philby Goes Native in a Middle Eastern direction, he is widely applauded.

Nobody yet knows whether it was lucky or perfidious when a visit by a powerful Middle Eastern head of state ended in a very strange event. But it shows that the English can feel so Eastern that they sometimes neglect their homework. Or do they? As I was there, I'll tell it in my own words: the more especially since no journalist seems to have covered the story.

The Head of State was not in the West to look at racehorses and the like, but to agree an aviation contract – if he so decided. Getting wind of the project, the president of a certain European country which wanted the contract invited him to dine at his London embassy. It is not usual for such a thing to happen: but there you are, it was arranged and the Foreign Office was not best pleased.

The European ambassador arranged for a sumptuous banquet, having asked a Foreign Office man for advice on the etiquette of such things. With the usual courtesy, the Englishman provided gave all the guidance he could.

I had been invited to the function, and I was impressed by the guest-list. Political and industrial leaders, members of the aristocracy, heads of universities and senior civil servants from the host country had flooded into London for the occasion. Together they represented every conceivable interest which might have expectations from the illustrious and well-heeled guest. The contract was worth nearly four billion dollars: 'That is equal to *four thousand* millionaires!' as one mathematically-minded functionary put it to me.

The British diplomat's *Aide-Mémoire* said: 'Careful attention. should be given to every word and action of the visitor. His customs are different from ours. If in doubt, the safest course is to emulate and reciprocate any sign or remark . . .' Copies of this document, in various languages, were circulated among the guests.

On the day of the function, we entered the ballroom to be presented in strict order of precedence to the man who, in the words of the briefing, 'could topple the entire Western econmic structure'. We were then seated by fawning lackeys. Two hundred of us: at low tables beneath garish trappings supposed to represent an Arabian tent. Very different from the life of the distinguished visitor, of course. But the effect, if bizarre, was not unpleasing.

Just before the food was served, a number of flunkeys in Ruritanian uniform brought bowls and ewers of water, so that we could wash our hands in the Eastern manner. This ceremony was not an absolute success. Everyone looked at the chief guest to see exactly how to perform the ablution. When they saw him wave the servant airily away, they all did the same. This was a distinct solecism, for they had unwittingly signalled that their hands were as clean as those of the visiting Ruler. He frowned.

But, thanks to intensive instruction, all present knew that everyone must finish eating together, and the meal ended in a dead-heat, with two hundred and one pairs of hands being folded, right over left, at exactly the same moment.

The foreign Ambassador beamed at his guest, and cleared his throat. He was about to start a conversation.

At that moment, with all eyes on him in eager attention, the Monarch stood up, his body twisting from side to side. Immediately everyone else did the same. The man next to me gripped my arm and pulled me up, signalling that I, too, should join the whirling dance.

My fellow guests were now tearing off their ties and rolling their heads from side to side: a glance at the Head of State showed why. Then, still mimetically absorbed, the tycoons, statesmen, men of science and the rest there assembled left their places and staggered, grunting, around the enormous room.

It was at that juncture that I was able to break free from my neighbour (the head of a Foreign Ministry department) – and run for a doctor. To my eyes the potentate was distinctly ill. Something was stuck in his gullet.

Later it emerged that the order of runners past the post was: me first, for I had 'saved the Ruler's life': the doctor second, for some good work retrieving the chicken bone (he did so well that he retired to a tax-haven on his honorarium) – and the European Embassy a very trailing third. The Ambassador, however, tried to get the decision reversed. I was sitting with the Monarch in his hotel suite when the envoy's letter arrived, setting out the grounds for his appeal. They were quite ingenious, blaming the whole thing on the English, who had made such an issue of the need to imitate the Ruler's every movement as to constitute a deliberate plot.

'What is this *Beek*?' the Monarch asked me, as the letter was examined, word by word, to plumb its deepest significances, as is the way of all Courts with official missives. Basking in the glory of saviour of the illustrious one, I had been honoured with the style of *Mustashar*, Counsellor. Now I had to counsel.

I looked at the paper, 'Oh, may thy life be infinitely extended', I was able to say, 'it is *pique*'.

'His Majesty,' a courtier hissed, 'has already said that. *Beek*.' P is pronounced like B in Arabic.

'Pique', I explained, 'I mean *Bique*, is the word used here by the Continental Ambassador, writing that the unfortunate incident was due to an English plot, rooted in rancour. That's another meaning of the word; it is commonly employed among the Inglizi. The equivalent is *istiya* or *ranjish*.'

'And the real word, the English one: what is that?'

I could only recall chagrin, resentment, annoyance – but they were all from French, too.

Shifting the emphasis, I said. 'But I think that the English are more lucky than perfidious, as one of their high war-leaders, who was also a Viceroy, once informed me . . .'

The King, in the usual Eastern way, and as the English also do, waited for me to amplify. Here was my chance to put in a word for my Angles. I said, 'May you live a thousand years! I intercede in the matter of the contract, in favour of the Ingliz. I support this with a quotation from our ancient classic, the Orchard, specifically the passage where the great Sheikh Muslihuddin instructs:

"Be brave, good-thinking and forgiving
As God scatters favours to thee, do thou to others scatter.
None came into the world and remained
But he whose good name remained."'

'I believe that they meant well,' said the Head of State, 'and your intercession is accepted. We shall give the contract to the Ingliz. They are lucky, in this; and, as for perfidy, what can be worse than this letter, which blames the innocent for an accident?'

25

Disinformation

The British Council

The council was started to spread 'British ideals' among foreign nations. One early torchbearer, Sir Eugen Millington-Drake ('tall, handsome and very rich') specialised in reciting Kipling's '*If*' to the natives of Montevideo: another lectured in Brazil on 'The Old School Tie'.

John Carey, in *The Sunday Times*

'You *are* loyal, I suppose?' The British Ambassador in Jeddah (British? you could have fooled me, he looked so *English*) was not looking at me. But he asked the question in that thin, rather high-pitched, far-away Anglean voice which I have come to recognise as signifying that the subject is important.

Now, there is a special, technical meaning to this word, 'loyal' among the English. The self-confessed Irish–Scottish D. W. (Sir William) Brogan has, perhaps, overstated things by calling it a 'curious phenomenon'. On the other hand, he is able, in *The English People*, to describe it:

> To be 'loyal' meant preferring English interests and sentiments to the interests and sentiments of your own country, or it meant a highly uncritical, superstitious and verbally servile devotion, not to the institution of the Crown, but to the Royal Family.

I wouldn't have put it quite so brutally, but I understand what he is trying to say.

This conception of loyalty is what made it possible for any number of unconsulted people in subject territories to feel loyal, or to be punished for being disloyal. Irrespective of nationality or origins, it is thus obvious that it is better to be loyal than otherwise.

In the Ambassador's study, I was reminded of the story of my compatriot, quite illegally conscripted in wartime Britain, who found that the possession of a foreign passport and neutral status did not impress the authorities. They constantly asked him what he would do if his wife were to be raped by a German, said they'd never heard of Afghanistan, and shipped him off to an army training camp.

When he got there and managed to secure an interview with the Commanding Officer, he was told, 'Even if, as you say, your country is not in the Empire, it *should* be.' What had been worrying my friend was that he would have to take an oath of allegiance: he wasn't averse to doing a bit of fighting from time to time; and the Brits seemed to place a high value on his services. He was finally reconciled when the form of the oath was shown to him. Typically English in its imprecision, it said 'I swear that I shall be loyal to "*My* King, *my* country, and *its* flag"'.

With these thoughts in my mind, I answered the Ambassador's question about fealty, 'Er, yes I suppose so'. In terms of Englishry, other considerations apart, it would have seemed unauthentic to be too definite.

We were having tea and Huntley and Palmer's biscuits in the rather rundown-looking Embassy not far from Sams (SAMS means Saudi-Arabian Mining Syndicate) Pier in the baking heat of the Hejaz summer. All the electric fans were broken. The Ambassador had just looked at my passport and handed it back to me.

'And you're going to Mecca, what?'

'Mecca, your Excellency.'

'Saw a bit of Arabic handwriting, as well as the rubber stamp, on your visa . . .' His voice seemed even farther away than before, so I was sure that he had read and understood it.

'It only says, "Visa issued on the personal command of the Crown Prince", Ambassador. Known him since he was Viceroy of the Hejaz.'

'You know his son, Abdullah Faisal, is Governor of Mecca?'

'Yes. I'm calling on him. After I have fulfilled the requirements of the Pilgrimage, of course.'

'Of cawse, of cawse, wouldn't do not to, would it?'

The Ambassador leant back with his eyes closed. '"Millions
of spiritual creatures walk the earth/Unseen, both when we
wake, and when we sleep;"' he intoned.

I recalled that the English papers usually referred to British
ambassadors in the Middle East as Competent Arabists: and the
words did sound familiar. I said 'Muhiyuddin ibn al Arabi, of
Moorish Spain, called Doctor Maximus, The Greatest Teacher,
by the medieval Schoolmen?'

His eyelids opened, slowly. 'Milton, actually, *Paradise Lost*,
Book Four, Line 678.'

I nearly said 'Of cawse, Line 678', but restrained myself. It
might have been a test.

'Loyal, yes loyal', continued the Head of Mission. He had
leant right back in his cane chair, and now his thin voice seemed
no higher than an anopheles mosquito's whine. 'Bein' loyal,
you'll keep your eyes and ears open, won't you? There's a good
chap.'

It's so often like that with the English, I thought. You don't
know whether they are trying to recruit you as a spy, or if they're
just keeping their hands in. Or perhaps, I reflected, he's only
being kind, making me feel at the centre of events. I left the
Embassy almost with a sense of having been honoured.

Mind you, the Saudis were not far (if any distance at all)
behind, in their subtlety and alertness. As I got into the long
Cadillac, upholstered in cut-up Persian rugs of great antiquity
and beauty, put at my disposal by Ba-Khashab Pasha on orders
from Riyadh, Habshi – the tiny driver – showed his toothless
gums.

'Mecca', he said, 'Holy Mecca is ringed with powerful anti-
aircraft guns, set invisibly into the mountains which surround
her. Ready for any attack: spies are numerous, but they are
always instantly detected, especially *Inglizis*.'

'I am *loyal*. Loyalty and fidelity, *ikhlas* and *wafa*, are my chief
characteristics' I told him.

'Allah support the truth and utterly destroy the liar' he rejoined, looking at me narrowly. 'Amen', we chorussed.

Spies are numerous; keep your eyes and ears open; the Inglizis . . . For a glorious moment I considered bringing the two,
the Ambassador and the chauffeur, together. They could discuss anti-aircraft guns. Then I remembered that spies were
always instantly detected, especially Inglizis. I left well alone.

I could not claim to be a diplomat, I reflected, as we took the
main road to Holy Mecca, much less that I understood English
ones. But life with them is seldom dull. Take Montevideo.

I had complained to a senior member of the staff at the British
Embassy there that I was always being stopped and questioned
when I took the ferry across the River Plate from Buenos Aires
to Uruguay. The Chancery people took my passport from
me. In a few minutes they returned it, stamped GOVERNMENT
OFFICIAL. 'That should fix things, old boy.'

It did indeed fix things. Every time they saw that endorse-
ment, Argentinian and Uruguayan officials were convinced that
I was up to no good. One lot of them even impounded my
passport and ruined the cover by stapling onto it a note: NOT TO
BE RETURNED TO THE HOLDER UNDER ANY CIRCUMSTANCES. I had to
go to the President of the Argentine Republic, and get him to
order its return, to get it back.

I got so fed up that I eventually stormed into the stronghold of
the heirs to the British Raj. If they didn't stop this tomfoolery
and get on with their work, I announced, didn't do something
sensible instead of their usual incoherent babbling and disas-
trous acts of absurdity, I'd kick them into the middle of next
week, that's what . . . And I threw in, for good measure, the old
Afghan challenge: 'Your moat may be deep, but I want to see
how much water's in it'.

The man I attacked was sweetness itself. 'Tell you what, old
boy: why don't you have a little talk to H.E. about it?'

His Excellency had already been told. No sooner was I seated
in his office than he said, 'Tell you what, my dear sir: why don't I
drop in for dinner at your place and have a little talk? Straighten
things out, as it were?' It was fixed for the following day.

'Uncommonly civil,' I said, returned to the apartment and
gave my secretary the evening off. He was American, and the
Embassy had hinted that the Yanks were making far too many
inroads into Latin America, as it were. ('Call it their own back
yard. What *is* a back yard, by the way?') Then I called in my

housekeeper. She was really a self-employed contract maid who looked after several foreigners who had apartments in the fashionable suburb of Pocitos.

Concepción was small and scrawny, with one brown and one green eye, was of indeterminate age, and spoke a sort of Spanish, though she preferred to talk Guarani and came from Gualaguachu. She had no English, if you except her *Khieve mi dha money*, which was accompanied by an open-palm, fanning gesture, when she wanted a pile of pesos for the market: or, more likely, for the cinema. She could spend all day watching the Japanese film '7 Bravos Samurayos Caballeros', even though she couldn't read the subtitles.

'Concepción', I said, uncomfortable as usual with the name, which evoked irrelevant associations in my mind, 'The place needs cleaning, and the food must be improved.'

'*Que dice, señor?*' I reached into my tiny stock of Spanish, still at the stage where I was adapting French words and adding o's to English ones.

'Concepción: as you know, I am not happy . . . that is, *Zho no soy* – what was the word for happy? In French, now, it was *hereux*. In Spanish, let me see: yes, "Hermoso" sounds near enough. *Yo no soy hermoso, Concepción, como sabe, pero,* but . . .'

Concepción was, as usual, straining to understand me, word by word: but, suddenly, she clapped her hands, danced a brief jig, and ran from the room shouting '*Hermoso – Carámba!*' And other words to the effect that those crazy, *loco, Ingleses, Madre de Dios*, were going crazier by the minute.

I had obviously done, more likely said, something wrong. But what was it?

I looked up the word: HERMOSO = Handsome, attractive. It didn't mean 'happy' at all. 'Concepción, as you know I am not handsome, but . . .' is what I had said.

When the time for the dinner had almost come, I was dressed informally. That's what the Embassy had said: 'Nothing special, old boy . . .' I wore my brown-and-white co-respondent shoes, then all the rage in Monte, my white two-piece single-breasted suit from Harrods de Buenos Aires, and a yellow tie with green stripes. All ready for Mr (later Sir) George Vereker, CMG (later KCMG).

He arrived, in black tie and dinner jacket, shook hands, complimented me on the flat and instantly, smoothly, asked if he could please see the kitchen. I sent him down the narrow corridor to Concepción, chuckling among her pans, and rushed up the stairs of the duplex to my room. Just time to change if I hurried. When I came downstairs, Sir George hadn't come back.

I settled into an armchair for an unconscionably long wait. Concepción peeped in from time to time and said various things with increasing urgency, but as I had tidied away my Spanish, Guarani (and French) dictionaries, I wasn't very sure what she was talking about. It usually sounded like 'The *matambre* is spoilt', but I did not really care. I had lost the initiative by my protestations that I was not handsome, and spoilt *matambre*, I was sure, could not be much worse than the unspoilt: fibrous meat, the kind which she loved and kept serving up. As I could seldom eat it, she usually had a bonus: she wrapped it up and took it away.

An hour had passed. Whatever was the Ambassador doing in the kitchen? There was a ring on the doorbell, just to complicate things, I thought, when I had this important dinner to solve my passport problem. I answered it, and there stood – the British Ambassador whom I'd assumed was still ensconced in Concepción's quarters, pursuing some purpose of his own. But no, here he was on the doorstep, looking like someone auditioning for *Our Man in Havana*.

He wore a broad-brimmed, white floppy hat, alligator-skin shoes, light green double-breasted suit and red silk tie. Vereker, no slouch at getting a non-verbal (if unintended) message, had been home to change. He knew this apartment building well, and had got out quite easily. My flat was typical of many in the block, with the back door opening straight off the kitchen. Handy for the ambassadorial escape.

I was impressed by the Ambassador's courtesy in refusing to be over-dressed. His coming back through the front door and not the back, I supposed, was intended to administer only a half-rebuke. He didn't bat an eyelid at the sight of my dinner-jacket.

Still, I reflected to reassure myself, he probably had to be like that. In this part of South America, people really lived it up, and were sticklers for etiquette. They looked to Paris, London and the Wild West for their standards: or, rather, they followed the customs which they imagined were pursued by American beef barons, French dukes, and English peers. I had recently been to dinner at a vast house where there was a footman in white gloves standing behind every chair; on an *estancia*, a cattle-station, where the women wore the ranch's brand in awful heraldry, picked out in glittering chunky diamonds on great platinum collars. Shirts were said to be flown to Paris laundries, that kind of thing. And lots of these people were – English. Or Anglo-Argentines.

The rolled-up, sinewy beef *matambre*, this time, was not as bad as I had feared it might be. The cries of '*Loco extrangeros!*' of 'Caramba!', and snatches of song, from Concepción, as she skipped in and out, almost added up to a cabaret. And we never did get around to the matter of my harassment by the local frontier Latinos. To be fair, I do not think that there really was anything that the Ambassador could have done about it: he was only showing friendliness.

It was against the background of such experiences with the Representatives of the Throne that I once approached the British High Commission in New Delhi with the optimism tinged with trepidation which such places are plainly calculated to induce in the visitor. The one was occasioned by the size of the building, the other by the snarling doorman just inside.

There was worse to come.

'Get out, *jaldi*, quick, *goonda*, hooligan, or I'll set the *chaprasi* on you!' said the sultry blonde beauty in the first room I walked into.

For a moment I had a vision of the great Queen Boadicea – Boudicca – the British heroine who fought the Romans and actually captured Verulamium, today's St Albans, from them. Although she was not an Angle, their descendants have adopted her to such an extent that they think of her as English. Dion Cassius described the lady as being

> of the largest size, most terrible aspect, most savage of countenance, most harsh of voice, having a profusion of yellow hair, which fell down to her hips, and wearing a large golden collar, a particoloured floating vest drawn close about her bosom, over this a thick mantle connected by a clasp, and in her hand a spear.

I looked at the High Commission lady.

A fair description, apart from the thick mantle and spear, which were probably not necessary indoors, especially in India. But, however terrible the aspect or savage the countenance, I had to face it.

'I say', I drawled, looking her straight in the face, 'I know that women never much take to me first off, dontcherknow: but isn't this a bit extreme?'

She lit a cigarette, fumblingly in her fury, threw the box of matches onto the table, and treated me to a look of smouldering contempt.

No progress.

Keep talking, I thought, and something will happen. That is the way you do it in England. Stand your ground. I simply had to get some papers notarised, and that very day, too. I continued:

'As a matter of fact, a member of my own family . . .'

Suddenly, as if some invisible force had intervened and had pressed a triggerpoint on her brain, her attitude changed. Stubbing out the cigarette, she stood up, ran her hands through her hair, looked wildly around, and licked her lips, saying, 'Oh, I'm *so* sorry . . .'

I waited. Paradoxical Reversal of Symptoms, psychologists called it, I reflected.

'You see', she went on, 'I thought that you were another of those dreadful men trying to immigrate: I'm full up to *here* with it. But You're *not*, are you? You're *British*!'

Then she revealed all. 'I didn't know until I heard you say "A member of my family", and not "One of my family members." My name is Rosalind. How can we help you?' A pretty name, which I later discovered to originate with the (Germanic) 'Horse-Snake'. But that is by the way.

I hadn't felt so *persona grata* since I was invited to join the English Club, the august Club Inglés, in Montevideo, when it leaked out that I had won the national lottery. Mind you, I was also boycotted by half the Islamic community (its total population was two) for gambling. The other half made up for it, though, by hailing my achievement as proof of my high spiritual attainments. You see, as a member of a Sufi family, I had prescience: to *know* what number would win, in advance, could not be called taking part in games of chance. Actually, it was someone else who bought me the ticket. An English friend.

And the visit to the Delhi High Commission achieved more than getting my documents attested: it solved a nagging problem.

As long ago as 1943, I had read, with some surprise, the reactions of the excellent D. W. Brogan in *The English People*, on his exposure to certain forms of English womanhood. 'A girl', he wrote, 'who doesn't mind appearing sulky or indifferent is no asset to the world.' Agreed; but there was more: the 'shopping voice' of some of them 'is one of the most distressing sounds in the world.' He certainly *had* been through it, I thought. I imagined that he was back-tracking when he went on, 'Fortunately, most English girls get over this stage' – but then he put the boot in – 'but those who don't recruit that large class of formidable middle-aged women with whom England is too well supplied. There ought', he declaims, 'to be a law about it'.

The girl was one of Brogan's viragos. The problem had been how to deal with them. Now I knew.

When I spoke the right words, perhaps in the right accent, the abracadabra which put all right, when I showed that I knew that 'family members' sounded to the English ear like something undesirable and perhaps anatomical, the viragoism evaporated. So, what I had learnt was that perhaps Brogan, (avowedly, remember, not an Englishman) had jumped to conclusions, assumed too much too soon, judged English womanhood on too short a run of acquaintanceship. Perhaps he had not said the right word. Perhaps, even, he had said the *wrong* words, like 'in back of', or 'hopefully', or even 'Have a Nice Day'.

I admit that, in both the New Delhi and the Montevidean instances of feeling accepted, the grounds may seem insubstantial. The sensation, however, did not.

'It's the glorious unpredictability, though, of the English diplomatic life which really fascinates me.

I spent most of an afternoon with Sir (John Henry) Eugen (Vanderstegen) Millington-Drake, KCMG, former ambassador and now a professor *honoris causa*, in Uruguay. He wanted, he said, to hear about the situation in the Middle East. It was too bad that the time (three hours) did not permit us to discuss more than his presentation of football boots to all the children of Carrasco. And some other things, such as the importance of my pronouncing the name of the place as CarraHko, and 'One must always say "Pocítos" as if it were spelt "Pussy-toes", d'ye see . . .'

British, and especially English, diplomats have a reputation of being very deep, perhaps because of the frequent difficulty of understanding exactly what they are talking about and, especially, why.

Among the Chinese, whom it is sometimes said the English much resemble in outlook, if a mandarin or envoy says 'Consider the blue of the butterflies against the azure of the sky', you may be sure that he is changing the subject. With English officials, however, such a remark *is* a subject of conversation; if one of them says that to you, you have met an amateur lepidopterist. *I* don't call that very deep: but then I have spent a lot of time among them, you see, had to learn to speak the lingo, that sort of thing, to get to this stage.

Sometimes this directness provides the perfect cover for indiscretions: the ailment being its own antidote, as it were. In Morocco, just before the Suez adventure, I was the recipient of a quite outrageous confidence, though admittedly from a fairly junior English member of the diplomatic staff at the Rabat embassy.

'Better out here than in London, do you see;' he said.

'Yes, I believe it's raining there', I agreed.

'No, no, it's Number Ten. Senses taken leave of, if you get my drift. Get amazin' signals from London all the time. Trying to cover it by sayin' all kinds of things dontcherknow.' He went on to be even more explicit.

No doubt when the statutory period during which British official papers are kept secret is over, we shall learn why the Suez business was kept even from people who should, surely, have been told that it was imminent.

I was in Cairo just before the attack, and the British Ambassador, Sir Humphrey Trevelyan, suggested that we might meet. We talked, or rather he did, for about two hours. The subject, covered in great detail, was his stint as a District Officer in the Madras Presidency of India, in the nineteen-thirties. I simply could not make out the purpose of the meeting, even if it did teach me that Madras *had* a Presidency. After the Suez Canal campaign, I concluded that he had kept to neutral topics in case anything about the impending Anglo–French invasion slipped out. Then I thought that couldn't be the reason, since he did not need to talk to me at all.

It was not until much later that I discovered that London had not warned him about it.

More recently, I had an opportunity of mentioning my conversation with Sir Humphrey to a seasoned diplomat. 'For my money,' he said, 'the purpose of the meeting was to fill out a dispatch with something about an 'informal conversation during which wide-ranging subjects concerning the East were discussed.' Such as presidential Madras, I suppose.

Of course, diplomatic stories are by no means confined to English dinner-tables and têtes-à-tête; and foreigners have many tales about the English which they tell among themselves. Adam Malik was one of the founding fathers of Indonesian independence, and, as its Foreign Minister for some years, he took a keen interest in the English. I met him a number of times when he was President of the General Assembly of the United Nations: and once he offered an example of Englishry for my collection.

A certain British ambassador to the United Nations, he said, was not whisked straight through Immigration at New York with the customary courtesy since the local officials (unlike those of Washington, D.C.) were not then used to dealing with diplomats. The Immigration and Naturalization Service man kept him standing there, filling in a form:

'You are a Caucasian, Male . . .' the official intoned, using standard US immigration terminology.

The Englishman bristled, remembering his time in Tblisi.

'My good man,' he rapped, 'have you ever *seen* a Caucasian male? I have. A dirty little podgy man, with a drooping moustache, on a filthy donkey, stinking of garlic.'

'They are, indeed, two countries divided by the same language', said Malik who had actually witnessed the scene; 'but the American boredom threshold is low. The official just said, "Okay, on your way, buster" – and His Excellency was home and dry, in God's Own Country.'

This ambassador had mellowed quite a bit by the time I met him myself. I ran into him in the huge garden of the Embassy in – was it Ankara or Tehran? His first words were, 'Oh, *there* you are. Don't suppose you know the rules of croquet, do you? Pity, understand it's becomin' popular again, at home. Must keep in the swim. After all, the locals might take it up, and then where would be we? Can't forget the time when that low-down Levantine game called *Tric-trac*, backgammon, caught on. Lost a lot of face, not knowin' how to play it.'

Anyone who says things like that simply has to be protected, so I'm not going to identify him.

The frequent, virtually daily, luncheons or dinner-parties, all at the expense of the government (*Anglicè*, the taxpayer = you and me) are held, of course, to keep the finger on the pulse. These occasions are often attended by important political, industrial and cultural figures, sometimes referred to as the Opinion-Forming Minority.

'The other guests? Oh, they're a leaven of camouflage, old boy', I was once informed, leaving me grappling with the mental picture of a mixture of yeast and painted canvas all round the ambassadorial table. Perhaps it was my fault for wondering, aloud, to the First Secretary, what all those people could possibly be doing there.

'Got to have the right mix, of course: goes without saying.'

Over the years I must have met a couple of hundred people of great interest, if not of any instantly discernible value to international relations, at such occasions.

There was the man whose dinner-table anecdote was about how he was shot by no less a figure than Picasso – I forget why; and the one who had met the man who killed Rasputin. There was the lady golf-course landscape architect who claimed, I did not discover why, that she had a wooden leg. 'Hollow legs, more likely', the Ambassador whispered to me.

There was an aristocratic foreign woman who was as compulsive a knitter as she was an over-confident speaker of English. Her patterns, she assured me, were not her own. She only 'aped them'.

An expert on hens had, I am sorry to have to report, little small-talk. I asked him whether brown eggs, preferred by English housewives, were more nutritious than white. All he said was, 'No'. But he had a good appetite for caviar. At that particular dinner I was able to contribute little and learn less. The lady on my left confided: 'I know so many people that you would be amazed, *M'sieu*. But you would not expect me to

speak of them, would you?' No, of course not, madame. Perish
the thought.

At one party I met a man who was trying to sell army surplus
hammocks to the British Embassy; a lady who had written to the
Ambassador from hospital because she 'was bored, but was now
pleasantly surprised, if amazed, to find herself on the Embassy's
invitation list', a lady in combat gear, who had come as the
photographer of the occasion 'but I have jacked that in, as I
prefer the champagne.' Quite, as the English often say when
faced with interesting, baffling, or even ordinary, information.

And once, perhaps, I actually got near to the real thing, the
heady world of intrigue and mystery, the work in which those
who are sent to 'lie abroad for their country' are perhaps really
engaged.

It was at the celebration of the National Day at a certain
powerful nation's Embassy in London. The Prime Minister, no
less, was in conversation with the foreign minister of the powerful nation, who was passing through London. I edged close to
the two great leaders. 'There are some pretty funny things going
on down there' one was saying to the other. 'Well, I'll certainly
have *that* investigated' was the cryptic reply; 'killings, you say?'

When I made enquiries of a friend at the Embassy as to what
the meaning of this exchange might be, I was met only with
evasion. That is to say, he told me 'Oh that! That was just about
predators getting into the trout-stream and killing the fish.'

But of course this kind of disinformation ploy is one of the
duties of the diplomatic staff.

A certain number of journalists, known as Diplomatic Correspondents, get invited to the thrashes which embassies throw to
celebrate National Days, Monarchs' Birthdays, Adoptions of
the Constitution, and so on. Such invitations are greatly prized,
and the writings which appear afterwards are generally quite
servile: for the diplomat, like the better class of Head of State,
has perfected the art of taming even the most arrogant at an
expense which is trifling when measured against its public relations yield. You don't bite the hand that feeds you, after all.

It has been calculated, with the great increase in independent
states and their worldwide missions, that every year some
124,800 parties and receptions are held, not including luncheons
and dinners – or even banquets – and excluding several tens of

thousands more given by international bodies like the United Nations and its subsidiary or associated organisations. And this does not include At Homes, to meet Visiting Dignitaries. The total, internationally, must far exceed a quarter of a million functions. That's getting on for seven hundred every day . . .

The journalists who get into the parties endlessly repeat, in print, the diplomats' refrain that such get-togethers produce valuable information, since diplomats, even when nominally opposed, can't help letting fall bits and pieces of fact and gossip. But the newshawks themselves are seldom involved in the diplomats' own talk, particularly at table. In these rarefied circles, only true literary figures are really seen as acceptable people. If this rule is neglected, difficulties can occur.

Ignorance of this caused me to come unstuck at an ambassadorial dinner, at a British Mission in one of the major European capitals. I was seated next to the Envoy's wife, while she prattled on amiably enough about how some journalist ('basically he's a novelist, of course') had been surprised by something said by King Hussein of Jordan.

'You see,' she said, 'Timmie was representing the *Bugle-Monitor*, and it was *incredibly* difficult to get the audience: it always is at that level, but Willie and Johnny, and even Billie, helped.'

'That was good of them'; I felt I had to contribute.

'Yes, I suppose so. Well, imagine Timmie's *surprise* when the *King* addressed him as "Sir"! You'd think it would be the other way about . . .'

From years of being asked by English people why Middle Easterners do this or don't do that, I slipped into my accustomed role of general specialist, as it is called in our country. I answered, automatically, taking her Ladyship's penetrating gaze as an invitation to comment on technical lines. I nodded sagely.

'"Sir"', I explained, 'in such a context, meant that the King was showing consideration, not servility. *Noblesse oblige*, and all that.'

She didn't say anything, and I failed to observe her stiffen: that was reported to me later. I went on, 'For example, in my own family, children are traditionally regarded as possessors of dignity. My father, as far back as I can remember, never called me '*tu*', thou: always '*shuma*', you.'

I should have been warned by the Ambassadress's bitter-sweet smile, as she enquired, 'And what has *your* family's behaviour got to do with the Jordanians?'

'Very little', I admitted, 'as Jordanians. But we are of the same, Hashemite, lineage. So we share these customs.'

I could now see that she wasn't very pleased, though I couldn't work out why. Not until later did I hear that the purpose of her story was to boast a little about the distinction accorded to Timmie – who was her son.

'Besides', said my informant, the Counsellor, 'She's always tryin' to compensate for Timmie bein' only a newspaper-writin' feller, and it seemed to her that you were puttin' him down.'

He looked at me gloomily. 'And it was *me* that got the flak for seatin' you next to her and not sayin' who you were.'

'What do you mean, who I am?' I asked.

'Accordin' to her, someone who'll go and blow the gaff to Hussein, and then it'll get around, all over the place.'

'I'd never identify her in such a churlish manner,' I assured him. Then (since she came from an English naval family) I added, from my treasure-trove of Englishry, 'tell her Ladyship that I'm more of a Jellicoe than a Nelson.'

'And what's that supposed to mean?'

'Just a reference to what Lord Fisher said, in his *Letter to a Privy Councillor*: "Jellicoe has all the Nelsonic attributes except one – he is totally wanting in the great gift of insubordination."' I told him.

'I'd better not do that: she likes both Nelson and Jellicoe,' he said.

You should remember that all these experiences of mine among British higher echelons are given only as I see them. They may, in fact, be using such behaviour-patterns to cover all kinds of other activities. Perhaps, for example, we'll be told that Burgess and Maclean, Philby and others were in reality planted on the Russians to confuse them, and that people at the highest levels never defect.

These people are undoubtedly capable of it. I once said to a British diplomat that he must be relieved that a certain anti-British politician had not been made prime minister in a country I was visiting. 'Not relieved; shall we say satisfied', he told me.

What was the difference, I wanted to know.

'Well, when the news leaked that the job was likely to go to that anti-British chappie, our Old Man sought a meeting with the dictator himself; on some pretext, of course. At the end of the meet, he said, casually, "Glad to hear you're considering X for the Prime Ministry, Excellency. We've always had a lot of confidence in him ourselves, you know . . ." That fixed him. Dictator's totally paranoid. Nobody approved by the British would do for him. Considered topping him, in fact, until we made further representations. Had to threaten to cut his aid . . .' He paused, and then continued, in the phrase seldom far from British diplomatic lips: 'It was Sir Henry Wotton who wrote, in 1604, that "An ambassador is an honest man, sent to lie abroad for the good of his country."'

The Russians may have coined the word disinformation: but the British have always known about it. As we say in my country, 'A fish does not need to know what water is.'

And it probably pays to be loyal, dontcherknow. But I can't help wondering who Willie and Johnny, and even Billy, are when they're at home.

26

The Mysterious Quaker

Peculiarity

There is a peculiarity in the countenance, as
everybody knows, which, though it cannot be
described, is sure to betray the Englishman.
George Borrow: *The Bible in Spain*

I rose, one morning, with trepidation, for I was due to visit one
of these people characterised, by Father Batista from London,
in a letter to Father Manzoni, of Rome, thus: 'Nothing on this
globe has half the arrogance of a Quaker'.

This, coupled with the fact that the Reverend Father had
noted that the English disliked literature but nevertheless produced great literary men, gave me furiously to think. That can
be a great mistake in England, as the Duke had warned: one
usually comes to the wrong conclusions.

The Quaker whom I was to meet was a celebrated historian,
Professor G. P. Gooch, a Companion of Honour and editor of
the *Contemporary Review*.

Perhaps, I reflected, he was not so dangerous after all. Eminent he might be, editor of a famous journal ('journal' really
means 'daily', but in England this more often signifies a weekly,
monthly or quarterly periodical) but perhaps he might have
been sobered by the English habit of taking no notice of
geniuses and literary men.

I could see few English-looking people in the number thirteen
bus which took me to Piccadilly Circus, and the streets were full
of Americans with light hats to protect their heads and lighter
plastic covers to protect their hats, so I took out *Letters on the*

English Nation (Volume One) to obtain a quick rundown on the Quakers from the Reverend Father Manzoni:

They were so named because they writhed on the ground during their religious ceremonies, I understood. Fair enough; but what was this? They meet in towns all over the country, for conspiratorial purposes:

> To those places of rendezvous one or more of the Quakers of the towns within two hundred miles always come.

I could sense the heightened tension behind the writing, even from small clues. Nobody in England travels two hundred miles without some very good reason; twenty miles is often thought quite enough.

Eagerly I sought the denouement. What were these sinister writhers up to? Here it was:

> At this time their real design of meeting is concealed, by praying and preaching; it is a religious act to the eye, but a political one at the heart; every Quaker who assembles brings the state of the trade of that town from whence he comes along with him; the particular business of every grocer, mercer, and other tradesman; his industry, manner of living, and expences: by this means the wholesale dealers of London, Bristol and other great towns, are acquainted with the characters and business of all the tradesmen in the kingdom . . .

Phew! Unnerving indeed, this conspiracy. Professor Gooch would probably appear to be a mild and sincere man, friendly even.

But I had been warned. He might ask me to find out the most intricate details of the character and business of the hamburger joint where I had eaten the night before. Did Herr Kurt von Stutterheim's *Those English!* not warn that 'the Englishman . . . assumes a look of innocence when he wishes to deceive. Anyone who hears an Englishman declare that he is a plain and ordinary man had better be on his guard. Such language is only employed by a man seeking to entrap his fellow'? He received me in the graceful rooms of the London Library.

Dr Gooch was calm, gentle and kindly in appearance. If I had not read about the dastardly habits of his community, I would have mistaken him for a thoroughly upright and trustworthy man of culture. He was old, and bowed with scholarship, though this may have been part of his front, his cover. I decided to try to blow it.

Was he, 'at the heart' one who had vital information about the English, painstakingly collected by Quakers as far as two hundred miles away, which would cast light upon this dark ('difficult to understand' – *Chambers's Dictionary*) people and their land?

'Tell me', I hazarded, 'something about the typical Englishman.'

As he motioned me to a seat, I noted that he was bareheaded, a sinister sign. Father Batista had unambiguously stated that Quakers never removed their hats for any reason whatsoever. Yes, Gooch was obviously playing a part.

'A typical Englishman', he began, conventionally enough, 'will rise from a Saracen bed, bathe in a bath invented by the Romans, and drink tea introduced here from China by the Dutch. He wears a signet ring on his left little finger, a custom originated by the Prophet Mohammed and emulated by the Crusaders from Eastern Emirs, who were the cultivated gentlemen of the time.'

I wrote all this down, and he kindly waited for me to finish.

'He will dress' resumed the Professor, still in the same even tones, 'in a jacket and trousers brought to us, I believe, by the Turks. But it may be in the black and white stripes which were first introduced from Italy.'

From Italy! I waited, in vain as it turned out, for his opinions on Father Batista, who had blown the sect's cover so dramatically over two centuries ago. But he was too wily for this; veering off the subject with what the good Roman would undoubtedly have realised was suspicious haste:

'Next the Englishman puts on a crash-helmet, a "bowler", designed for the country, to show that he is a city man, and picks up his umbrella. Though this has an Italian name, it appeared in the 1700s from the Far East, and – as we know from the Persepolis carvings – it was in use there thousands of years ago.'

The Professor paused, and looked at me over his half-moon glasses, with the ghost of a smile.

'In London, Jonas Hanway – well known for his Persian travels – created a disturbance by using one, in 1786.'

The Far East, Persepolis! Verloren Hoop would have been as downcast at the news of the origins of the Englishman's favourite appurtenance as Commander Saif Al Haq, my Afghan friend who thought everything comes from the East, would have been delighted. Racing to get the words down, I felt almost out of breath as one revelation after another struck my ears:

'The Englishman may be educated, at great expense' he pursed his lips, 'at a "public" school, originally founded for the destitute; and at a university whose roots are traced to those of Moorish Cordoba and the Cairo of the Middle Ages.' Again the Eastern link. When I came to write my book, surely I would be a hero from Casablanca (Dar al Baida) to Kota Kinabalu (formerly Jesselton).

I looked at the walls of the beautiful, panelled room in which we sat, in the silence of that great library, and could hardly believe that I had at last attained access to the great and mysterious secrets of the English. Quaker or not, Professor Gooch was delineating the character of what they used to call 'Our Race'. Collect what you will, from where you will: give it any name you like – or keep its old one – and carry on doing whatever you like . . . I rubbed my hands with glee.

'He works', continued the Professor imperturbably, 'in a building whose facade is imitated from the work of the Greeks or Romans, and eats food, in the day, believed to have been introduced by the French, or perhaps it was the Americans. In the evening he may sup in the style of the Japanese, Indians or Italians.

'He washes with soap called Russian Leather; his wallet is Moroccan; he delights in Caspian fish-eggs. And', here the slight tinge of disapproval was plain, 'he decorates, at Christmas his home with holly, continuing a habit which originated at the Roman Saturnalia.'

Nothing on this globe, Father Batista had said, has half the arrogance of a Quaker. But where was it in Dr Gooch's case? Hidden deep, by centuries of dissimulation, perhaps; the English character itself being no more than a mask concealing its true, Machiavellian nature.

Ms Anne Sofer, a Social Democratic Party member of the Greater London Council, in a *Times* article, writes that she has been reflecting on the English national character. Compounded of eccentricity and sang-froid, with pottering complacency: that is how she sees her people viewing their image abroad. From Dr Gooch I had not been able to find out what the Quakers were really up to. I had no chance, as it happened, to steer the conversation around to some really sensitive questions, like what the business of every mercer actually was. But he projected no complacency, pottered not at all, showed no eccentricity; yet he was totally English. Perhaps that was his sang-froid.

I stepped into the mysteries of St James's Square (named after the patron saint of Spain) and thought about his multicultural references. Why, if so many things in England are so foreign, does the Englishman remain the same? Suddenly, when I had, English-fashion, allowed these ideas to interact in my mind, the answer came out pat. It was in a word-sequence almost eerily close to the style used in the Professor's exposition:

'On all these alien things', I told myself, 'the Englishman has put his own stamp. And the world gapes at him, because he lives and works with flair, ingenuity, and savoir-faire. These are foreign-rooted words, of course. Since the English actually have these qualities, they need no native words for them.'

Funny, though, that impatience keeps breaking through. As a foreigner I know that, no matter what the impacts, the importations, the crises, the English will absorb them. Yet, un-Englishly, the papers are full of questionings. Article after article asks whether the English are changing. Ms Sofer's article is even titled *The Rose that has lost its Bloom*. Talking about the English character, she asks, 'Is it true now? Was it ever?'

Yes, it is, and yes, it was. Just look at what the English have absorbed in the past, at the pathetic remnants of once-proud systems, groups, convictions, brought in from abroad – and you will be looking at what many of today's threats will seem like in future years. 'What is a devouring fire today', says the Afghan poet, 'will be a mere heap of ashes tomorrow.'

Perhaps the greatest misconception about the people of these islands is that they themselves never change, and that they never change anything.

Imagine – if you can – a people who would not eat chicken because they thought it holy, who revered hares and kept geese for a pastime and made pacts and then broke them. Conceive of a people whose marital arrangements involved ten or twelve men having wives in common. These major characteristics were noted as those of the people of Albion when Julius Caesar observed them. They have changed all that. Of course, it was Anglean immigrants and others who changed it. But that is the English way.

Or, if you prefer the Anglo-Saxon, it is the *Lifbrycgung*, the Way of Life.

27

Foxas Habbath Holu

Paradise

England is the paradise of individuality, eccentricity, heresy, anomalies, hobbies and humours.

George Santayana: *Soliloquies in England*

The Angles are so hard to get to grips with that you might well imagine that there is some kind of conspiracy about them. They came here, working for the Saxons. There are said to have been only 1500 of them. They depopulated their own country, effectively moving it over here. How, when and why did they effect this transition?

Professor Otto Jespersen's authoritative and much-revered *Growth and Structure of the English Language* was the book most often quoted by scholars when I went to them for help. 'You'll find it all there; highly regarded, major sourcebook, standard reference work . . .'

Well, just have a look at the facts.

Before I consulted Jespersen, I had collected these statements from simple, less splendid but unanimous books:

1 There were fewer Angles than Saxons;
2 Yet the country became England, not Saxonia;
3 And the Saxon language took the Angles' name.

Anyone could collect these scraps of information. Now all I needed was a great scholar, honoured and recommended by his fellows, to fill out the picture, and to give the whys and wherefores.

Naturally, I opened *Growth and Structure* at its historical section with due respect and in a spirit of proper anticipation.

The sum total of the illustrious Professor's learning – or as much of it as he was prepared to impart – is this:

1 The Angles were less numerous than the Saxons;
2 But they were 'influential enough to impose their name on the whole: the country is called England,'
3 'and the language English'.

As with so many English books, often the highly-regarded ones, it petered out – just like that. After telling you what everyone knows, or could learn by spending ten minutes in a public library.

Afghan persistence would have to be brought into play; but, just in case there was any security ingredient, something that should not be divulged to the layman, I cast around for a high-ranking Civil Servant. Mr Geoffrey Charles Veysey, CB, seemed a good choice. He not only belonged to one of my clubs, but *Who's Who* listed his extraordinarily English qualifications, earned during thirty years in harness. Successively, he had been

Private Secretary to Parliamentary Secretaries and Permanent Secretaries of Ministry; later Assistant Secretary, Principal Assistant Secretary and Under-Secretary.

'Barking up the wrong tree' he told me, kindly enough; though the analogy with dogs is not the one most appealing to an Afghan ear. 'See the only man worth talking to.'

That's how I got a letter from the multiple Secretary to a Cambridge don.

There didn't seem to be any secrecy about the matter. Like the Secretary, the don was helpfulness itself. Built like a rugger blue and impervious to the paralysing damp chill of the river area favoured by the founders of their more ancient English universities, he got straight to the point.

'Jespersen's *Growth and Structure* uses the university lecturing approach. Stemming from the attitude of the teaching monks of the Middle Ages, this technique is rooted in the habit of authority. Over the centuries it became standard practice to declaim truisms and banalities with a profound dogmatism originating in the presumption that the professor is always right. Or, at all events, always being believed to be right. Not being answerable. Not having to be highly relevant.'

'Thank you', I said, 'but I'm not after Jespersen. What I essentially want is to find out what is really known about, say, the English language in its Anglean form.'

He filled a pipe, lit it, and gave several slow nods of donnish sagacity.

'There are, none can dispute, numerous statements to the effect that the Angles, when they came over here, brought the English language with them.'

He gave me a benign smile. 'Just do a little reading on that, will you?'

The don stood up and held out his hand with the vague smile of dismissal that undergrads know so well.

'I *have* been reading', I said, a little wildly, 'reading anything and everything. Talking to experts. What I need to know is where I can find hard facts.'

I saw at once from his expression (pursed lips, screwed up eyes) that this was no way to address a man of learning. But he was a Cambridge don, and his courtesy, faced with an impatient foreigner, was stronger than his feelings of disapproval. He smiled.

'I shall be glad to be of service to you.' He sat down, leant back, and recited, melodiously:

> *Tha cwaeth se Haelend to him, Foxas habbath holu and heofnan fuglas nest, sothlice nannes sunu haefth, hwaer he hys heafod a hylde.*

Then he wrote it all down, in a beautiful hand, and gave the paper to me. I took it with trembling fingers. Here, in my very grasp: Anglean – at last!

But I could only understand the words 'to him', and then 'nest ... he ... a.' Less than a quarter of it. Not enough to understand what it was about. But it was a beginning.

'So, this really is the Anglean language?' I asked. Rhetorical, of course, but there wasn't anything else to say.

The don passed a huge hand over his thinning hair and frowned. 'One of the functions of a university is to teach people not to jump to conclusions. Did I actually *say* that that passage was, as you term it, Anglean?'

'Sorry, Doctor,' I said, though I was sure that nothing was really my fault; 'but I failed to note what you said it actually was.'

'It is in the language of England, spoken here three or four centuries after the Angles arrived.'

Three or four centuries? I was still struggling with that one, remembering the saying 'academics tell you what they want to, not what *you* want', when he said, 'Now see a passage from Wycliffe, written in 1389, some centuries later.'

'Nearly a thousand years after the Angles arrived?'

'Quite. And note, too, that although it's called Wycliffe's Bible, he had no hand in the translation.'

He recited:

And Jhesus said to him, Foxis han dichis, and briddis of the eir han nestis, but mannes sone hath nat wher he reste his heued.

'From Matthew 8: 20, of course – "And Jesus said to him, 'Foxes have holes and birds of the air have nests; but the son of man has nowhere to lay his head'."'

But which extract, I wondered, was English? The Venerable Bede of Jarrow is the greatest figure of Old English. He says that the ancient English, including the Saxons, came from Scythia, in Asia, somewhere not all that far from Afghanistan. I asked the don whether the original tongue would resemble its Iranic cognate, Dari, more than all that about Foxis in their Holus did.

'First get the matter of the Angles and Saxons straight' said the don. 'They were related tribes who did indeed hail from Asia and were living in western Europe when they set off for England.'

I told him that I knew that. 'I suppose that's why they called themselves Anglo-Saxons.'

The man of learning sniffed. 'It is no function of an university to teach elementary facts. But please register that there is no support, anywhere, for the view that they *ever* called themselves Anglo-Saxons.'

I had to interrupt. 'But everyone in England knows that they were Anglo-Saxons. Surely it's their oldest name for themselves?'

'Everyone may think that he knows something, but your statement is wholly misconceived. They were not called Anglo-

Saxons until eleven or twelve hundred years after they got here. We even know who named them!'

Hard facts at last, even if they seem bizarre. More than a thousand years' residence before they even had a name, and an ancestral one at that! That must have been in the fifteenth or sixteenth centuries, virtually in modern times. I held my pen over my notebook, anxious not to miss a word.

'Our term *Anglo-Saxon*,' said the Doctor, 'is derived from William Camden, antiquary, 1551–1623. The first usage of the word is found in Holland in 1610. That is, let me see, 1181 years after the proto-English came here. Three hundred and seventy-five years ago. Yes, we may safely say that the phrase is only 375 years old.'

So why were the early English given this name at all? I asked.

'Merely to distinguish them from the German Saxons. Bede called them Germans. As this book has it' – he opened one and showed me – '"Anglo-Saxon was just a device to differentiate them from the Saxons still in Germany".'

'Look it up for yourself in Hadyn's *Dictionary of Dates*.' There was a copy, a book of a thousand double-columned pages, on his bookshelf. Under ANGLO-SAXON it said 'not in any native historical record is it once to be found.'

'You fascinate me', I said, but he corrected me, 'I hope that the *information* fascinates you.'

'Yes, of course. That's what I meant.'

'And are you now satisfied about the English?'

I hadn't really got anything about their origins, but the Anglo-Saxon language bit had given me an idea.

'Up to a point', I said; 'but I am still puzzled by something I noticed some years ago. Did you know that there are affinities between modern English and my own language?'

'It is true', said the sage, 'that English is an Indo-European – formerly called Indo-Aryan – language, like German. But I doubt whether it is much like the Dari of your Afghans.'

'Wanna bet?' I asked, for only an Americanism seemed strong enough. 'Why, coming from one and a half millennia and four thousand miles from the Angles, we have whole sentences which look much more like modern English than "heofnan fuglas nest" does.'

'Such as?' he enquired acidly.

'Such as this,' I said, 'in fairly modern English: "Is it thunder? No, O brother, it is thy mother and father."'

'And how, pray, would you render that in Dari, so that a present-day Englishman might understand it?' He was not at all convinced.

'Maintain the appropriate position of your head-covering', I paraphrased; and then translated:

'"Thunder ast? Nay, O barodar, mother o pidar-ithu ast".'

He said nothing for a moment, working it out, so I continued:

'Whatever the original language of the Afghans and the Angles, there has obviously been a parallel evolution. And Dari, incidentally, had reached the stage about a thousand years ago, shedding case-endings and so on, which is only recent in English.'

This had given him time to think. 'Assuming that your Dari contains no loan-words from English . . .' I shook my head. He danced up and down, though quite prettily, with annoyance, and gave me his closely reasoned explanation. I do not propose to subject you to it, apart from saying that it spoke of 'proof by selected instances'. Let academia pay for its own typesetting.

But the Cambridge interlude had put me onto something else, another oddity, of English: the concept of loan-words. There are so many of them, taken from other languages, that whole volumes are devoted to listing and explaining them. The point is that, as with so many other things English, the phrase does not mean what it says.

The words may have been taken from other languages, but I am absolutely sure that they were never lent, to the English or to anyone else. I can confidently say that there is no evidence that any authorised person has ever said to an English person 'I hereby lend you this word . . .'

In our own language, we say, 'This is an English, a German, an Arabic, word': and leave it at that. Neither borrowers nor lenders, we. And, as an Anglophile, it is sad to have to record that there is no movement afoot to return these many thousands of words, captured cultural property, like the 'Elgin' Marbles, to their rightful owners.

These thoughts made me realise that this may be read as an overt or implied criticism. If this were so, I remembered, there would be a record of an English person who had said it first, due to the English pre-emptive habit of getting in first in case a foreigner might aim a dart. Sure enough, I soon found it, in John Florio's *Firste Fruites*, published in 1578, over four hundred years before:

> it is a language confused with many tongues . . . so that if every language had its own words again, there would be a few remain for Englishmen.

The habit of borrowing has enabled the English to claim that they have more words than anyone else. They never point out how few of them are English, apart from the single, statutory example of Floris, which enables them to say, 'There's nothing new in that. Why, an Englishman said in 1578 . . .'

In the matter of the restitution of linguistic property, unfortunately, many other countries are actually ahead of the English. France has an Academy which does its best to give back words, especially to Albion. It has already surrendered *Le Weekend*, *Le Smoking*, and *Le High-Life*. The Turks have worked hard to jettison all sorts of foreign rubbish – like Persian words – and the Persians, not to be outdone, have expelled much Arabic. Modern Persian has started to acquire a curiously semi-teutonic look. The equivalent of *Knowledgeplace* is currently its word for university, and *Learningseeker* is a student. The struggle to unload *Merci*, however, is still in an active phase.

I spoke to an English industrialist who had been to Afghanistan to seek his roots. He was fascinated to find that the Afghans called both their Nuristani minority (the original inhabitants of the country) and also the English by the same name: *Kafir*, even if it does only mean Infidel. British officers of an invasion force, he was excited to learn, had identified with the Kafirs. Like him, they were surprised to find wine-bibbing, blond, blue-eyed people who sat at tables on chairs and carried beautifully ornamented daggers which might have been Saxon. And did the Kafirs not send deputations to welcome their 'kinsmen', when the British invaded and were not over-popular among the other residents of the country?

The tycoon was almost incoherent as he reminded me that the Venerable Bede (died AD 735) had said that the forebears of the English came from Central Asia: and there was more.

My English friend had collected Kafir legends. One of them

told how their migrating forefathers had gone west, ending up 'in a green country with wide beaches and soft walls of white rocks, jutting straight up from the fierce cold sea.'

I could not help wondering, aloud, how the Nuristani bard who reported this could possibly have made the round trip in the fifth century – and why . . .

But you know the English: he was not to be gainsaid. 'These Afghans of yours', he told me, 'are what our own ancestors must have been like. We have changed a lot, of course, what with industrialisation and so on.' I asked him to be more specific.

'Well, *we* revel in good jobs with fringe benefits. *They*, like our ancestors, are sorry for people who have to work for others. Perks, after all, are only things given to servants here!'

He looked so doleful that I felt it my human duty to give him a quick fix. 'But your computer programmers are the envy of the world', I said. He agreed, but then plunged into the linguistic question.

'You know, there may be a way in which we can recapture some of the elements which we have lost. Through a study of the Afghans. We could find out a lot from their language. Why, lots of words used there are the same as English ones, and not imported, either!'

I said, 'I'm studying the English. I see them in a rather similar way to that of Sir Olaf Caroe, who told me himself that he was "a bit of an expert"'.

'Oh yes?' said the industrialist, without much interest, 'what did he say?'

'He says', I went on, '"we have here what John Morley calls a congeries of peoples engaged in a long march through the centuries from the fifth to the twentieth. To be in a position to observe all this, relatively undisturbed by the influences of our complex life, is a vastly exciting experience."'

'Sounds pretty dull to me, but I suppose it reflects the English panorama well enough', said the Englishman, obviously itching to get back to the Afghans.

'The *English*?' I asked; 'I am talking about us. That's a passage from Sir Olaf Caroe's book on the Afghans!'

I wondered, then, whether Pierre Danois was really right when he said of the English 'they exist without anyone being able to explain them.'

And, after all, according to Ibn Khaldun, the first social historian, 'Man is the child of his customs, not of his ancestors.'

Good old Ibn Khaldun. Without him, I would be stuck with trying to explain how it is that half the English historians claim that Englishry's forte is the existence of a pure and undisturbed race, while the other half positively revel in the title of mongrel. They contradict one another, too, on the matter of whether English is efficient because pure, or flexible because it is composite.

They are, therefore, inexplicable to foreigners because of their, shall we call it, agility. Horses for courses, say the English. After my Cambridge experience I can rephrase that as Foxis for Dichis.

28

Confidence Trick

They have a Sense of Humour

Nothing corrects theories better than this sense of humour, which we have in a greater degree than is to be met with, I believe, in any other people.

Sir Arthur Helps: *Friends in Council*

Well, Perhaps Not . . .

That the English are, except for their humorists, particularly distinguished for humour, an Englishman (but no foreigner) may be permitted to doubt.

H. W. Garrod, in *The Character of England*

I had gone to visit my Albanian friend Qazim Kastrati, to learn what I could from his researches into the English. Qazim had just handed me a cup of tea, and I was looking into the moonlit, frosty night through the window, when a figure – whom I had not noticed before – sprang from the fireside chair and shouted: 'Moon through glass! Very unlucky. Quick, go outside, turn three times widdershins, then bow deeply.'

When I had obediently completed the ritual, Qazim introduced the speaker, his English friend Ralph. I noted that his name's meaning, in the ancient English tongue, was Counsel-Wolf. That sounded promising; at least, the Counsel part did.

'He's my expert on local customs, quite a good fellow, but given to excitement;' Qazim said, 'Did you know that the

English, as an affectation, follow the Greek habit of spelling some words with "ph" instead of their own, perfectly good, letter "f"? That's how the name "Ralph" came about.'

Ralph was tall, thin, bespectacled and pale, with a long, stringy moustache, and not at all wolfish. 'How do you do? Never look at the new moon through glass. Should be all right now, though, touch wood. Not that I'm superstitious.'

'Are you sure that the turning and bowing averts the evil?' I asked, nervously. 'Oh, yes, promise. Look – now it's wet, now it's dry, cross my heart and hope to die.' He licked a finger and passed it across his throat. 'You didn't walk under that ladder outside when you came up the path?'

'No.'

'That's all right then.'

We had another tea all round.

Alas, Qazim is no longer with us: he got an elegant and well-deserved obituary in *The Times*, proof enough that he had made his mark. He had been an aide to King Zog and later was a well-liked figure among the Liberals in London.

'I have to admit', he told me, 'that I started nosing around them when I heard that some were mixed up in a mystical school. Based on the dervish philosophy, which is popular in Albania. Found that that was just a bit of English wierdery; they'd completely misunderstood the ideas. Liked the Liberals, though.'

The things you hear in England . . .

My father had put Qazim up for membership of his London club, and Qazim became quite a leading light there, after an initial hiccup. This was when he insisted on reminiscing about his 'idyllic days at the Gymnasium.' Several of the stuffier Members felt that he was lowering the tone of the place, until they discovered that a gymnasium, on the Continent, is a word for a school.

His bequest, his rhetorical yet cryptic enquiry, will long ring in my ears. He often spoke directly into one's ear, in that low tone and with that confidentiality which are the mark of the courtier the world over. His constant refrain, while in exile pending the restoration of the monarchy to Tirana, was 'How do they *do* it, Brother Idries Pasha?'

He meant, of course, the *they* whom all foreigners mean: the

English. The whole phrase decodes, by common consent, as
'How do the English do all those things which they do, and
which nobody else can?'

Qazim was not only an educated man, accustomed to linear
thinking; he often had flashes of inspiration. One day, sitting in
the Club's immense smoking room, he turned to me and said,
very low but with an underlying sense of certitude: '*They* will get
out of their economic problems, just you wait and see. I
wouldn't be surprised if they actually found an oilfield here in
Britain!' And that was years and years ago. Nobody else suspected, then, that one day Britain would be the fourth largest of
the world's oil-producing nations.

'A confidence trick?' I enquired. This was one of Qazim's
favourite terms. He had discovered it in England and liked it so
much that he used it for all kinds of things. So, as I knew, in his
vocabulary 'a confidence trick' could mean lots of things – such
as 'something which will bring back confidence.'

But he also liked puns. 'Trick? No', he riposted, 'not that.
More of an oil *trick*-le . . .' And he laughed, that long, gurgling
from the front of the mouth which I associate with the Albanian
Court. Once, when I went to see His Majesty, Zog I, in Buck-
inghamshire, I said 'Your Majesty may be pleased to recall that I
was presented to you, on one occasion, in Geneva.'

Ahmad Zoghu (for that is the correct form of his name) at
once replied, with the affability usual among monarchs, 'Oi
remombir', and gave that very same gurgle, though naturally in
a suitably abated, regal manner.

The British, with their customary hospitality, gave the Shqi-
perian monarch asylum after the Italians invaded his country
one Good Friday. True to the tribal testing-by-buffeting process, however, tribute was exacted by the Press. They tried to
make fun of Zog. But the English respect a survivor; and it is
good to know that his son and successor, H. M. King Leki
(Alexander) I of the Albanians is officially recognised in
London by this title.

From time to time journalists have a go at him, in a kind of
low-key way; but His Majesty knows English well, and realises
that the mickey-taking is affectionate. Albanian students of
Englishry like Qazim have been well positioned to advise Leki
why pressmen seem fascinated by his great height and liking for

guns. Qazim himself gurgled to me, 'It's probably because so many of them are pint-sized and would like to have guns themselves, if they knew what they were. Clear case of a confidence trick.'

Whether a king has effective control over a country is not of special interest to the English, because *territorial* sovereignty is something of an innovation among them. The country wasn't even called England until Egbert named it in AD 829, and *his* title was not geographical. It was 'King of the English'. Or did another monarch, Alfred, name it in 901? The English are not sure, so presumably nobody else is. It depends which books you read. Some historians even say that the naming took place as late as 925 (or, again, possibly in 934) and may have been done by Athelstan. These points were made by Ralph-Counsel-Wolf, who was trying to find out who *had* named his country, and why. I could not help him in that, so I switched to something I did know.

'Of course,' I said, 'there were kings before the country was named. Offa struck a gold coin in the 8th century, describing himself thereon as King: but not of anyone or anywhere in particular. Perhaps there was some difference of opinion.' There is one of those coins in the British Museum: it is an imitation of an Arabian dinar. In addition to the inscription (upside-down) of OFFA REX, it also says (right way up) 'No God but God, Mohammed the Prophet of God'. At the earliest, the country was named thirty-three years after Offa died in 796.

I wonder whether Offa knew that, in using the Islamic creed on his coins, he could have been regarded, legally speaking, as having placed himself and his subjects (and his country, if it existed by then) under the suzerainty of the caliphate of Cordoba or that of Baghdad?

In Offa's time, and for some time after that, there was still no England. The Venerable Bede (672–730) says that the English 'are still called Germans by the neighbouring nation of the Britons.' The English, he notes 'are the Freesons, Rugians, Dans, Hunni, Old Saxons and Boructarians'.

Even in the twelfth century, the language spoken by the English was a form of German. Thierry, writing of the flight of Richard the Lionhearted through Germany, notes that an Englishman accompanying the French-speaking king spoke a language 'exactly similar' to that of the Germans, and was thus able to interpret. Nearly eight hundred years later the Hitlerite Germans trained special troops to fight the British in – Schleswig-Holstein . . .

I have felt some affinity with Offa's people since I learned of the dinar. The original of which his is a copy was minted by the great Caliph Abdur-Rahman of Cordoba, whose ancestry our own family shares, as Sir Iain Moncreiffe reminded me when he was in Spain.

On the evening of my gaffe about the moon, Qazim, Ralph and I were also concerned with matters rather more remote in history. Ralph had done some research into English origins, from the best published sources.

The Angles, he explained, were named after the angle of land which touched the Frisian country on the west, Saxony on the south, and the Wendish tribes of the Baltic coast on the east. They had been mentioned by Tacitus. Their country was given in English sources (he brandished T. W. Shore's *Origin of the Anglo-Saxon Race*) as 'somewhat larger than Rutland'.

'Rutland was the smallest county in England', I remarked, 'so they made a good bargain when they immigrated en masse. But where, exactly, did they come from?'

'And how did they *do it*?' breathed Qazim.

Ralph adjusted his spectacles. 'They did it in Asiatic chariots, like previous invaders here. And like the Saxons, S. R. Clarke, in *Vestigia Anglicana*, says that *they* came from near the River Jaxartes, in Central Asia. North of present-day Afghanistan.'

Professor K de B Codrington and Sir Mortimer Wheeler, I recalled, were also convinced, and had told me themselves, that this was a fact: but who *were* the ancientest Angles?

I wondered what they had been called before they came to take up residence in the Angle itself, just across the sea.

'Interesting that you should say that', said Ralph, with great animation, 'because I have a theory. *They always were* called Angles, or something like it.'

Qazim and I looked at one another. Here was something new.

'The *Oxford English Dictionary*,' he went on, eyes glistening, 'says that "Angle" is from the Aryan root *ank*, to bend. It is related to the Indian word *ankus*, the crooked iron elephant goad.'

He looked up from his notes, triumphantly, as I recalled the Persian word *anga*, 'a bent spade' – and, for that matter, ankle, in English.

Unable to pursue the English beyond Central Asia, our talk drifted to other topics. But Ralph has kept up the contact. Years after the conversation, he wrote to me. He enclosed a clipping of a news item which 'indisputably' linked the Angles with an Oriental patrimony. The passage read:

A rare tropical trigger fish weighing nearly two and a half pounds was caught at the weekend by Mr Toby Ward, a member of Boscombe Sea Fishing Club, Bournemouth. There is no record of a trigger fish being caught by an angler along the South Coast.

The clipping was meticulously marked '*Daily Telegraph*, 3 Sept, 1984, p3.'

Even in my pre-Kastrati days, I am sure, I would have noticed this story and its oddness. But, just to illustrate the difference between my mentality and his, I'll give you what would have been *my* reactions to the news:

If there is no record, as the paper says, of such a fish being caught, then this one wasn't either. So it would not have been in print. That is, unless a careless printer has allowed the word 'hitherto' to drop out of the paragraph.

You will observe my rather Continental method of reasoning. And Kastrati's? He was far too Albanian, or Englishised, to have reacted like that. He would have telephoned me to arrange a meeting, would have sat down at a table in the club, looked around, taken the clipping from an inside pocket, and murmured, low but with cold emphasis, 'How do you think they *do* it, Brother Idries?'

Ralph has approached the matter much more specifically. His letter says, *inter alia*:

Angling is undoubtedly connected with the origin of the English. The OED distinctly says that the word ANGLE stands for a fish-hook. It can also mean a fisherman. ANCHOR must be connected, too. Since our forebears bore this name before they became known as fishermen or seafarers, their maritime tradition following their occupation of these islands may confidently be attributed to a desire common among tribal peoples, to turn their name into its physical expression.

Does he mean that we have Central Asia to thank for Raleigh, Drake and the rest?

I read that the country where the ancients placed the settled progenitors of the English was called – by the Hon Mr Keppel, who visited it – 'Karabagh'. Although this area is in Central Asia, seventy miles north of Baku, we, too, have a Karabagh in our ancestral Afghan domain of Paghman . . .

Talk about confidence, whether tricks or otherwise. How *do* they do it?

Qazim's English, though excellent, sometimes came and went in a disconcerting way. One day he brought me the news that underpants (he pronounced the word 'panths', and I thought for a moment that this could only be the diminutive of panthers) were selling cheap at Harrods. I had the temerity to say, 'How do you think they *do it*, Qazim?'

His answer came pat, 'Bought a job lot, I shouldn't wonder.' Was he just stringing together two English idioms, perhaps recently learnt, and had thus scored an accidental hit, or what?

That could have explained his next remark – but so could Balkan mysteriousness: 'Plenty more where that came from'.

At other times, Qazim seemed involved with people without the slightest interest in how they did, or claimed to do, most extraordinary things. He once brought me a mysterious-looking, saturnine Englishman who was 'going to restore the rights of the Throne of Albania'.

I looked at his visiting-card. His surname was Persis (Greek for 'Persian'): and his Christian name was an old English pagan one – Randolph, which means Shield-Wolf. The card further described him as an International Consultant. I said that I supposed he did a lot of that kind of thing.

'Average amount', he told me, fingering his Etonian tie; 'I'm putting the Turkish Imperial Family back into Istanbul, too.' He was now inspecting my furnishings, suit, shoes and watch, discreetly but with care. They evidently passed muster, for his next remark was, 'When I've got through the present work-load, I'll put *you* back, if you like. Meanwhile all I ask is the usual retainer.'

It was then that I blurted out, in Qazimean wonderment, 'But how would you *do it*?' The International Consultant leant back in my best armchair and looked interestedly at the ceiling, a slight smile playing about his lips. Qazim, however, far from leaning forward to find out, at last, how the English *do* things, hacked at my shins with his impeccable brogues, his broad shoulders hunched, his blue chin bristling with courtierly affront at the brashness of the enquiry.

There is said to be a secret society in England whose strength is that is has no secret. The English way (though this would have disappointed Qazim Kastrati) may actually reside in their own esoteric slogan, By Guess And By God. This is used even in the best ordered professions. The *Guardian* Newspaper (15 September 1984) blows the whistle on medical men. The 'average General Practitioner and Neville Chamberlain have one thing in common – a little piece of paper and a pious hope.'

Is it a Confidence Trick if they claim that they have more, these GPs? Qazim asked me that, when he was patched up by his own doctor after being duffed up by muggers. I said that I thought not . . .

Be that as it may, we could look at the Confidence Trick which features in Qazim's favourite story. Now that I have more experience of England, I am inclined to think that it was attempted by foreigners: but you can decide for yourself.

As he told it, Qazim was walking, quite innocently as was his wont, through the streets of London, when three men jumped him. They hustled him down a flight of steps into a basement area: then they beat him about the head and tore off his jacket, stealing his wallet.

Finally, they fled. 'It was,' Qazim said, 'definitely a confidence trick.' Certainly the men had the confidence to do the job. They had more than paper and a pious hope.

Then there is another way in which they 'do it'; though the event which illustrates it happened too late to consult Qazim about it.

When I had written about twenty books, I was flattered to see that my name, and a couple of things I'd written, were included in the *Penguin Dictionary of Modern Quotations*. Great. Perhaps I had arrived at last.

Then I looked at the nature of the extracts chosen to represent my work in the English language. The first was to the effect that if it took all sorts to make a world, where were they? The second claimed that someone might have a wonderful presence, but also had a 'perfectly delightful absence.'

See what I mean? At one stroke (or, at the most, two) I was characterised as someone who didn't like people very much. Or liked to be alone . . .

Perhaps I am too sensitive, and it is not so much that they are 'doing it' to me, as that they are applauding what look like Anglean tendencies.

Qazim would have found yet other meanings in this selectiveness. Out of my three million published words, the choice of those particular fifty-three, because they appear in such a distinguished volume, may well be a confidence trick in the Qazimean sense.

Angling, whether in fresh water or in the sea, is one of the most popular activities among the latter-day Angleans: who would have expected otherwise? And who but an Englishman would have written, and made into a part of the national literature, *The Compleat Angler*? Not just a textbook on fishing, Izaak Walton's classic is everywhere regarded as a work of greatness which shows 'how the humblest object may be ennobled by the spirit in which they are pursued'. The English spirit.

It was a thousand years and more after his forebears came here that Walton wrote the book, and it just over three centuries since he died. Angling, among the Angleans is more popular than ever, with specialist magazines, books and radio programmes of its own, not to mention clubs up and down the country – and tropical trigger fish turning up.

Even Kastrati, I fancy, would have found it a challenge to work out how this strange people from Asia, though named after their penultimate location in Schleswig, also carried the Indo-European word for 'angle' with them and turned it into an obsessive hobby and even a philosophy. A coincidence – or was the Jutland angle actually named after *them*? Persuasive theories have been built on less.

I wondered aloud once, when talking to Qazim, whether,

someday, someone would discover an ancient land in Central Asia called something like Angalistan.

'More than likely,' he gurgled.